Projections 13

in the same series

PROJECTIONS 1
John Boorman fires the starting-gun for the series; includes interviews with Michael Mann, Gus Van Sant by River Phoenix and Demme on Demme

PROJECTIONS 2
Interviews with George Miller, Willem Dafoe, Jaco Van Dormael, as well as Altman on Altman

PROJECTIONS 3
The diaries of Francis Coppola, interviews with Quentin Tarantino, Chen Kaige, Sally Potter, as well as Kasdan on Kasdan

PROJECTIONS 4
James Toback's diary, an interview with Gene Kelly, Lindsay Anderson's tribute to John Ford, Walter Murch on sound design, Arthur Penn on Arthur Penn and poetry by Viggo Mortensen.

PROJECTIONS 4½
What is your favourite film? Answered by Clint Eastwood, the Coens, Elia Kazan, Mike Leigh, Stephen Frears, Steven Soderbergh, among others

PROJECTIONS 5
Animation issue. Also includes Jamie Lee Curtis talking to her father Tony Curtis, Quentin Tarantino and Brian De Palma, and Jimmy Stewart's last interview

PROJECTIONS 6
Pieces by Mike Figgis, Eleanor Coppola, Tom DiCillo, Robert Towne and interviews with Vittorio Storaro and Stanley Donen

PROJECTIONS 7
Scorsese issue; also includes Jamie Lee Curtis talking to her mother, Janet Leigh, Willem Dafoe with Frances McDormand and an interview with Robert Mitchum

PROJECTIONS 8
International critics answer the question: Does film criticism have any value today? Also, Christopher Doyle's diary of his work with Wong Kar-Wai and interviews with Abbas Kiarostami and Abraham Polonsky

PROJECTIONS 9
The legacy of French cinema from Robert Bresson to Matthieu Kassovitz's *La Haine*

PROJECTIONS 10
The Hollywood issue. Mike Figgis explores the System in conversation with Mel Gibson, Salma Hayek, Paul Thomas Anderson and others

PROJECTIONS 11
The New York issue. A companion issue to the Hollywood one in which Spike Lee, Tim Robbins, Jim Jarmusch, David O. Russell and Wes Anderson provide an alternative to Hollywood film-making

PROJECTIONS 12
Are film schools necessary? Former film students such as Lynne Ramsay discuss the pros and cons. Interviews with new directors: François Ozon, Pawel Pawlikowski, Bruno Dumont and Walter Salles; Peter Weller's diary of working with Antonioni; images by Richard Linklater and a story by Ethan Hawke

PROJECTIONS 13
Women Film-makers on Film-making

Edited by Isabella Weibrecht, John Boorman and Walter Donohue

ff
faber and faber

First published in 2004
by Faber and Faber Limited
3 Queen Square London WC1N 3AU
Published in the United States by Faber and Faber Inc.
an affiliate of Farrar, Straus and Giroux LLC, New York

Typeset by Faber and Faber Limited
Printed in England by Mackays of Chatham, plc

A CIP record for this book
is available from the British Library

ISBN 0–571–22047–9

10 9 8 7 6 5 4 3 2 1

Contents

Farewell to Karel Reisz (see page 263)

Foreword by John Boorman

It is thirteen years since Walter Donohue and I published the first Projections. The aim and purpose was and is to explore the process of movie-making with its practitioners. But it has evolved. In the early editions the spine was a diary of the previous year written by a director in the thick of it – bulletins from the trenches. I wrote the first, followed by Bertrand Tavernier, Francis Coppola and then the anarchic James Toback (who will live in film history as the man who filmed Robert Downey Jr making a pass at an astonished Mike Tyson). We still include diaries (there's one in this book by Rebecca Miller) but they have become less central.

Projections 5 was the first to be devoted to a theme – Animation. Then we did one on Critics; another on French Cinema; there was a Scorsese issue; a Hollywood special edited by Mike Figgis; and balanced the following year by one on New York movie-making; and last time out we covered Film Schools.

This present edition has been edited by Isabella Weibrecht on the subject of Women in Film, to recognise the welcome growth of female input to movie-making.

But tucked away at the back of these themed editions we always tack on unrelated pieces that we can't leave out, that force their way in: obituaries of loved directors and actors; lost films rediscovered; pieces by art directors and editors and screenwriters. So it is here. How could we pass up this wonderful rant by Ingmar Bergman? At 84 he no longer finds it necessary to be polite or politic – if he ever was. He takes us on a rhapsodic journey through the films he loves, from the silents up to last year's releases. On the way, he side swipes Orson Welles as a phoney; hates Godard's films; says Antonioni never learned his craft. He revels in Carné, Kurosawa, Fellini. His appetite for film is prodigious and undiminished. At the time of writing the whole of Sweden has just watched his positively, final and last film (he's said that before) *Saraband*.

Then there is the production designer, Gene Allen, giving an extraordinary insight into the films of George Cukor, and particularly how he developed his techniques when colour came in. He was perhaps the first to introduce a restricted palette to keep scenes in a narrow spectrum to modify the garishness of early Technicolor emulsions.

Finally, Mike Leigh lovingly remembers Katrin Cartlidge, Gavin Lambert writes about Karel Reisz and the early days of Free cinema, and I pay tribute to my dear friend the great Conrad Hall.

Introduction by Isabella Weibrecht

Today the Iranian reformist lawyer and women's rights campaigner Shirin Ebadi is in Stockholm to collect the Nobel Peace Prize. By coincidence, I spent last weekend here with my friend Michelle Bohana, Aung San Suu Kyi's most ardent supporter. Aung San Suu Kyi won the Peace Prize in 1992, but to this day remains under house arrest in Burma where she has spent most of the past fourteen years, sacrificing her sons' childhood and separated from her husband during his illness and death. Michelle was in Ireland to meet with Irish ministers, journalists, and human rights campaigners to plead Suu's case prior to this country assuming the presidency of the EU in January 2004. Her commitment to this woman and her cause is indefatigable. In an ironic twist, we were obliged to watch the Miss World competition on television, held, of all places, in the People's Republic of China, since my next door neighbour's niece was competing as Miss Ireland. Michelle wondered acidly whether the show was being beamed into Tibet.

The juxtaposition of these two icons of womanhood: one rewarded with the most prestigious human rights award (mind you, Henry Kissinger bagged that one once too), the other, a competition based solely on looks and sex appeal, had us alternately horrified and in fits of giggles. How do we regard an achievement by a woman? Does it necessarily need to have a different sensibility from that of a man? Are women expected to be sexually appealing and twice as clever as men in order to succeed?

The same duality is constantly argued in film. Can one catergorise them in such a simple way? Women are now involved in all aspects of film-making. More and more we see women's names credited as DP, gaffers, designers, writers, directors. Sherry Lansing has been head of Paramount for nearly a decade. She doesn't make 'womens' films. She makes blockbusters, like all the other studio heads. While she was making the shareholders bucketloads of money she was lauded, now that they are not, she is being criticised as having lost her touch, implying that this frailty is because she is a woman. But would a male studio head go before the CAA agents and admit his errors, as she did? Kathryn Bigelow confounds critics in that she can turn out an action film that would shame most so-called action directors. We tried to interview a female studio executive in a top position to see if being a woman in any way clouded the 'business'. Our set of questions had to be submitted to a studio lawyer and we never heard from her again.

In this issue we have tried to engage with as many women film-makers as possible, from as varied a specialty as possible and collected their stories from across the world. There is the witty fairytale diary of Rebecca Miller about the chaotic making of her Sundance award winning *Personal Velocity*. It shows someone pursuing her vision with steely determination. Allison Anders romantically resurrects the shamefully forgotten Mrs Wallace Reid, the silent film director, whose masterpiece, *Linda*, was described as a Hollywood 'quickie'. (Some things never change: Rebecca too shot her film in sixteen days). Mrs Wallace Reid is perhaps the archetypal female director, with her 'very liberal, Quaker-like, anti-racist, anti-sexist, humanistic view of the world'.

What all these women talk about – and men don't – is the importance of collaboration. Men tend to be insistent on everyone being a servant to their vision. Rebecca is continuously amused by her crew and their personal eccentricities, and is thrilled at their contributions. Ramona Sanchez, production supervisor, describes her job as fundamentally being 'able to keep lines of communication open' between the various warring factions in the crew and the minefield that is the Hollywood Studio. Heather McGowan successfully juggles the solitude of novel writing with the team effort involved in screenwrting.

The UK's only senior female entertainment lawyer, Libby Savill, describes her role as 'trusted advisor, to have that rapport with a client, set a goal, and help them achieve it'. The multi-talented Anna Karina falls into the traditional artist-muse relationship with none other than Jean-Luc Godard. And then there is the collaboration gone a bit sour: Katia Lund's co-directing credit on the Brazilian hit film *City of God* being usurped by her collaborator once success is assured. Frances McDormand, Emily Mortimer and Lisa Cholodenko discuss nudity in an open frank way, which they might not have done if one of the participants had been a man.

But, ultimately these women are all film-makers who want the films to be seen, just like men do, and that requires an enourmous effort in itself. As Rebecca Miller comments when hearing Robert Redford dampen the importance of film awards and assured distribution: 'to those of us who struggled so hard to make our films, getting paid nothing or next to nothing, the idea that someone might actually see them is appealing.' Denise Breton describes the complicated and manipulative world of publicising a film and how film-makers hate it. John Boorman often tells the story of meeting Fellini and Mastroianni in NYC, all of them crossing paths on their press junkets. As they commiserate, Fellini comes up with the idea that they should make films for free, because that is what they love doing, but distributors should pay them for doing publicity. I'm sure many would agree. These women's stories are their own, the way they tell them is varied, but ultimately their hope is that there is an audience out there to discover them.

By the way, Miss Ireland went on to win the competition and become Miss World, and her itsy-bitsy bikini clad photograph was on the front page of every Irish and UK newspaper the following morning. Talk about publicity . . .

Annamoe, Ireland
10 December 2003

'If you obey all the rules, you miss all the fun.'
Katherine Heburn

WOMEN FILM-MAKERS ON FILM-MAKING

Lisa Cholodenko discusses a scene with Christian Bale and Natasha McElhone (photo by Neal Preston)

Talking About Women: A conversation between Frances McDormand, Lisa Cholodenko and Emily Mortimer

Frances McDormand: Lisa Cholodenko and I worked together on a film, and with us is Emily Mortimer, who is a new friend of ours. She has just worked with Nicole Holofcener on *Lovely and Amazing*.

Lisa Cholodenko: She is going to be our referee.

Emily Mortimer: I'll stop you when you stray too far off the post.

FM: It's inevitable that we're going to talk about being women, though we don't have to.

EM: I suppose it'll just happen, won't it?

FM: Our voices are women's voices.

LC: Remember that article you did about a year ago for *Première* magazine? You said such great stuff about feminism – about what makes a film by a woman different to one by a man. It went right to the essence of the issue.

FM: You have to talk about it in personal terms. You can't talk about it politically because it's not a political question. I don't think films are political. Documentaries are political.

LC: There's a tradition of women making esoteric art film, films with a feminist agenda – film-makers like Chantal Ackerman and Sally Potter, for example. They had a political feminist agenda. They want to subvert.

FM: I think that the problem with those movies is that either their entertainment value is limited or their audience is limited. Whether it's different being directed by a woman instead of a man came up a lot in the press when we were in Cannes with *Laurel Canyon*.

LC: Really?

FM: 'Do you like it better, do you want to work with more women?' But the best directors I've worked with – male or female – are collaborative, so I would think that one of the major pluses of working with a female director is that they would be more collaborative and not dictatorial – although you have to be somewhat monomaniacal when directing a film.

LC: Emily, you've worked with male directors, so was there a difference in the collaborative nature of your work with Nicole?

EM: I felt that there was a difference from most male directors, but I agree with Fran that, when you feel it's been successful, it's not a question of whether the director is a man or a woman.

LC: My guess is that collaboration is more likely with a woman.

FM: Yes, I just assume that, in a weird way.

EM: My feeling about *Lovely and Amazing* is that it wasn't so much about it being a female director; it was more about it being a female writer. It fundamentally changed the storytelling, so that by the time it got to the collaborative process between actor and director, so much had already been established because of the script. I definitely felt that way with Nicole's script.

It's just a different way of storytelling: the resolutions aren't as tight, it's not as packed, there's more dialogue, and the dialogue is much more specific, the voices stronger.

LC: Have you ever worked with a woman director on a Hollywood project that was not written by that woman?

FM: I feel that the women of my generation are much more about being for hire. They might not originally have been, but gradually through the process you find yourself becoming that. Lisa, you are a director for hire for television stuff. What's the difference between directing something you've written and something you've been hired to direct?

LC: You feel like you've much more authority when you've written it. TV and film are radically different.

FM: But you've done work for HBO, so that's a little different.

LC: Yeah, it's a little different, but you still have to deal with the time constraints and that particular structure of work. In my experience, when you are the writer/director, you have much more insight into the characters, so you can make creative choices much more fluently. There is the potential to be collaborative because you are working out something that you understand, instinctively, as the writer, so you can sense what the actor is feeling about it, their instinctual take on it, as they are performing it. So it's much more gratifying because you have a clearer vision of how the thing should be. I prefer to direct my own material. I feel I can climb under the skin of it.

FM: Also, it's a non-gender thing. The conversations I've had recently with actors have been about their having had more satisfactory experiences with directors that are writing and directing their own material.

Emily, I was talking to Ewan McGregor yesterday about a film you're doing with him for a young Scottish director called David Mackenzie.

EM: He's adapted a fifties beatnik Scottish novel by Alexander Trocchi into a screenplay and then directed it. It's called *Young Adam*. Instinctively, you think that when somebody's written their own script they're going to be so obsessed by it that it's going to be hard for them to adjust to other people's visions when they come in and have new ideas, but I think that when you've actually written the script you feel a kind of security: it's your text, so you feel more confident about changing things, about working other things in. He was incredibly open to just going with what happened in the moment.

LC: I think it obviously helps with the directing too, because you are not only thinking about what the characters are saying, you've actually created this whole world, you've seen the spaces and how people move through those spaces and their gestures. I've never talked about it, but I think I tend to overwrite, put too much direction into the script – you know, *She moves her hand and scratches her hair and she looks over at her when she does that . . .*

FM: But isn't some part of that a kind of protection against the people who are reading it, the people that you are trying to raise money from – studio people or producers – so that they can understand it? You write it more novelistically, when in actual fact further down the line a visual image is going to be enough.

LC: I think my stuff is kind of literary anyway. The two films I've made are not big on plot, they're not big visual-effects films. I feel that all I have going for me are the psychological underpinnings of the characters, their behaviour. I think a great screenwriter can express that in a few words. I've read scripts when I say, 'Fuck, I see the whole thing,' yet there's hardly any text there. It's just one line of dialogue and a setting, but I've got the whole thing.

FM: In *Laurel Canyon* the voices of the characters are really specific, male and female. You can't check off any of them as 'supporting characters' in terms of the dramatic arc of the film. For instance, Sarah, Natascha McElhone's character, was full and complete, and you wonder what went on when she went home.

LC: I wonder if women are instinctually more invested in fleshing out their characters, whether that's sort of a female instinct . . .

FM: That is what I mean about the storytelling.

LC: . . . and men are more plot than character.

FM: And archetypes, those iconic archetypes in male genre films. In a lot of cases, it's the personality of a movie star that feeds into the character, and that has nothing to do with the writing. What's interesting to me about *Laurel Canyon* is that your voice is really present. Sometimes that worked for characters and sometimes it didn't; there is a real dry, acerbic quality to your voice and to your humour that worked in my mouth, it worked in Alessandro Nivola's mouth, but it couldn't really work in Christian Bale's or Kate Beckinsale's character . . .

LC: Right.

FM: . . . because they haven't exercised that side of their communication skills.

LC: As Christian and Kate, or as those characters?

FM: As those characters, so that when they do, it doesn't feel right.

LC: That's funny, because your character and Alessandro's character were the two characters that came first. They were so much easier. They wrote themselves, whereas the other ones felt much more laboured because they were unfamiliar to me personally.

That's what's hard about being a writer/director – you don't want everybody to be, you know, an acerbic lipster. You want them to have a full palate, and that's the challenge.

FM: Both your movies have two sides to them pulling in different directions: one is this yearning for freedom and abandon and for people to just do what the fuck they want; and then there's another side which is that life can't always be like that and it doesn't necessarily induce happiness or security or whatever. So Kate and Christian's characters must have been part of your psyche, in a sense. I guess they don't represent the most flamboyant side, so it's kind of less fun.

LC: I think of them more in terms of embodying a concept that I'm interested in, fascinated by or engaged in, so it's easy to extend that and say that situationally this is the dilemma, this is what's up; but I think that, just in terms of the texture of personality, hands down I identify much more with the character that I wrote for you. That's just more my personality. I'm not a shut-down, non-communicative, non-emotional person. I'm the opposite of that.

FM: The other thing that I thought connected the two films was the question of integrity – at what point does your integrity come into question.

LC: Yeah.

FM: It was more of a sub-plot in *Laurel Canyon*; in that film it was the music, and which side of the music to play, which way to go with it. Unlike *High Art*,

Top: Having communication skills . . . (Alessandro Nivola and Frances McDormand)
Bottom: . . . or not (Christian Bale and Kate Beckinsale)
(photos by Neal Preston)

it wasn't so much about the transition of the character. What I loved about the character in *High Art* was that it wasn't just about a young woman's sexual awakening . . .

LC: God forbid.

FM: . . . it was about ambition. She was an ambitious person, and her journey was about questioning how far she would go to fulfil her ambition, how many compromises she would make and how many people she would compromise. In fact, in her situation, it was a dangerous compromise, right?

LC: Yeah.

FM: And, in that sense, it's the perfect subject for a first film, but *Laurel Canyon* has more of a sub-plot. The song was going to work either way, so it wasn't really going to be devastating for my character if it didn't work; my character had gone through a lot, so it wasn't going to be the end of the world, but it worked as a sub-plot, it injected something of a personal crisis into Christian and Kate's characters.

LC: Well, they never questioned their integrity. I think my position was that you can't really be a full person until you question your integrity. Actually, there is no moral agenda with this movie at all, but there is some stuff in it that I'm sure people look at and go, 'That's way out of hand, that's totally over the line.'

FM: When we first met, you asked me if I thought the character was unsympathetic.

LC: I did?

FM: Is that because you were working with another actor on it and she had?

LC: I developed it for a while with another actor – a very different actor from you in terms of personal image, star image – and she wanted to justify the character in every aspect, to make sure that the character was sympathetic to a much greater degree than . . .

FM: . . . was dramatically necessary.

LC: It made me feel insecure because I was creating a character which, if you read it on paper, would make you go, 'Whoa, that was really fucked up,' but I knew when we met that you were going to humanize it, that it wasn't going to read like that at all on the screen.

FM: There is no moral question in the character. A movie can open a little window on to a couple of days in people's lives – and they don't even have to be

'My character has gone through a lot.' (photo by Neal Preston)

interesting people. Just the fact that you peek in on them for a certain amount of time . . . and if there is some progression, some series of dramatic events, it doesn't have to be conclusive in any way . . . That's the way I feel about Nicole's movie too – you've got the thrill and the joy . . .

EM: . . . of seeing inside their lives from really close up.

LC: Really close up is the thing. It has the most shelf life. You know, the movies that I remember are ones where I can say, 'Oh my God, there is a moment in that film when this or that happened and it altered or confirmed my thinking or feeling about something.'

EM: I was thinking that a lot about Nicole's film as well. Some people have watched the movie and said that it's really uncomfortable, or that there are

Emily Mortimer and James Legros in *Lovely and Amazing* (photo by Eric Mas)

moments which seem so uncomfortable that they don't seem real. However, when you actually think about it, they are super-real; they are reality, but we don't often admit to it. Both movies are about families, as well as all sorts of other things, such as how you can't admit every day of your life to the shit that is going on in your life, so you have to make it all seem like: 'I've got a lovely mum and a lovely dad and a lovely boyfriend and a lovely sister.' If you were honest, there are moments when you feel you hate your mother and you wish you weren't anything to do with her.

LC: You're going to break up with your boyfriend every five minutes . . .

EM: Exactly.

LC: You're out the door . . .

EM: Exactly. Then suddenly the sun will shine, and you'll think your mum is the best thing that ever happened.

LC: That's a really interesting point. I think we spend the majority of our life questioning rather than in contentment.

FM: Exactly. I think it comes back to female storytelling too, because how often have you found yourself, maybe while having your pedicure or at the grocery store in the checkout line, hearing a woman reveal some kind of naked truth that blows you away, leaving you standing there thinking, 'Oh my God'? Well, I know I've done that. This just doesn't happen honestly in male dialogue.

LC: Do you think women are more susceptible to revealing themselves?

FM: I just think that it doesn't happen in male dialogue. It doesn't happen as anonymously. Maybe it's just men of my generation, and I think, just from becoming friends with Sandro Nivola and men his age, that there is something different happening.

Men of my generation set up important dates to talk about things. Male friends have told me, 'I had to get really drunk before I brought up what I needed to talk about,' or 'I could barely eat after it happened' or 'We talked about it for five minutes then we spent three hours doing something else.' These conversations can take place during sporting events, where there is a certain release and a certain kind of anonymity to the confidential situation. You throw a ball, hit a ball, play racquet ball – 'I'm having a rough time at home' – and that's the extent of it. But it's not anonymous; it's not a constant part of the daily grind.

We don't see it like a male does, it's not as shocking. I mean, it is shocking, it always shocks you when somebody reveals something, but it's like watching a movie: it's sometimes a trivial, innocuous thing that happens and only later when you put it all together do you think, 'Oh, something was revealed.'

LC: What's interesting is that there have been great male film-makers who have made great character films – I mean American movies from the seventies.

FM: Yeah, you keep talking about movies from the seventies.

LC: I just really love them.

FM: Is that because those were the films you watched when you started tuning into movies?

LC: No, I really didn't tap into a desire to make movies till I was in my mid-twenties. It wasn't a 'cinefile' growing up; I was just an average film person, so I got to film school when I was, like, twenty-eight and all of a sudden I was exposed to world cinema. I took a class with Andrew Saris called 'Cinema of the Seventies' and I was exposed to all these Bob Altman, Bob Rafelson and Mike Nichols films. And the temperature of those films was just totally different. They were character films, and the male characters were investigated with a real intimacy, I thought.

FM: Do you think there was a style to the acting in those films? That was something that came up in this discussion I had with Ewan McGregor yesterday. He is doing a movie, *Down with Love*, that is kind of based on the sex comedies of the sixties, kind of farcical, but he said it was really hard for everybody to get together on a style of how to do it. Like, how do I act that sixties-sex-farce style? The actors couldn't find the technique for it. It just comes down to technical things like doing it fast or funnier or just trying to get the timing right. In a rehearsal of a play you get to work out the timing and you often have preview audiences to find out where the laugh lines are, which you can't do in a film.

LC: It's called timing and lighting.

FM: There was a little bit of that in *Laurel Canyon*. It does end up feeling like there are two styles of acting going on, because there are two styles of life that are represented. Sandro and I talked about it and we kind of represent one element of that world, even though there were a lot of other people in that world, but the other people in that world weren't actors, so we went along on their ride or they came along on ours – it's hard to tell.

LC: But when I think about it, there always were two styles in that movie, weren't there?

FM: It's like a split screen. You did it technically too: one's a lot bluer and cooler, and the other is warmer and yellowier, it's got more gold.

LC: Yeah.

FM: I think that helps to place it. And then, when it crosses over, all of a sudden Missy is in the warm golden and her head is in the cool blue . . .

LC: Well, the DP, Wally Pfister, talked about that a lot. I don't know what it's like with Joel [Coen] and his DP, but I find that the problem with TV is that you don't really get the time to prep with your cinematographer, and I find that relationship so critical . . .

FM: Major . . .

LC: I can't tell you what Wally brought to this picture . . . almost as much as I did, I think.

FM: And the operator, Mitch, as well. Wally used to be an operator for other DPs, and to have somebody like Mitch, who works only with top-drawer people, say to Wally, 'You're now a DP and I want to operate for you . . .' That was another thing: the crew were an amazing set of people, and I think the strength of the script roped them in.

LC: . . . and, I think, the strength of the strike . . .

FM: Yes, but they still have choices.

LC: They were largely people that live in LA and have families in LA, so it was no trouble to be able to stay there, but I think they appreciated an LA story that they felt had some realism to it.

FM: Something just developed that wasn't there at the beginning. The crew just showed up for a nice decent job during the strike in LA, but because we were all hanging out at that house for three weeks straight, nobody went back to their wagons, nobody went back to base camp. Everybody was hanging out by the pool – and that meant the crew too – and everybody started personally vesting themselves in characters or different parts of the story. Regardless of what they thought the whole story was gonna be – you know, from make-up and hair to props – everybody had a personal investment, and that's what I see happen on Joel and Ethan's movies. I think the movies that really work are the ones that the crew has invested in beyond a job.

LC: Maybe it's when they know the film-maker has invested something of themselves, that they're not there just for the buck but for the art.

EM: Which, you know, should go without saying, but unfortunately I don't think it always does.

LC: It would be insane for me to say that it's all charity, that I work for free, but I kind of did. But you know you guys did; I mean, why would you guys do a movie where you're making God knows how much less than a Hollywood film?

FM: You know exactly why, and that is something that would be interesting to talk about. You know why I did that movie: it answered, exactly, a need and my own personal agenda. And it was so much more beyond the superficial idea of wanting to do nudity. I mean, that was kind of the heading of my essay, which was all about being forty-five and wanting to do something I hadn't been able to do before, even when I was younger, because I wasn't offered or because I couldn't from my own insecurity or my own modesty. I wanted to show a forty-five-year-old woman strutting around, and this script offered me the opportunity.

LC: God, you must have been really happy when it came your way.

When I think about it, that's a real 'feminist' kind of take on things, because she is such an unconventional forty-five-year-old. But it was so unconscious. It goes back to that first question: I do not have an agenda and it doesn't come out of any 'This is gonna be my cause. Now I'm gonna write a forty-five-year-old character who is a free spirit.'

FM: I don't think it is really that unusual. If you looked around the set, most of the women were my age and . . .

EM: Have lived the life.

FM: . . . have lived through life without any problem.

LC: I agree with you, and also, when you look at the context of the film, it doesn't seem exceptional. I mean, it's odder that Catherine Keener is making out with Jake Gyllenhaal in your movie; it makes your situation with Alessandro seem banal in a way.

FM: We're seeing more of that kind of relationship.

LC: There's an article in the *LA Times* about older women and younger men and it actually mentions four different films. By the time my film comes out it's gonna be passé.

EM: It'll be old hat.

Chapter Two: After lunch, over cookies and coffee, overlooking the Pacific Ocean. We are going to talk about body image.

FM: When I go to England or Ireland, I feel great about my body. I don't judge it against people that are genetically different from me.

LC: Emily, what about you? You're the kind of babe who looks good in anything you put on your body.

EM: It would be a lie to say I went through life blithely unaware of my body or whether or not I should do exercise or not eat certain things or whatever, but I remember saying to someone before *Lovely and Amazing* came out that if the scene where Dermot critiques my naked body, analyzes it from top to bottom and tells me all that is wrong about it had been about something else, like if the speech had been analyzing my character . . . I mean, I have pathologies but they're not necessarily about the shape of my body; they're more about whether or not I am a good person.

FM: You see, that's what's great about that scene because, at the end of the day, that's exactly what does feel like is being said . . .

LC: That's what I loved about that scene. We live in a culture where being lean is the way to be right, so we look at you and say, 'Wow, Emily's got a beautiful body and she has nothing to worry about.' It is really interesting to see you up there having someone deconstruct your body and you feeling weird about it, but not for the conventional reasons of like, 'Oh man, I got extra fat on my stomach . . .'

EM: But what's interesting is that, when it came out, the reaction I got to it – specifically in LA – made me feel much more exposed than I did before and much more embarrassed about my body. And it is such a nonsensical thing to have got obsessed about, but I was in the gym the other day swimming, and this friend of mine came in whom I hadn't seen for ages. She had just seen the film and she shouted across the pool to me, 'Jesus, your bush is enormous.'

FM/LC: Ow! Oh my god . . .

EM: You know, 'Did you grow it specially for the film?' I mean, she was so . . .

LC: Was this in public?

EM: It was in public but, luckily, I don't think anybody else heard, and afterwards she rang up to apologize because she knew it had been a weird thing but that was the only way she could think of to react to the scene. It had really obviously affected her seeing me put myself in that position.

FM: It was an intimate gesture and now people are probably going to be a lot less proprietorial with you . . .

EM: I know, that's the thing that I was saying.

FM: . . . and it's not just the nudity, but that it was characterized by another character looking at you.

EM: Right.

FM: It's fascinating to me that to this day, no matter what else she's done, journalists still mention Julianne Moore's red pubic hair in Altman's *Short Cuts*. And that was ten or twelve years ago.

LC: Of course there was Sharon Stone's crotch shot – the whole nine yards.

FM: I mean, how often do you see men or women's pubic hair? I got quite a lot of 'You're so brave for doing this character . . . at your age blah blah blah.' But at the end of the day you don't see me naked. I don't stand . . .

EM: Naked . . .

FM: . . . and have a camera go up and down my body the way it did yours, right? I'm not even sure I could do that, even though I really want to do that . . . I think that the character would have gone out the window for me.

LC: Right.

FM: I don't know if I could have kept up the bravado in that situation.

I had no trouble being naked getting into the pool and being naked around the people that were working on the movie, but when it actually came to shooting it we didn't show my character Jane naked. We covered up the parts of my body that are suspect – you know, the dimples don't show. Wally lit it beautifully. In fact, I talked him into lighting a scene badly because I thought she should look worse than in the bathroom scene.

LC: You did! I think that's your sexiest scene.

FM: It's that whole, you know, dark like three o'clock in the morning thing, but I talked to him at lunch the day before and I said, 'Listen, I haven't seen dailies but I've watched lighting on movie sets enough to know you are making me look really good in this, but in this scene I think it's really important that she is coming to terms with herself and, almost as important, is that her younger lover has to look at her in the harsh light of the bathroom saying, "I can't do it any more, I'm not going to do it."' And Wally said, 'I have never had an actress come to me and say, "I want to look bad."' But you know, it's not about looking bad; it's about looking good bad – so bad it looks good – which is how it ended up looking.

LC: I didn't go out of my way to cover up your body or anything. I just felt like I'm not going to have you parading around like a nudist and then have Kate in her padded bra. That just wasn't going to work for me.

FM: I know that you were concerned about that, but her not completely going naked I thought was completely right for that character,

EM: Because it was such a step for her to involve herself in the first place, you felt that for her to be totally abandoned at that moment wouldn't have . . .

FM: . . . it goes against the grain.

EM: Yeah, she had to keep a bit back, you know. We all have to. When you put yourself in compromising positions, which the best of us do – as in your film – it's like a little trick you play with yourself. You think, 'Well, OK, I'll kiss this person but I won't go inside their house,' or . . .

FM: But it's also about integrity . . . your own integrity and the integrity of the character.

After seeing *Laurel Canyon* three times now, what Kate was doing very subtly with the character was . . . like, there is a door that does not open for a character like that; or the door cracks open, they see a little light come through, but they don't cross the threshold, and then it shuts again – and that's what happens for the rest of their life.

LC: You know, we were talking before about being a writer/director and how to get out of your own narrow vision of the thing and let the actor bring what they are going to bring, and the circumstances of shooting and all that stuff. That was a huge hurdle for me because I wrote that Kate's character *does* sort of strip down and go for this kind of total abandon. In the end Kate didn't want to do that, and I had to respect that. I had to re-orient myself and say, well, in terms of the trajectory of her character that makes better sense, but it was hard having to reconceptualize it.

FM: You know, for me it was a step forward in my experience of film because I did really embrace the idea of being nude or being in more revelatory sexual situations than I normally am.

LC: You were a sexual character.

FM: Sex has been part of other characters I've played, but it's not been as dramatically important as in *Laurel Canyon*. Everyone was celebrating a forty-five-year-old woman. It was the same with Nicole casting Emily, knowing that that nude scene was implicit for the dramatic progression of her character. In both of our situations it was a cinematic use of a female body.

LC: I had, as a director – and I don't know if it's as a female director or as the writer/director – a very specific response to you, directing you in the more intimate scenes . . .

FM: Which was?

LC: It brought out this part of me that was really shy, like I had overidentified with you. I was also wondering what the experience was like for Nicole, saying, I wrote this thing where you have to take off your clothes and stand there, and I'm going to point the camera at you and go up and down your body . . . You know, it's a test.

FM: Nicole also gave you Dermot Mulroney.

EM: She gave me Dermot, which made a huge difference.

FM: And I feel that way about Sandro. There was something in the casting of the people which you could play with. I couldn't have done it by myself. I could pretend a lot of it by myself, but that's basically a projection.

EM: Yes, something happens between you and somebody else; it's not just about you doing this.

LC: Well, the thing about shooting is that you're not chronological so I've got you for those four weeks at the beginning of the film, and there you are with this guy who is not a friend of yours; you've never done a film with each other before, you're bonding with him, you know how to make that happen. He's great at that, but I'm off making a movie and I've no idea how intimate you've gotten at this point. It's now a week after we've started shooting and, for all I

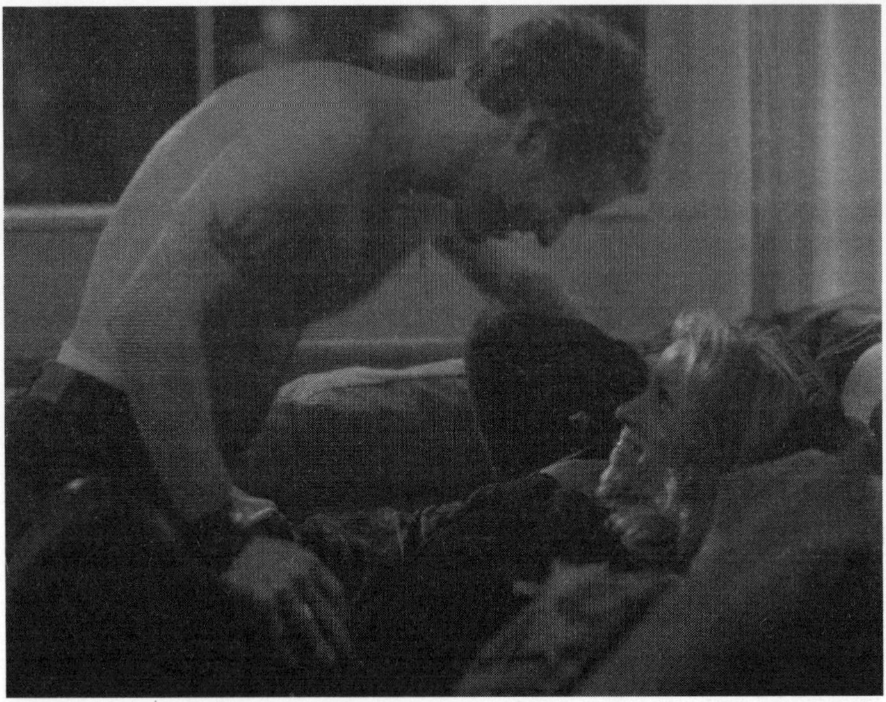

Getting intimate (photo by Neal Preston)

know, you've talked to each other, like, four times, and you're on the couch and he comes over and he spreads your legs and unbuttons your shirt and then he kisses . . . And I'm sitting there thinking, 'Oh my god, is her skin crawling, is this just totally mortifying for her?'

FM: No, it wasn't like that at all. Was it for you?

LC: I don't know, maybe a male director might sit back and say, 'Yeah, let's see some more, I want to see her breasts . . .'

FM: Maybe it was because you were more sensitive to it that it became more specific, which made it a lot easier for us so that whatever emotional element came into it came into it within those parameters – but the task was technical.

It's something you make a dramatic part of the writing. You say at this point they are doing this and then they're doing that, and it's not just randomly improvised. Often a male director will say, 'OK now, pretend to have sex,' and it's impossible to project any kind of intimacy that way. The only thing you project is a fumbling, desperate thing; you don't get any layers to it. When you go to kiss somebody that you're in a long-term relationship with, you go to one side of the nose or the other, you just go automatically, or you go to the bottom lip or the top lip. You don't move around a lot; you go in where it fits. You know your spot.

When we did the scene with the three of us, it was really important to know exactly what was going to happen so that within those limitations we could be a lot freer and more spontaneous.

LC: Oddly enough, I've done these two movies that are really sexual, yet I'm really shy and this stuff is really hard for me; I'm not at ease with it. We were up at the Château Marmont and were going to do this aborted threesome scene. It was pretty intimate and you were going to be making out with Kate Beckinsale and all kinds of other nonsense was going to be going on, so I thought it was great that you said, 'Let's go to a room and map this out.' It just made it a lot easier on everyone.

EM: What was interesting for me – and I think that's where the two films are similar – is that our nude scenes, although totally disparate in terms of why we are naked and what is happening in our trajectory through the film at that moment, are totally integral to the film and our journeys through it. It's about using our nakedness to make that moment more raw, intense and real.

FM: Right.

EM: The naked element of it helps project something which is, in both of our cases, both vulnerable and strong, through being able to stand there naked at the same time.

FM: Yeah, to get in that situation in the first place, you have to have a kind of inner strength.

EM: In both cases we are using nudity in a way that is different from things that you've seen before: there's a woman with a much younger guy who is sort of facing up to something in herself; and a girl who is obsessive about her body and facing up to her obsessions. Our nakedness in both instances just makes those moments more interesting and intense.

LC: I think so. I have a question for you guys about the translation of a screenplay to the actual film. You are given something and you are reading it and you are considering it, and it demands that you put yourself in various scenes that will compromise you or whatever . . . I mean, how do you determine whether it's worth it? What are the odds that the film is going to come out good enough that you are not going to be ashamed of having done that? It's such a crapshoot, in a way.

FM: It's not completely a crapshoot. I mean, it wasn't necessarily just what was being asked of me in *Laurel Canyon* as the character, because it was something

I was looking to do, like I said.

LC: Right, but how do you know what it's going to be like on the screen?

FM: I researched it; *High Art* was the only thing I could see, but I saw that it was clearly made by a film-maker, not by somebody who did it as a hobby. You clearly knew how to make a movie, so whether or not it was going to be completely successful as a film, you at least knew how to go about doing it, so I could trust that the foundation was going to be solid, so that whatever I came up with was going to be protected.

LC: So I guess that leads me to the question of how important it is for you guys to know the director that you are working with, or do you feel you can pretty much go on a script and trust the material? Or is it some combination of both?

EM: It's a combination.

FM: It's each thing.

EM: I loved the script of *Lovely and Amazing*; it was really clear. I don't know how much changed from your screenplay of *Laurel Canyon* to the finished movie, but very little in *Lovely and Amazing* did.

LC: With a lot of scenes, a lot of fat went out the door. And there were a few places where you put your own spin on it.

FM: Definitely, definitely, because, as you know, I was worried about the last scene when I first saw it, and I'm so glad we went back in and dubbed it . . .

LC: Yeah.

FM: . . . making the voice not quavering, so it would then complement my quavering face. And I found the same thing in *Fargo*; it was a similar technical thing. I'd worked on the accent with a great dialogue coach, and basically the work on the accent gave me the whole character. And the script . . . it wasn't something I was intrinsically interested in doing when I first read it. It was kind of like, 'Ah fuck, is this really the part you have written for me?' But then I got in there and by working on the dialect it gave me the whole character; with that accent I had to smile a lot and my face was in that upturned thing a lot to get the phonetic sounds. We got into a scene really early in the filming where she is interrogating Bill Macey's character and she gets confused and possibly angry. I couldn't remember any of my lines in the scene. I could tell that I wasn't getting it because Joel and Ethan were pacing a lot and going 'mmmmmmmm' and then finally I figured that I had no idea what to do with my face when it wasn't smiling – it just felt out of character.

LC: So what did you do?

'Ah fuck, is this really the part you have written for me?'
(photo by Michael Tackett)

FM: Well, Ethan finally just made a sentence longer so that the rhythm of the speech helped it propel itself so I didn't have to do anything, except just try to get through the line. And I felt the same way in the last scene in *Laurel Canyon* between Jane and her son. Jane was contrite, but not apologetic; she was saying it's not anybody's fault that our relationship's messed up. She was searching for the words, and I made suggestions for changing the lines because it felt like some parents' magazine . . .

LC: Yeah.

FM: . . . because you're not a parent and I am – though I've only done it for seven years. Even though Jane's not a good parent, nor even thinks of herself as a good parent . . .

EM: Though she is.

FM . . . there were phrases like, 'I'm not a good parent, I'm not a good parent' that had to be balanced by something more – I can't think of the word – more colloquial . . .

LC: Yeah, Yeah.

FM: . . . for her mouth, that's why saying, 'You're my baby, man' to Christian Bale balanced it for me, and when I looked at my face in that scene, it didn't feel right, because I was trying to get my face to look like I cared; I was trying to project vulnerability.

LC: Well, that's weird, because in directing you I wanted you to feel vulnerable.

FM: Right. You see, that's what's interesting – I still don't know if I can do that scene. I think that I could do it now more than when I was younger, but one thing that I can't do as easily as I did when I was younger is allow my vulnerability to be manipulated . . .

LC: That's interesting.

FM: . . . to be used gratuitously, because I feel that in much of my younger work I was taken advantage of and got stereotyped that way: I was the victim. I was vulnerable and, even though I always brought something else to it, that was what I was being cast for and that was the money shot when I cried or when I got beat up.

LC: I felt that way with you and it was really a head wreck for me because the work had been pretty seamless, yet here we are in this last scene and I don't know how to work through this. We are obviously at an impasse – I don't know how to make it work, and you're not giving it up, and I feel like I'm failing as a director.

FM: Somebody comes up to me and they use the word 'vulnerable' – 'I need you to be vulnerable.' So I cried in that scene and I felt vulnerable.

LC: When we finished that scene, I thought, 'Wow, this is bringing out Fran's defence zone like she ain't giving this one up easily.' And, you know, it was one of those instances when I felt shy again. It's interesting that it was your crying and emotion and nudity that made me feel shy, like I was pushing you into a territory that was uncomfortable for you. I didn't like making you feel uncomfortable; I'm not someone who works in that way.

I remember that I wanted Fran to be just a little bit more emotional in that scene. We walked away not feeling right and then worked in the editing room. Then we came back in and you did some ADR and this and that, and in the end I saw it really is appropriate to the character.

EM: It is, totally.

LC: You get a little choked up, you say something uncharacteristically sentimental, and that's where the character should go . . .

FM: Yeah, yeah.

LC: And had you been fucked up, it would have been gratuitous.

FM: She's not going to change that much.

LC: You hope that people will look at it and think it's a slight movement forward, because in a conventional Hollywood film it starts here, it goes there, and then there's the big pay-off and she rips off her shirt and has a sob-fest at the end and it's *Terms of Endearment*. And in this film we are tailoring it to the degrees to which people move in reality.

EM: It'll be interesting to see how the critics respond because although, on the whole, *Lovely and Amazing* has been very well received, I think that the one criticism supposedly intelligent critics made was that no big conclusions were reached, you know, that there hadn't been some epiphany or some moment of . . .

LC: . . . resolution. I felt the opposite.

EM: But insofar as those characters were able to resolve anything, they sort of did – or at least there was a moment, a little chink in the door, a little ray of sunlight . . .

LC: Absolutely.

EM: . . . and then probably the clouds come over again and they are chasing their tails the next week, but at least they had that redemptive moment. You know what I keep thinking about during this whole conversation about women and men in terms of film-makers? Chekhov. He's the dramatist I'm most familiar with because I studied Russian at university, and I think both these films, in their way, are kind of Chekhovian.

FM: His work has lasted because he studied behaviour.

EM: Yeah. His characters are people who are self-involved, self-obsessed, chasing their own tails, can't listen to anybody else, on their own little jag of life. Nothing ever happens in his plays and yet everything happens; you feel some sort of peace at the end which isn't to do with anything having changed from the beginning really, it's just . . .

LC: Illuminated.

EM: Yeah, a little moment of illumination, and the other thing about his characters, which I think is true of both these films, is that although they're deluded and irritating, they are intelligent and not stupid, and I think that's rare in films today.

LC: It's interesting that you say that, because I think people have said this about *High Art* and will probably say it about *Laurel Canyon*: that there is a pretentious quality to it, because I'm trafficking in people that are from a bourgeois type of culture.

EM: Cultured and well-read.

FM: What's wrong with that?

LC: That's half the people that I hang with and I understand and I'm interested in; I mean, I'm interested in all types of people, but that's what's most readily accessible to me. But I'll be called pretentious, no doubt about it.

FM: Unfortunately, so many of the connotations of 'pretentiousness' are negative but, in fact, if you expand on what they are actually saying, if your goal is to lift us out of something and your hope is to illuminate something a little bit brighter . . .

LC: Well, that's the essence of what I'm trying to do.

FM: I've done Chekhov's *Three Sisters* three times and what's fascinating to me is that at some point during every rehearsal process I've ever been through for that play we have been on the floor laughing because of the behaviour of the characters in the play – and then you get in performance and it becomes so heavy . . .

EM: But Chekhov said they were comedies, and it was Stanislavsky who tried to make them into these heavy-handed melodramas.

LC: Well, it's kind of like laughing and crying – there's a fine line. These things are so intersected – which is what I was trying to do with *Laurel Canyon*, to show that there is absurdity and ludicrousness and also tragedy in the same breath.

FM: It's a hard thing to do in cinema.

EM: Yeah, the genre-crossing thing which definitely happens in Chekhov and also happens in your movie is difficult for people to stomach in films. They get nervous.

LC: They don't know where to position themselves.

FM: But it's also a hard thing to pull off from a film-making point of view, and it's a style thing a little bit, I think.

LC: I don't know.

FM: Because it's not as if you can't do gags in behavioural comedy. But then, there are some visual gags in *Laurel Canyon*, and sometimes they work and sometimes they don't, because they're almost separate from the more interpersonal communication type of humour that's in it. But there is a lot more of this kind of humour in it than there was in *High Art*.

LC: Yeah, there is. When I see dramas now, the first thing that will register with me is that I liked it, but it was humourless. People need to laugh.

FM: They need to relax; the best way to get an audience off-guard is if you can get them to laugh, and then you can slap them so much harder, when they are not expecting it. It's a theatrical device, but it's an editing question more than it is a writing or directing one.

LC: If you can get the timing right.

FM: Yeah, one frame to either side of a moment can change something. If a casting director says to me a director is really good with actors, it's like, well, I don't care if they are good with actors – tell me if they know how to use a lens, if they know what a 250 is or if they know how they are going to edit it. More importantly, do they have a collaboration with an editor? I love to be manipulated well on a set. If something comes up – like that scene where I don't know my own defences – at the end of the day I would much rather be sure that you know what we can do with it.

LC: We can fix it in ADR.

FM: Do you think in your kind of storytelling and in Nicole's type of storytelling that that kind of collaboration with an editor is invaluable?

LC: I have only worked with one editor. I've done some TV stuff, but with all the material that I've originated I've just worked with this one person. We know each other really well, and when we are in the cutting room, I can really trust her; I can ask, 'Is that over the top?' or she'll cut something together and we'll both laugh.

FM: Could you make a movie without her?

LC: Yeah. I think I'm conscious enough of what I like and what works for me and what doesn't that I could form another relationship with a different editor, but I feel it is really comforting to have that kind of reinforcement; it's not dissimilar to working with Wally. We are just totally on the same page: what makes him laugh makes me laugh, so I trust his weird ideas because I think they are going to be good. We've looked at the same type of movies together and we've both admired them in the same way, which is similar to the way I've worked with my editor, Amy Duddleston.

FM: Joel edits all of his movies because he started as an editor, and I think when he and Ethan are writing, he's editing in his head. They've always had people assisting them because Ethan is in the editing room too, but the one time they were trying to get a movie done faster and they worked with a proper editor, they couldn't even come up with a way of talking about it because it had become such an intuitive process. Joel couldn't articulate.

LC: Yeah, it's very frustrating. You sit there and say, 'No, I want to . . . um, um . . .' You really have to work in this strange language.

FM: Did you do it on an Avid or did you do it on a Steenbeck?

LC: We did it on an Avid, only your guy does it on Steenbeck . . .

FM: They're talking about trying it.

LC: It's just simpler.

Anna Karina
interviewed by Graham Fuller

Even the most cerebral director of them all couldn't keep rhapsody out of his rigorous cinema of ideas when he turned his camera on the woman he loved. Anna Karina, born in Copenhagen on 22 September 1940, illuminated seven features directed by Jean-Luc Godard – The Little Soldier *(1960),* A Woman Is a Woman *(1961),* My Life to Live *(1962),* Band of Outsiders *(1964),* Alphaville *(1965),* Pierrot le fou *(1965) and* Made in USA *(1966) – as well as his episode, 'Anticipation', in the anthology film* The Oldest Profession *(1967). Implicitly charting the couple's 1961–7 marriage, these films vibrate with the tension between Godard's implacable intellectualism and Karina's sublimely poetic femininity. One wonders whether the very act of catching Karina's lightning on celluloid made the everyday business of sharing a life with her so much harder for Godard.*

Watching Karina do her goofy, high-kicking spin around a billiard table in My Life to Live *or insouciantly dancing the Madison with Claude Brasseur and Sami Frey in the recently released* Band of Outsiders *is to see, if not a Ginger Rogers, an innately musical actress at work. She was also capable of injecting a film with detached erotic melancholy, as in* Alphaville, *or her own brand of mercury, as in* Pierrot.

As well as Godard, Karina has been directed by, among others, Agnes Varda, Jacques Rivette, Luchino Visconti, George Cukor, Andre Delvaux, Rainer Werner Fassbinder, Raul Ruiz and, in 2002, Jonathan Demme, contributing a song of her own to his Charade *remake* The Truth about Charlie. *In 2000, she issued a CD of her throaty torch songs called* A History of Love.

Graham Fuller: What are your memories of growing up in Denmark?

Anna Karina: I grew up first with my grandparents, but my grandmother died when I was four so then I went back to my mother. I only saw my father once, when I was around four and a half or five. I don't know why my mother and my father didn't stay together. I guess I was a happy little girl in a way. I was into sports, and one day when I was running I fell and broke my right arm. After two or three months they took the cast away and my hand was bent; I couldn't move it. But everybody said, 'Don't worry. It will be fine in a few years.' I had to write with my left hand. Anyway, I started to run again and broke the same arm again. This time I went to a clinic and the nuns there said, 'What luck! Your arm mended so badly that you would have been infirm for the rest of your life, but now we can repair it properly.' And I must say they did it so well it has never hurt since.

GF: How old were you at the time?
AK: Twelve. It took about a year and a half for them to fix it and by then I had become very lazy. They told my mother I wouldn't be able to go far in school. I was upset about that so I started to work and work and work just three weeks before the Certificate Etude examination. I did better than anyone and the professors couldn't understand it. They said I must have cheated. So I went to the director and said, 'I'm leaving school because the professors told me I cheated.' He said they'd take me back if I changed my mind, but I didn't. I was fourteen and had to get a job. I was hired in a big store like Harrods as the elevator girl who says, 'First floor – shoes.' It was a nightmare because I wanted to be an actress. You couldn't go to acting school until you were twenty-one, and seven years was a long time to wait. And all these old men were trying to touch me in the elevator all the time. I hated it. So after a few weeks I stopped going in. I'd run around by the harbour in Copenhagen during the day and go home every night at the right time. Of course, the store's director wrote to my mother. The day she got the letter she said to me, 'How was work today?' I said, 'Just normal. I go up and down in the elevator with all those guys I don't like.' So she got very angry and sent me back to the store the next day. The director asked me why I didn't want to work there, and I told him I wanted to be an actress. He said I was pretentious and threw me out, so I had to look for another job. In between a man had seen me on the street and asked me if I wanted to make a test for his first movie. I said, 'Yes, but you have to ask my mother because I'm underage.' At that time, if you weren't twenty-one, you basically didn't have the right to talk. My mother said it was OK, so I made this test with many other girls, and he chose me for the lead. I did the picture [*The Girl and the Shoes*] and five years later it won a prize at Cannes.

GF: What was it about?
AK: It's about a girl who's got this amorous appointment with her boyfriend but feels her old shoes are not nice enough. So she buys a pair of high heels but they hurt her feet. Then her old shoes come dancing after her and she puts them on and throws the new shoes in the canal. A few months ago I went to a festival of some of my films in Copenhagen. The guy who played my boyfriend was there. He was so sweet and didn't want to leave. He told me he plays the trumpet now. I was very touched by the whole thing.

GF: How did you know so early you wanted to be an actress?
AK: It started when I was a very little girl. My grandfather told me I was already singing 'Lili Marlene' when I was a baby, if you can call that singing. And then I saw a lot of movies, all the American musicals.

GF: Who were your favourite stars?
AK: My favourite was Judy Garland because she could sing and dance. And I also liked Ava Gardner, Edith Piaf and Charles Trenet.

GF: How did you end up in Paris at eighteen?
AK: After making the film, I got a job working for a painter because I have a little talent for drawing. I didn't make much money, but this painter knew a lot of people and helped me get work as an extra in some bad Danish movies. I earned about a hundred kroner a day, which was more than I earned for a whole month working for the painter. So I did both, but after a while I started having problems at home because my mother left my first stepfather for his best friend, who started hitting me. I moved in with my granddad when I was sixteen. But I didn't want to wait any longer to become an actress so I went to Paris. I had one dress and one pair of shoes and a little suitcase, no money. But the priest in the church at the Champs Elysées helped me find a room close to the Bastille.

GF: How did you make a living?
AK: I'd draw on the street. You couldn't make much, but I could get a piece of bread for seven centimes. I was very skinny. I'd go by foot all over Paris. One day I came to St Germain des Prés. I thought I looked like the other people there and I felt at home in the Latin Quarter. Then this lady approached me and asked me if I wanted to make some pictures for a magazine. My grandfather had said, 'Don't talk to strange people in Paris, because you can end up in South America.' I was a bit scared but in a naive way said, 'If there are going to be a lot of people there, then maybe it's OK.' So we did the pictures, and I said, 'Can I have my money right away?' She said, 'No, you can't be paid before the pictures are published in *Le Journal France*.' But she gave me some addresses, and I went to *Elle* magazine where I did some more pictures. A lady in a smart dress and a big hat there said to me, 'I heard you say in the make-up room that you want to be an actress.' I said, 'Yes, Madame.' And she said, 'What's your name?' I told her it was Hanna Karin Blarke Bayer. She said, 'That's no good. You've got to call yourself Anna Karina.' I asked afterwards who she was, and they said, 'Oh, that's Coco Chanel.'

GF: So you started modeling full time?
AK: Yes. I said to myself, 'If I can earn 50,000 francs in six months I can stay in Paris for at least three years if I eat very little each day, and then I can learn French.' I calculated all this in my little head. And that's what I did. I didn't even take the Metro, so I could save money. But I did go to the movies because it was cheap and you could stay from noon until midnight, and that's what I did on Sundays. I saw films starring Jean Gabin and Gerard Philipe, and I began to understand that if Gabin said, '*Salut la vieille*' – 'Goodbye, old lady' – and Philipe said, '*Bonsoir, Madame*,' it meant the same thing. One was talking in

street language and the other was talking perfectly good French. Little by little, I picked up all those phrases.

GF: How did you meet Jean-Luc Godard?
AK: I did a lot of publicity for soaps and things like that. Jean-Luc saw a couple of them and asked me to come and see him because he was preparing *Breathless* [1960]. He said, 'There's a little part in the film. You have to take your clothes off.' I said, 'I don't want to.' And he said, 'In that case you don't do the film.' That was fine by me and I left. Three months later he sent me a telegram saying there might be a part for me in another film. I showed it to my friends and said, 'This guy wants to go to bed with me or something. I don't want to go there.' They said, 'You must be crazy. He just did a picture called *Breathless*. It's not out yet but everyone says it's fantastic. You absolutely must go and see him.' I went back to his office. He said he wanted me to do the part and that I should sign the contract the next day. I asked him what the picture was about and he told me it was political. I said, 'I could never do that. My French is not good enough and I know nothing about politics.' He said, 'It doesn't matter – you just have to do what I tell you to do.' And I said, 'But do I have to take my clothes off?' And he said, 'Not at all.' I told him I couldn't sign because I was underage. He said I should come back with my mother and that the production would fly her down from Copenhagen. I hadn't spoken to her in six months, but I phoned her and said, 'Mother? I'm going to star in a picture in France, and it's very important you come.' 'In a picture – you?' she said. 'Yes, and it's a political picture, Mother.' She said, 'You must be out of your mind. You have to go to a hospital to see if you're OK.' And I said, 'No, Mother, you have to take the plane tomorrow because if you don't come they might change their mind!' She hung up because she didn't believe it. I phoned back and swore on my granddad's head it was for real – she knew he was the person I loved the most. So she took the plane and we signed the contract. That's how I got into *The Little Soldier*.

GF: How did you and Jean-Luc get together?
AK: That happened while we were shooting the picture in Geneva. It was a strange love story from the beginning. I could see Jean-Luc was looking at me all the time, and I was looking at him too, all day long. We were like animals. One night we were at this dinner in Lausanne. My boyfriend, who was a painter, was there too. And suddenly I felt something under the table – it was Jean-Luc's hand. He gave me a piece of paper and then left to drive back to Geneva. I went into another room to see what he'd written. It said, 'I love you. Rendezvous at midnight at the Café de la Prez.' And then my boyfriend came into the room and demanded to see the piece of paper, and he took my arm and grabbed it and read it. He said, 'You're not going.' And I said, 'I am.' And he said, 'But you can't do this to me.' I said, 'But I'm in love too, so I'm going.' But he still didn't believe

The Little Soldier: 'Mother, I'm going to star in a picture in France.'

me. We drove back to Geneva and I started to pack my tiny suitcase. He said, 'Tell me you're not going.' And I said, 'I've been in love with him since I saw him for the second time. And I can't do anything about it.' It was like something electric. I walked there, and I remember my painter was running after me crying. I was, like, hypnotized – it never happened again to me in my life.

So I get to the Café de la Prez, and Jean-Luc was sitting there reading a paper, but I don't think he was really reading it. I just stood there in front of him for what seemed like an hour but I guess was not more than thirty seconds. Suddenly he stopped reading and said, 'Here you are. Shall we go?' So we went to his hotel. The next morning when I woke up he wasn't there. I got very worried. I took a shower, and then he came back about an hour later with the dress I wore in the film – the white dress with the flowers. And it was my size, perfect. It was like my wedding dress.

We carried on shooting the film and, of course, my painter left. When the picture was finished, I went back to Paris with Jean-Luc, Michel Subor, who was the lead actor, and Laszlo Szabo, who was also in the film, in Jean-Luc's American car. We were all wearing dark glasses and we got stopped at the border – I guess they thought we were gangsters. When we arrived in Paris, Jean-Luc dropped the other two off and said to me, 'Where are you going?' I said, 'I have nowhere to go any more. I have to stay with you. You're the only person I have in the world now.' And he said, 'Oh my God.' We took two rooms at the top of a hotel and he went to the cutting room every day. Some days I wouldn't see him at all. But I guess at that time he had his own life. He was ten years older than me – he still is, I can assure you [*laughs*]. One day he came in during the afternoon. I was sitting waiting in the hall; I had no money to go out. And he said, 'You have to look for an apartment for us.' And I found one behind La Madeleine, the first of many we had.

GF: Were you anxious to make another movie as soon as possible?
AK: Well, *The Little Soldier* was banned for a long time because it was about the French war in Algeria. But there were private screenings and the director Michel Deville came to one of them. He later phoned Jean-Luc and said he wanted me to play the lead in his first film, *Tonight or Never*. I went to see him and he hired me. It was a comedy so I was happy. And Jean-Luc said to me, 'How are you gonna say all those funny words? You could never do that.' I said, 'Yes I can.' And every day he would take me to the studio where I was filming and he'd say he didn't like this, didn't like that – he was jealous, I guess. But when he saw me singing and dancing in *Tonight or Never*, he asked me if I wanted to be in his next film, *A Woman Is a Woman*. He said, 'You'll have to sing and dance with Jean-Paul Belmondo and Jean-Claude Brialy.' I loved that, of course, so I did it, and I got the first prize at the Berlin festival. I was the youngest actress to win it. Everybody was talking about me, and my mother was very proud. After that I did some more films, then Jacques Rivette asked me to do *La Religieuse* on stage.

GF: Was the play as controversial as the movie version you made with Rivette?
AK: Oh, no. Everybody cried, they all loved it – even Brigitte Bardot, who came to it with Sami Frey. Nobody screamed about it like they did when we made the movie.

GF: Were you happiest being directed by Jean-Luc?
AK: I guess so. We had fun, but he was tough. Sometimes he would tell us, 'You cannot even read the first page of the most stupid magazine in the world without going wrong' [*laughs*]. It was much easier to work with other directors after you'd worked with Jean-Luc, because at that time they would just do a master shot, like in American films, then go into a close-up. Jean-Luc would do a lot of long shots that would sometimes run three to five minutes. Also he'd write the dialogue at the very last moment. Sometimes we would get it five minutes before shooting and there'd be a lot of things to say, but we'd always get a chance to rehearse.

GF: Were you aware that he was reinventing cinema?
AK: We knew we were doing something special. We'd take the films around

Top: *A Woman is a Woman* – with Belmondo
Bottom: With Godard – 'You're the only person I have in the world now.'

Paris and out to the provinces and talk to the audiences after the screenings. And some people loved them and some people hated them. One day Jean-Luc and I were sitting in a café in Boulevard St Michel and we heard these two students talking about *My Life to Live*. One was screaming, 'I love this picture!' and the other one, who had his back to us, was saying, 'I hate spending my money on this kind of shit.' And Jean-Luc tapped him on the back, gave him ten francs and said, 'OK, you didn't like my picture. Why don't you go and see a picture you really like?' The guy was very red-faced and apologetic.

GF: I'm sure he's still dining out on that story. Tell me about your hair in that film.
AK: We'd done *The Little Soldier* and *A Woman Is a Woman*, and I said to Jean-Luc, 'I want to look very different next time.' And he said, 'Yes, I would like that too.' So we went to see a hairdresser, and little by little Jean-Luc decided we would cut my long black hair shorter and shorter to get this Louise Brooks style.

GF: Do you remember doing the dance in the billiard hall?
AK: I improvised it. Jean-Luc said, 'Do what you want.' Michel Legrand [the film's composer] decided he would call that dance 'Swim'. Maybe it's because it looks like I'm swimming.

GF: Were you ever going to play the role Brigitte Bardot played in *Contempt*?
AK: No. Jean-Luc really wanted to do that picture with Brigitte. I think it's one of his best movies – it might even be the best one he ever did.

GF: Is it true some of the lines in *Contempt* came from your relationship?
AK: Well, when I was little my granddad loved to make me say bad words, and I'd always said, 'No, Granddad, I don't want to say all these terrible things!' And he'd say, 'Yes, just say, "I hate you, Granddad. Fuck you!"' He'd torture me about it, but he really loved me the most in the world – it was a big love story between my grandfather and me. But later I would say things like 'fuck', 'shit' and 'asshole' in front of Jean-Luc just for fun, and he'd say, 'Don't talk like that!' And then he made Brigitte say them in the film. And when she says, 'I only want red curtains. If not, I don't want any curtains' – well, I'd said that when we moved into the apartment. We all do that anyway – I wrote three novels and sometimes I'd put things into them that I'd heard on the street.

GF: But it's a bit different when you're married, isn't it? Didn't it bother you that Jean-Luc was reflecting on your marriage in his films?
AK: Not very much has to do with our private life, only the dialogue once in a while. I mean, come on – I haven't been a prostitute, as I was in *My Life to Live*. I haven't killed people like I do in *Pierrot le fou*. I have never been a stripper like in *A Woman Is a Woman*. I've never been that kind of naïve person like in *Band of Outsiders*. But, of course, when you are married you discuss things like that.

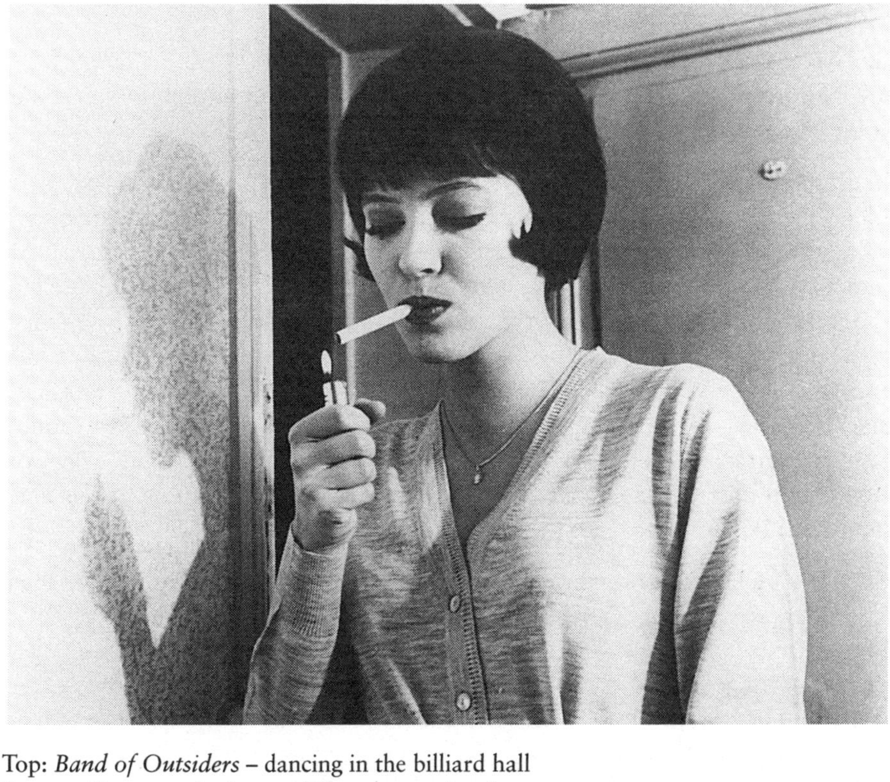

Top: *Band of Outsiders* – dancing in the billiard hall
Bottom: 'I want to look very different next time.'

Top: Godard shooting . . .
Bottom: . . . Anna Karina in *Pierrot le fou*, with Belmondo

GF: What was it like hanging out with the New Wave crowd?
AK: Very exciting, but I didn't talk that much – I listened. I was the little one because they were much older than me and much more intelligent. Jean-Luc taught me everything. He made me read and he gave me culture, but on the other hand he was not very easy to live with. Sometimes he would say, 'I'm going to buy some cigarettes,' and he'd come back three weeks later.

GF: Do you think his films became too political in the late sixties?
AK: In a way, I would rather he had told stories. Once he started working with [screenwriter] Jean-Pierre Gorin, I thought, 'It's not his cup of tea really.' I think his films were more political when he didn't talk about politics in them. That's just my point of view.

GF: Some critics have said his films lack emotion, but there is tremendous love in the way he filmed you. Do you agree?
AK: Yes, very much. It was a great love story. I guess it shows on the screen. I mean, for me it does. But most people don't know about my life. It's only now that I'm getting older that I've really started talking about it.

GF: Which is the favourite of your films together?
AK: They're all so different. It's like having children – sometimes one is a little more touching or more crazy, but you can't choose between them. The young people I meet at film festivals tell me their favourites are *My Life to Live* or *A Woman Is a Woman*, but mostly *Pierrot le fou*. In England and Brazil they love *Alphaville*, and in Germany they prefer *A Woman Is a Woman*.

GF: When do you think you became a good actress?
AK: When I was around five because kids aren't scared.

GF: Were you less confident later on?
AK: I am always a bit nervous before shooting but not once I am into it. The same when I go on stage with my little sextet.

GF: Are you going to record another record?
AK: Yes, Philippe Katerine and I are writing the songs. We talk a lot together, and we're very close, as we are with all the musicians. We've never had any problems. Everybody loves everyone.

GF: Do you play an instrument?
AK: I used to play piano a bit, but I've forgotten. I'm going to try to learn the guitar. In the show, I dance a little bit, as well as sing.

GF: Do you want to do more films?
AK: I guess. If I have a small part, if it's interesting, I want to do it. If not, I can write another book or I'll try to do a musical comedy.

GF: We've talked a lot about the past, but do you think you're somebody who lives in the present?

AK: What else can you do? If you sit down and cry because of the past, you go nowhere. Sometimes journalists ask me, 'Aren't you tired of talking about all this?' But I'm not. It's good to know you did something that still moves people. How could I sit there and say, 'No, I don't care'? I'm really honoured. It's too much!

(Part of this interview was published in *Interview* magazine in October 2001.)

Graham Fuller is the editor of *Potter on Potter*, *Loach on Loach* and the forthcoming *Mike Leigh on Mike Leigh*.

On Writing *Tadpole*
Heather McGowan interviewed by Tod Lippy

Tod Lippy: Weren't you a production assistant on Hal Hartley's *Trust*?
Heather McGowan: Yeah, I was.

TL: How did that come about?
HM: Well, I'd always been interested in films, and I was curious about how they were made. I had just lost my job for a photographer – it was really bad economically in 1989, 1990 – and I ran around pestering about a hundred production companies before I ended up there.

TL: How was it?
HM: Absolutely gruelling. We were shooting in Long Island, in two brand-new houses in this suburb; the production office was based in one and we shot in the other. There were four PAs and we all slept in these empty houses. There was no furniture, nothing but equipment. We had sleeping bags. I grabbed a walk-in closet; the other three slept in rooms surrounded by camera gear. It was pretty much nineteen-hour days because, after the rest of the crew had gone home to their hotels, you would still be cleaning and getting ready for the next day. We were also security, making sure no one stole the cameras, which was ridiculous because all four of us were kind of undernourished punky kids. I think we secretly hoped the camera would get stolen if it meant we'd get a day off. It was back-breaking.

TL: I assume that was the last PA job you had.
HM: Yep. The first and last. And then I was a camera assistant for a little bit.

TL: What did you work on?
HM: *Pushing Hands*, Ang Lee's first film. And also commercials and music videos, and some shorts. I worked for a documentary director for a while. We did films for the BBC and Channel Four, one in Kosovo at the very beginning of the war, on Albanian blood feuds.

TL: Did you shoot anything?
HM: Once: I shot the women in a Muslim family. That's a strange sentence. I wasn't really interested in shooting; I was only interested in hanging around the camera. I thought, 'If I'm camera assistant, and I have the slate, they can't throw me off set.'

Heather McGowan (photo by Tami Reiker)

TL: When did you begin writing?
HM: After about three years in film. I was disenchanted with New York. It was expensive to live there – I was working all the time just to afford it – and I just wanted to do something of my own. It was time to start making something. So I moved to San Francisco, worked on rap videos – kind of Oakland gangsta stuff – and started writing. Then I went to graduate school. I started *Schooling* there, and then did the Fine Arts Work Center in Provincetown fellowship, went to Yaddo and MacDowell, stayed with my brother or my parents, made money writing book reviews and doing the odd camera job. I think I lived for about three years without paying any rent.

TL: I read that the writing process for *Schooling* took six years.
HM: Five years, really.

TL: Was that a constant process or were you writing other things concurrently?
HM: Well, I wrote a play. When I was getting my master's at Brown, I was also taking the graduate classes in playwriting with Paula Vogel. So I wrote a play in her class while I was there. She was an incredible teacher, everything you hope for in a professor and mentor.

TL: This was *The Return of Smith*?
HM: Yeah. But mostly I was just working on the book. I threw out so many pages. The book is about three and change – 320? – but I wrote all the time, so there are probably another three or four hundred pages in the garbage. People think if your book took five years you weren't working on it all the time, but I was, I swear!

TL: There are several 'play-like' chapters in the finished novel.
HM: I've always been interested in dialogue. The novel started off having much more dialogue than there is now. I had always wanted to write a screenplay. I called a friend of mine from Brown and said, 'Let's write a script together.' So we did our first script, called *Go See Rome*. Good Machine optioned that, and they actually sold it to Universal, where it languished . . .

TL: Turnaround?
HM: Yeah. We realized immediately it was never going to have a life, because it was kind of a throwback, an updated *Roman Holiday*. But a friend of mine knew Gary Winick was looking for a script, and suggested me. Gary read *Go See Rome* and he knew that a friend of his, Niels Mueller, and I both needed money. So he decided to pay us each to write a draft.

TL: So you each went off and wrote first drafts of *Tadpole*?
HM: No, the three of us got together at Gary's father's house, and we outlined the story and the scenes. One night we were playing Pictionary and Niels and Gary got the clue 'tadpole'. They won, and Niels jumped up and started singing this funny victory song, which became our theme song during writing. So there was only ever one title for the movie.

TL: Whose story idea was it?
HM: I think it was everybody's. We were sitting around wondering, 'What's the easiest story we can write?' You know, one that wouldn't involve any research and that took place in New York. So I wrote the first draft, and then Niels wrote the second – which wasn't so much rewriting what I wrote, but cutting and then adding.

TL: The script I read, which is your first draft, seems quite close to the finished film, which is pretty unusual for a first draft that another writer has worked on before shooting.
HM: It is pretty close.

TL: How long did you have to write it?
HM: I was given two months, but I did it in nine days.

TL: Wow.
HM: Because I was working two other jobs. Between the time one ended and the next started I only had three and a half weeks. And I procrastinated until the last possible moment, so then I had ten days. We had a pretty clear outline.

TL: So it was more like filling in that outline than writing from scratch?
HM: Exactly.

TL: Did you write a rough draft and then go back and edit afterwards?
HM: No. I wrote it and I handed it in. I actually went to my parents' house in Ann Arbor, because I knew that I wouldn't have to do things like go get food or toothpaste. They were so great. My father plied me with tea, and I would crank out nine or ten pages a day. I wore headphones – Gary had made me all of these tapes to listen to . . .

TL: What kind of music?
HM: Early Stones, Simon and Garfunkel, Van Morrison – music he grew up with. Seventies stuff. When you're writing a first draft there's so much freedom. I never tell people that it took me nine days to write the script, because it's really irritating, you know? I guess I'm outing myself here. But that seems to be the only way I can work – get it out really fast, at least the first draft. It's like a free-form spew. I think that most screenwriters would tell you that the dialogue is the easy part. It's the structure, how to make it work and function as a story that's really difficult and time-consuming.

TL: It's probably a tired question, but can you talk about the differences between writing for film and writing for the page? Is it a situation where, with novel-writing, you're spending much more time getting a particular sentence absolutely perfect, whereas with screenwriting that's less important?
HM: No, it's just a different kind of perfection. Sentences have to be perfect in scripts too, because time is so precious. Film narrative is so compact, every word counts so much in a script. That's why nobody except Woody Allen ever says 'um'. There just isn't time. Character, plot, subtext, relationship in every single word . . .

TL: That reminds me of something in your *Tadpole* first draft, where one of the parenthetical directions for Diane reads: '(*so?*)'. Screenwriters would commonly use an adjective – '(*lackadaisical*)', or . . .

Tadpole: 'I think it's really good to feel uncomfortable when you're watching a movie' Aaron Stanford and Sigourney Weaver)

HM: . . . '(*confused*)'. Right.

TL: It's not only economical; it's very playful, and it makes the script much more fun to read.

HM: I noticed in a script that I was doing some work on that the original writer had given hardly any parenthetical descriptions, which I liked. It shows you trust the reader to get it. I tend to be way too directorial, shove in a lot of parentheses. When I first saw *Tadpole* I was so surprised because I had imagined that the dialogue would be rapid-fire and overlapping, but the finished film seemed so slow. Now I think I'm trying to direct from the parentheses.

TL: I was wondering about a few discrepancies between your draft and the finished film. In your script, Oscar walks around the entire time with his schoolmate's scarf, which is a nice textural detail, but in the film it becomes Eve's scarf and takes on an almost fetishistic role . . .

HM: That was a Niels addition.

TL: I guess it was meant to provide a better excuse or motivation for Oscar's dalliance with Diane . . .

HM: Yeah, that's exactly what it was. But I didn't use the scarf as a plot point. For me, it was more about character. I think Gary felt he really needed a device to lead Oscar into sleeping with Diane. He was very happy to have found that.

One thing that's very different about the script is that I wanted it to be a little darker and sicker than Gary opted for. I wanted more *Murmur of the Heart* terrain, which I don't think American film-makers, unfortunately, tend to delve into. American indie films sometimes seem like less expensive versions of Hollywood movies. They really aren't riskier, and they aren't doing something incredibly different or difficult – at least the ones that get funding don't. In my version, I had Oscar and Eve rolling around on the floor after the kiss. You know, let's make this a little sick and uncomfortable. I think it's really good to feel uncomfortable when you're watching a movie. I think when you're confused and unsettled, you think about a film more.

TL: Have you seen anything recently that affected you in that way?
HM: I liked *Roger Dodger* a lot – it's so well written. Jem Cohen's *Benjamin Smoke* is tremendous. The Dardenne brothers' *The Son* I liked a lot, but it's not as good as *La Promesse* . . .

TL: One could argue that while all three of their narrative films – *La Promesse, Rosetta* and *The Son* – are brilliant, each successive film seems to have a little less punch . . .
HM: Exactly. *La Promesse* is incredible. Here's the thing about the Dardennes: I'm finding more and more that I like films where the script isn't that . . . *interesting* on its own. The truth comes from what the director does with actors and silence. I guess I'm putting myself out of a job. I mean, the truth is that I don't want to watch the movies I write.

TL: Really?
HM: Yeah. If I went and saw *Tadpole*, I wouldn't think it was a great movie. I would think, 'Oh, that's kind of fun. My parents would like that movie.' Or, 'Good plane movie.' You know? I think I like to leave a movie theatre agitated or a little uncomfortable or confused.

TL: Would you want to see *Schooling* as a movie?
HM: This is what I was asked at a panel at the 92nd Street Y that I was on recently. And my response was, 'If I'm doing my job right, my book can't be made into a film.' I want to write books that aren't so much plot-driven, but more concerned with style and language. So, no. But it's also because I wouldn't want that central relationship between Catrine and her teacher, one which I hope is subtle, made into a crass or predictable sexy-schoolgirl movie.

TL: Can you imagine yourself writing a movie that would give you the same emotional or creative engagement as producing a novel?
HM: Sometimes, but I think the lack of control would drive me insane. And I've seen friends go through the process of trying to raise money to make their films,

nearly raising it, then having it taken away, and having that happen over and over again. It's a tenable form of censorship in this country.

TL: But for now, you don't feel like any scripts you've written have approached that level?
HM: I can't imagine anything could give me the same emotional and creative engagement as writing fiction, but I did write a pretty twisted movie with a friend of mine, a nasty comedy. It's the script I've liked best because it has nothing to do with appealing to an audience. I was told it would never get made. Too dark. After that, well . . . I write fiction without thinking of who it will appeal to. I'm trying to find worth in writing something people will have access to, and that's where screenplays come in.

TL: Would you say that you're writing screenplays for the money at this point?
HM: Wow, that sounds crass, but yeah, I guess it's more job than vocation. At least for now. I fantasize about collaborating with a director I admire, to make something outside the mainstream. But most directors I admire don't need me.

TL: Have there been any attempts to option *Schooling*?
HM: I just told my agent, 'Say no to everything, and don't even tell me.'

TL: What if someone like Cohen or the Dardenne brothers approached you?
HM: Well, yeah, I would definitely talk to them. Actually, after I saw *Morvern Callar* – the book I loved, but when I first saw the film, I was upset, because the ending was very different. After the screening, though, I ended up speaking to Lynne Ramsey, and she was so incredibly intelligent and precise about the choices she had made. And then I went and saw *Ratcatcher*, which I loved.

TL: Hers would be a great sensibility for *Schooling*.
HM: Yeah, of course, if someone like that were interested in doing it, I'd be interested.

TL: What screenplay are you working on right now?
HM: The script is called *Ratbastard*. After *Tadpole* did well at Sundance, suddenly everyone was very interested in Gary, so he called me and said, 'Do you want to do another project together?' And initially I said, 'No,' but then I thought it could be fun if I could collaborate with someone. So I brought in my friend from the *Go See Rome* project. We came up with a story about this kind of working-class British 'rat bastard' who goes to find his partner who left him. And she's tried to go straight – she's working as a cook for this Park Avenue family – and he manages to infiltrate the family as a nanny, and high jinks ensue. I said to a friend, 'It'll be this provocative examination of class in America . . .' and he was like, 'For Disney? Oh, honey, you're going to get hurt.' We actually just handed in the polish.

TL: Do you have any sense of what's going to happen?
HM: No sense. A friend of mine read it and said it's clearly not a studio movie because they can't imagine the poster. I get it – I mean, the kids are smoking and swearing and playing poker. There are a lot of concerned mothers in Hollywood. You know, that stupid comment a while ago about the Jewish Mafia? Or was it the Gay Mafia? Well, I was talking to these executives about doing a project which involved a woman who doesn't want to have a child, and these women said, 'We don't understand that woman. Our families are everything to us.' I thought, 'Oh my god, it's the Momfia.'

TL: [Laughs] That's good.
HM: I'm never going to work in Hollywood again after this comes out [*laughs*].

TL: It's an interesting point, though. There is something markedly 'soccer mom-ish' about a certain kind of Hollywood product now – very safe, kind of skin-deep liberal and completely devoid of any edge.
HM: Yeah, there's no edge. Think about a movie like *Paper Moon* . . .

TL: That wouldn't stand a chance of being made now.
HM: Never. It will be interesting to see what happens, whether it ever gets made.

TL: Do you find dealing with the whole film industry apparatus different from dealing with the publishing world? Do you have different agents or managers for each?
HM: Completely different. I'm actually in the middle of changing my movie agent. I guess one of the major differences is that, with publishing, I don't talk to my agent regularly.

TL: Except to say, 'Book's done – here's the manuscript'?
HM: Exactly. And for movie stuff, it's an ongoing thing of trying to get work and trying to decide the best way to go: Will we set something up? Should I write a spec?

TL: What about the whole publicity angle? Is that similar for both?
HM: I think a movie is seen as the director's vision, not the writer's, so there isn't that much interest in interviewing the screenwriter. But when my book came out and it was time to publicize it, I was really paralysed. I had been in this little hole for five years, and I did not want to come out and talk to people and have to tell them what my book was about and all of that. And I also wanted it to exist in a vacuum: No picture on the book. Don't want to talk about what writers I read. Don't want comparisons. Don't want to talk about my childhood or my parents. My writer friends all gave me the same advice: 'This is how you handle an interview: prepare your answers and no matter what they ask, just give them the

answers you prepared.' I thought, 'I can't do that phoney thing.' I had no idea how difficult I would find it. I wanted the book to succeed and to do that you have to do publicity; it's that simple. One interview was just a description of me trying to avoid this guy's questions. But my experience in England was completely different: you could tell the interviewers had read the book and they wanted to get into it with you about Nabokov or Joyce – they didn't care what my father had done for a living or where I went to school.

As for the apparatus, I think the trick to writing scripts is to feel committed enough to care and detached enough to step aside for the A-lister breathing down your back. I did some rewriting for the project Gary's shooting right now, and the producers would call me up and say, 'We need this and this; we're shooting tomorrow.' And I'd say, 'OK, well what about this line?' 'No, not funny.' 'Hmm, well what about this?' 'Better. Can it be funnier?' It's so strange to be a little computer that spits out ideas on command. You can't be offended that so much you come up with is quickly rejected.

TL: There's a line in your script that didn't end up in the film where Eve, speaking of living alone, says, 'It's nice to wake up in your mood instead of another person's.' Writing novels really seems to be about living, in a creative sense, in your own mood, as opposed to this collaborative process you're talking about with regard to film-making.

HM: Well, it depends. I've been fortunate. I've only worked with Gary, and his ideas about story and structure and how a film works are solid. When he says, 'We have to get rid of this scene,' I immediately get defensive: 'Are you kidding? My God, the writing in that scene – you're killing me.' As soon as I finish saying that I realize he's absolutely right and the scene has to go. I love cutting, because if you can do it then it has to be done, and immediately it feels better and leaner. The thing about cutting is that up until that moment, you thought that every scene was crucial, and then to suddenly discover it's not, that the information or emotion you need is already there – there's something really exciting about that.

The other great thing about Gary is that if I really fight for something, he'll let me have it, even if we both know he's going to cut it in the edit room [*laughs*]. For example, what I really love – and this kind of relates to the scarf thing – are the extraneous things that don't do any expository work. In *Ratbastard*, the woman comes home from a date, and the rat bastard is in the kitchen, listening to her say goodbye to her date. So I've thrown them in the middle of an anecdote that has no application to anything else in the script. It makes me laugh because it's the second half of an anecdote, but you have no idea what the first half of the anecdote could possibly be. And then you can imagine the life that these two people have that's beyond what you know of them in the film. Gary keeps saying, 'Shouldn't this relate to something?' Anyway, he let me keep it, but he'll cut it in the editing room.

TL: When you're writing a script on assignment, you must be pretty aware of your audience – both the people you're writing for and, in a larger sense, the audience who will eventually see it in a theatre. Are you second-guessing yourself more than when you're writing a novel?
HM: Absolutely. I never think about an audience when I'm writing fiction. And it would be too difficult to pull myself out of the novel and try to see it objectively. That's what's great about screenwriting. For example, in *Ratbastard* I began with the guy getting off the plane carrying a guitar. And Gary said, 'You know, if we see a guitar in the first scene, people are going to think he needs to end up fulfilling his ambition as a musician.' It wasn't just the whole 'gun on the wall' thing, either. It was that by putting that detail in the first scene, I was establishing something important. I wouldn't have thought of that.

The people Gary and I worked with at Disney – the two executives – gave excellent notes. They know that sometimes it's more a matter of asking the right questions and letting the writer solve the problem.

TL: So you don't mind it, as long as the notes are relevant?
HM: No, no. God, I'm hungry for it. When I'm writing fiction I have no one I can call and say, 'Why isn't this working?' It's just you in the tunnel.

TL: But if you got those kind of suggestions about your novel . . .?
HM: Oh, I do, but I'm allowed to ignore them. You're the director of your own book.

The other thing is – and this relates to your earlier question – I pretty much always felt that the books I was going to write weren't going to have an enormous audience, and that's OK, because I tend not to gravitate towards those books myself. In fact, my friend and I used to joke about this – the way to be a good megalomaniac is try to get subversive ideas on to the big screen.

TL: What are some of those ideas of yours?
HM: Well, let's face it, the truly subversive ones aren't going to make it – even the slightest tackling of class and wealth didn't survive in *Ratbastard* – but I'd love to write a movie about work. I'd also like to get better women characters on screen. Right now, the women we see on screen, if they're smart, they never smile – that's how we know they're smart, apart from their glasses. You either have a sense of humour and you're warm, or you're cold and smart. Approachable women have careers at fashion magazines. Cold women are lawyers. Warm women are photographers – that's an allowable career in Hollywood. A woman can be a photographer.

TL: The two lead characters in *Tadpole* survived their transition to screen.
HM: But Gary made that movie at InDigEnt. I don't know if *Tadpole* would have survived Hollywood.

TL: You talked in some of those *Schooling* interviews about wanting to convey the sense of 'shifting ground' one experiences as an adolescent in your novel. The way you did that so viscerally with language reminded me of how Olivier Assayas does it visually in *Cold Water.* That film, like so much of French cinema, manages to convey that inner turmoil in a really resonant way.
HM: Did you see *The Dreamlife of Angels*?

TL: I did. I loved it.
HM: I did too. There's a really nice moment in it that he does with silence. It's when the girl who eventually kills herself – the blonde – has just gone back to the rich but sadistic guy. She's sitting in bed, and they've just had sex, and he's asleep, lying on his stomach. She's smoking a cigarette and looking down at this man's incredibly beautiful body. And you just get the horror of how tyrannical beauty can be. How she's going to have to jump out that window because this guy is going to slowly kill her [*laughs*]. That's such a great movie. But you hardly ever see that – women objectifying men. Although it's not really objectifying; it's more about how beauty just enters you on a different level and how you can suffer from it. The other great thing about that movie is Elodie Bouchez's character at the factory at the end, again, slowly being killed. The French are good at the slow deaths. That and work. The Dardennes have a similar moment in *Rosetta* when she hands over her first waffle with a big smile. She fought for that job, it's the first time we see her smile, and it's brutal.

TL: Are you working on a new book now?
HM: Yeah, in fact, it's kind of a slow-death novel. I've been working on it for a while and going back and forth from fiction to scripts. I might do something else with Gary, or maybe a spec. I think it could be pretty freeing to do that. Just kind of see where you end up.

TL: Would you be more inclined if you're writing on spec to do something more along the lines of *Schooling*?
HM: No, something a bit more conventional. I think the challenge would be how much I could write something I like, something a bit serious or with a bit of an edge that would also possibly get made. But sometimes the whole pursuit seems so frustrating; you hear about a lot of movies that began edgy and ended up pabulum, and you know it's going to happen to you. When I was out in LA recently I was talking to a producer about a script. She kept going back to this one idea and said, 'But I really love this idea. I don't know why . . . maybe because I've seen it before.' It's like McDonald's, same thing every time, no scary ingredients.

TL: The industry is run for the most part now by huge corporations whose focus tends to be mostly on the bottom line. And certain formulas tend to have proven success.

HM: But it's not just the formula; it's almost down to the exact scene and lines of dialogue. And sometimes the films that are strange do really well. They can't predict that; they don't have that on their charts.

TL: I think they're probably viewed as flukes, as lucky breaks. It doesn't mean you want to throw a lot of money into something so risky. I'm reminded of something David O. Russell said about the inept studio marketing of *Three Kings* –

HM: I read that interview with him [in *Projections 11*]. I'm a huge fan of *Spanking the Monkey*, which really *is* an agitating independent film. I thought about it when we were talking about *Tadpole*. Then I saw *Flirting with Disaster*, which I didn't like as much.

TL: What about *Three Kings*?

HM: I had mixed feelings. I was really happy that somebody was going to make a film about the Gulf War, and David Russell's an interesting film-maker, so I'll always go see what he makes. I had pleasant feelings towards him as a film-maker until I read that interview with him. He was talking about the test groups that they did for *Three Kings*, and he said, 'Well, it actually tested really well with women. I don't know why, maybe because of George Clooney.' That was annoying. I thought, 'God forbid you might think that women liked it because it was political, or complex, or because they're smarter than men' [*laughs*]. It's kind of depressing to see a good film-maker think that way.

TL: So far, it seems that your film work has fallen kind of loosely into the comedy genre; will this spec be a comedy too?

HM: Yeah, well, a serious humorous film. I guess my ambition would be to write a comedy in the way *The Graduate* is a comedy. I mean, the ending to *The Graduate* is so unsettling. People see that movie again and again because that character, Ben, is real and complicated, and what he's going through is real and strange *and* funny. But when he finally gets what he wants, it's not a happy ending.

Unresolved endings can be really satisfying. Most Hollywood movies wrap it in a bow. You dust the popcorn off your hands and leave smiling – it's all finished, the work's been done for you. But what happens is, people don't give it a second thought, and they don't want to go back and see it again.

Heather McGowan is the author of *Schooling*. Tod Lippy is the editor of *Projections 11*.

Rebecca Miller (photo by Erin Wyle)

Making *Personal Velocity*: A diary by Rebecca Miller

Introduction

In 1999, having spent the three years following the release of my first film trying to raise money for the next, and having had two financed films collapse for various reasons (actors pulling out, crooked producers), I reached a point where I could no longer stand asking permission to tell my stories. As all I did all day was write screenplays which weren't being produced, I thought perhaps I should try to write prose. At least then all my efforts would not be in vain. A short story need not be published to be a short story. An unproduced script, however, is basically very low-quality toilet paper.

So, for the next two years, I wrote short stories. Then I got a phone call from my old friend Gary Winick. Gary had formed a company, InDigEnt, and was producing a series of low-budget features shot on mini-digital video. He asked me if I would like to direct one of my scripts. None of the scripts I had ready were right for the super-tight schedule or for the video format. And I wasn't about to write a screenplay just in case he might like it.

So, I sent him two of the short stories in my collection – 'Greta' and 'Delia'. He loved them and had the idea of making a trilogy. I wrote the last story in my collection, 'Paula', knowing that it might be the third part of the film. Gary and the other people at the Independent Film Channel – who were financing his venture – green-lit my film only about a month after I found a publisher for the stories. So I had the strange, but exhilarating, experience of having shot the film of my book before it was published.

Here is a synopsis of the three stories:

'Delia': Delia used to be the school slut. Now she is a thirty-four-year-old woman with three children, in love with a husband who beats her. One day she escapes. We follow her on a journey back to the original source of her power: her sexuality.

'Greta': Greta is a cookbook editor who is inexplicably summoned to lunch by the most talented writer of her generation. The dream editing job which ensues unearths her stifled ambition and ultimately propels her out of a loving, but slightly unreal marriage.

'Paula': Paula is twenty, about to have an abortion, when one night she switches places with a man she barely knows; seconds later, he is run over by a car. She flees the scene and drives Upstate in a state of shock, searching for signs of some meaning to this apparently random series of events. An act of charity to a young hitchhiker breaks down the walls of apathy she has built around herself.

26 January 2001

I am worried about condensing the script to fit into what Lemore (Syvan, my producer) tells me is at best a seventeen-day schedule. I am trying my best to feel optimistic. Spoke to Michael Ballhaus (cinematographer and friend) who said, 'You'll be fine! We shot *The Bitter Tears of Petra Von Kant* in ten days, and that's two and a half hours long!' They had two or three locations in that film. I think we have forty. I saw *Chocolat* last night. One beautiful image: a black-and-white photographic still in which one person moved – blinking her eyes – and then disappeared. I think anything I do on the Avid could go right into film, it won't be an optical, so I may be able to have a lot of freedom with the idea of having still photos. Ellen K. (Kuras, who shot my first film, *Angela*) was against it in principle, I can't remember why – mixing stills with moving pictures. I figure anything can potentially work – or not. Gary Winick has given me total freedom. The thing is to be bold – who is there to be afraid of with this budget ($150,000)? I want to make a film where the viewer needs to find out what happens because they don't know already – unlike most films, where the message and resolution are telegraphed in the first twenty minutes. Anyway, the point of the stills is the many flashbacks, especially in the 'Greta' portion of the film, and the fact that we can't afford them. Yet they are necessary to understand her character – without that, understanding the film is nothing. In 'Greta' now the biggest problems are the dream and the Ohio sequence. I have made the dream something she tells Lee, and Ohio is stills with voice-over. Probably good that I condense because 'Greta' is so much more complex and longer than the other two films. I need to speak with an Avid- head, maybe Steve Silkinson, about the potential for manipulating images with the Avid these days. All right, I have to go downstairs and build an airport with my two-year-old son, Ronan.

I am so worried that there won't be enough shooting time, that this will be a botch. The casting is so crucial. I like the idea of sharing cast members between the three films – even the central characters?

29 January 2001

Have been thinking of 'intermission films' between the stories. Definitely not documentary footage. It ruins the fiction that follows. The opposite is the way to go. My mind is drawn back to the earliest films I made – dream-like, non-narrative images which embody the idea of the following film. Paula: flight, or baby, also dream life, life of signs versus life of the body; the fact of the body. Greta: impossible to kill/alter one's own nature once it is chosen; fish – or animals fighting – sharks. Delia: plants growing underground – too trite – would be nice to have a time lapse of a pair of tits growing but I don't have time for that.

I am working on ways to manipulate the images on screen – like Truffaut did for a moment in *Jules et Jim* when he has the screen go black around her, and she exists in a little rectangle all her own. (Am studying *Jules et Jim*, *Shoot the Piano Player* and *Two English Girls* for the way he uses V.O., as well as *Taxi Driver* and *Mean Streets*.) I want to do that a bit with Greta, especially in the opening sequence – a way also of pin-pointing moments and condensing time. I am being optimistic about what I can do on the Avid. Think of Greenaway – just a little. But I figure I should take advantage of DV, rather than treating it like film – be playful, not pretentious.

Spoke to Ellen Kuras, who is now free and interested in shooting, though understandably concerned about getting the crew together. I told her about everyone owning a part of the film (the InDigEnt deals are structured in such a way that all the key positions own points in the film, so, when it is sold, they all make money). I need to get more into that aspect, it will be especially important in attracting crew. Need to talk to Lemore again about the contract. Anyway, Ellen was just in Sundance on a panel about digital video. She is the new, reluctant DV queen because of her work with Spike Lee. The truth is she thinks it still looks like video, feels like video, the transfers are more expensive – she is still pro-film. So am I, in terms of what it looks like, but I have to take the opportunity as it is given. Somehow, everyone has it in their head that DV is cheaper. That may be a myth. Anyway, she is reading the stories. I'll get the script in shape by the end of the week and send her that as well. It would be good to work together again. I am thinking no lights. See *Celebration* (*Festen*). On *Angela* we thought a lot about shots, we changed our minds, we had seven weeks. I think this time I have to have talked things over with her enough so I can be very decisive on set and just get on with it. Story-boarding, stick to it within reason.

1 February 2001

I rearranged 'Delia'. Tore the skin of the narrative so we see through the wound, down into the past squirming around beneath the present like internal organs. Freeze-frame on her head about to be smashed into the table (narrator: 'Wait! Let me explain!') and go into flashbacks – live action and stills. Should Inge (Morath, my mother, photographer) shoot these? I suppose we would shoot them on a digital camera. Maybe Ellen should. Could be wonderful pictures. Fay being tortured by the railroad tracks – shoot the scene like Mary Ellen Mark would – like it's really happening. I have also been playing with stills which transform into moving pictures. D. (my husband) had a horrible case of the flu; and I was sick too, so I feel terribly behind. I need to finish the script. It may be in good enough condition to send to Ellen. One more read through, probably. Am getting nervous about casting. Call Lemore today. Ask about what kind of cameras they are giving us to use. Also find out where we are on casting and if there is any money at all for that yet; Cindy (Tolan, casting director) needs a contract. We need to start sending the stories to the women, make the offers, have the script ready. I think it's a good policy – sending the stories first – though I am not sure at this point. I feel a little funny about sending the stories around now that they are going to be published, as if I should keep them secret.

13 February 2001

Ellen K. wants to shoot the film! She read the stories and loved them, is free, wants to work together again. I must say she is a good sport, given the money she must get these days. Lemore will be sending her the newest script. I hope the script is all right. It seems that way to me now, but scripts have a way of turning bad over time. In a week I'll probably read it and think it stinks.

Ellen has worked a lot with DV, and she says there is a very high-end digital camera made by Panavision – which we will probably not be able to use, but you never know – with a digital still camera built in, and you can manipulate the images as with Photoshop. Alternatively, Ellen owns a digital camera, for all the still images. She seems sold on these now that she's read the script. Of course, we can probably do a certain amount of manipulation of images with the Final Cut software, which is what Gary Winick uses for these films; it is compatible with Apple computers, so I could rent one and have it in Roxbury, and edit in the Silo (my parents' barn).

Spoke to Danny Talpers (production designer on *Angela*), who, as always, sounds fairly desperate – about finding locations, pre-production time, money. But there is no one more loyal than Danny or a better designer for the things I want to do. Danny, Cindy, Ellen, Lemore – the family is getting back together. Ellen mentioned John Nadoe maybe gaffing, but she was uncertain because he'd had a bad experience on a DV film in which the director kept turning off all the lights. I think it would be overkill to have a great gaffer when I want to use available light all the time. I don't even think they have gaffers on these crews.

26 February 2001

Offering Delia to either Kyra Sedgwick or Catherine McCormack. Will see reel on latter. Cindy is sure Sedgwick is right, says she is that tough.

Gary Winick loved the script, but is still worried about how we are going to do it in the time. So am I. Next thing is a schedule so we can see just how absurd seventeen days is for the script. Then I will have to go over things with Ellen, see if we can consolidate images, think about what I can't live without. I think the main thing is to remember that if we get good actors – we have to – they are our best production value. Go in, live in their faces. Long shots and close-ups and forget the world of medium shots, for the most part. That way it won't matter so much that we can't afford to dress any of the sets. Shooting delayed till 15 May at the moment.

5 March 2001
Letter to Ellen Kuras:

Dear Ellen,

First of all, I am so happy we are making this film together. I feel like we'll really be able to take off with it. I feel I didn't make myself clear at all on the telephone the other night. I don't want the film to look like a documentary – no, but I am afraid of too much stylization. I think we need to save the obvious stylization more for the memories – all that past which can be poetry. I just know the present sequences need to seem absolutely real yet not straight realism – be very carefully designed to show what the protagonist is feeling, what she is going through at that moment; if we can design the shots from the inside out that way, emotionally, then we can eliminate a lot of coverage and hit the heart of the scenes.

The thing I don't want to lose in the stories is the sense that these are real women with real dilemmas. All these three women are in a state of emergency; even though Greta's dilemma is not life or death like the other two, it feels that way to her – she is in the process of losing/throwing away her husband – the film needs to have velocity, drive, urgency, a sense of inevitability – it should be lyrical without being languorous – unlike *Angela* where we were exploring childhood where time expands – for the women in this film, time is contracted, life is speeding by, they are confronted with choices they barely have time to acknowledge before the landscape of their lives shifts – these stories should really MOVE – not that there won't be tranquil moments but they should be chosen and very precise. The pace should be built into the way it's shot – it should feel like it's fleeing. Crafted, but REAL in the present sequences. In the stills – if we keep them as stills – especially in the 'Delia' section when she hits the kid who is torturing Fay, I keep seeing Mary Ellen Mark-like photographs – as she would have photographed the scene – and I guess that is reportage, but her work always echoes outwards into symbol. I see a lot of close-ups and long shots. I don't see so much in-between yet. I was watching *The Passion of Saint Joan* – let's watch it together. The simplicity, poetry – it is perfect. We should think about it when we design the memories.

Then there is the question of tone shift in the three stories. 'Greta' is more comic; I see a slightly different style for the camera in the present sequences than for 'Delia' or 'Paula'. But maybe if the memories for all three have the same quality, we can get away with a slight stylistic shift?

The movie, the stories, are about class as well as other issues – look at Greta's middle-class dilemma versus Delia's; when Delia rises look where she ends up compared to Greta – just something to think about.

I'm not sending you the drawings. They aren't right yet. I just wanted to give you a sense of what I'm thinking. I'm open as always and I can't wait to start the collaboration. One more thing – I am going to try to double in the casting – have actors play more than one character in the different segments, except the main girls. This will lend a surreal quality, a sense of the characters living in parallel universes, and I think if it works could be terrific.

Let's talk soon. Love, Rebecca.

7 March 2001, NYC

Spoke to Danny Talpers. Incredibly, he is turning down the chance to production design this; he feels the budget he would be working with is impossible, and also he is doing some renovation job. Though I am trying hard to think whether we can work together again, this feels like a betrayal.

19 March 2001

Met line producers Jenny and Brian. Just out of NYU, have made an $80,000 feature on DV. They seem perfect, very organized.

20 March 2001

Met Judy Becker, production designer from Rhinebeck. Good book. Realistic style. Understands budget constraints and isn't scared. Gave her the job.

Had first location scout – Ellen, Lemore, Jenny and Brian, Judy. Brownstone in Long Island, good for Greta's apartment, Paula's apartment, Max's dormitory – very good, free (friend of Jennie and Brian's). Furniture wrong for 'Greta' but you can't have everything. Nice drummer lives there. Then went to free restaurant location – perfect, modern. Then to free municipal building for the publishing house. A bit of a stretch, but I think we can make it work. It is, after all, free and, with tons of books around, it will be convincing. Saw pics of a good Tavi (change from Toshi because Toshi is Japanese) loft, free. Belongs to André Gregory's son, whom I have met a couple of times. Monday, we look at Ellen's for Mimi's house and masturbation bathroom. Early next week Ellen and I will get down to work. I am encouraged by the locations. Will have to consolidate some – see one room instead of two in certain locations.

Have script out to Kyra Sedgwick. Have to make a decision about Greta.

23 March 2001

A girl named Avigail Glazier-Schotz wrote to me saying how she was moved by *Angela*, she's coming to NYC, do I have a job for her. I called her to offer a job as my assistant without pay, which she miraculously accepted – she just sold her car.

I dyed my hair; it was free – the girl who cut it is about to get her licence and was desperate to practise. Sort of blondish, reddish light brown. Looks a bit like I'm wearing a hat. I'm hanging on to the doubling idea with the casting. I think I see a way. Offer parts to actors and say I want to talk about also playing another part. See what they say. So far we are offering to people who could play more than one role.

27 March 2001

Have begun to work with Ellen – semi-distracted hours yesterday in Nyak: she's buying a house and kept having to talk to mortgage brokers, then the dog needed attention, but we managed to slog through half of 'Greta' anyway and there were even a few inspired moments, flashes of shouting out the same thing at the same moment – we are beginning to find our zone again. A style is emerging – keeping to what I had in the script, of the blacking-out of parts of the screen, the stylizations and crispness and TV reference of some of 'Greta' juxtaposed with very documentary sequences, scenes where the camera floats, observes, passes over the characters' faces like a breeze. A lot of long lenses, seeing through doorways and past people. A lot of dirty close-ups, and then a lot of real e.c.u.'s too. Long shots on wide lenses do not hold up in mini-DV. Always keeping to the inner life of the character, liberate the camera to follow her inner life, don't worry too much about consistency – consistency will emerge.

We'll use Ellen's house for several locations (poor, generous Ellen!): Greta's country house, Lee's childhood bedroom, Paula's hallway, Paula's bed, maybe Mimi's party, the bridal shop. Judy Becker is worried it will start to be too obviously the same house. We have to be careful, but I think we can manage with those locations – Ellen's upstairs feels different than her downstairs and the mouldings aren't that distinctive. We have to consolidate or we'll never make the schedule.

Cindy T. (casting director) is right about the doubling idea – I hung on to it as long as I could. Have abandoned it because inevitably at least one part will be miscast that way. Am back to the idea of Chris Penn or James Legros as Kurt. No word on the offers yet.

30 March 2001

Greta: sexually voracious, intelligent, insecure, ambitious, guilt-ridden, funny. Parker Posey? But will it be clear she is less attractive than her husband; he is more powerful, and then as she attains power in the world his power is diminished, she can't respect him any more? Or are looks irrelevant? Lili Taylor would also be very good, a terrific actress. But as funny? Both great. A different Greta either way.

4 April 2001

Here's where we are: Kyra Sedgwick wants to meet Monday. Ron Leibman wants to play Avram, which is wonderful.

The crew is shaping up. AD, Paul – very solid, enthusiastic, a writer, seems a little emotionally constipated, but that's none of my business. Not a lot of DV experience, but very much wanting to be part of the team. We met with another

Kyra Sedgwick: 'A natural swagger, a toughness.'
(photo by Inge Morath)

woman with more experience, but she said she needed a couple of days, and that for me is a complete turn-off. So she's out, he's in.

Today my son Ronan said, 'Pardon me for being a bee, it was not me – it was my pee.' Also: 'I'm going to buy a new dishwasher. A silver one!'

10 April 2001

I met with Kyra Sedgwick in a Starbucks uptown. I watched her walk across the street through the plate-glass window. She has a natural swagger, a toughness I hadn't expected. Cindy was absolutely right. And what a body. She doesn't want to cut her hair in a shag, but you can't have everything. At the end of our talk, as I tried to sell her on the part, she said, 'But I want to do it' – like that had already been determined! Of course, her agents didn't present it that way at all. Anyway, she wants to; it's a question of working out the schedule – she has to work on another film till the very last minute. No rehearsal, but we will be fine. I am so pleased.

Greta meeting coming up – with Lili Taylor.

15 April 2001

James Legros said he would play Kurt! Referring to Kurt's single sentence in the script, he said, 'Well, at least I don't have to worry about remembering my lines.'

16 April 2001

Just met with Leo Fitzpatrick (*Kids* lead) – I think he'll be great. Need to read a few more – already made the appointments – plus he may baulk at the money, though I don't think so; he seems like a really terrific, truly original person who will take Mylert out of the clichéd dumb hick department.

Waiting for Liv Tyler for Paula. She'll never do this, but her agent is being so very positive.

Met with Ellen twice, drawing out everything, making shot lists. We are really hitting our stride. She thinks we will definitely have to light, though minimally – so John Nadeau is a must as gaffer, of course. Fuck Dogme. The very word gives me hives. Isn't the point of making art to be free, not live by some spurious set of rules like a religious devotee? The looks for the three films are emerging. 'Greta': clean, acid, organized, intellectual. 'Delia': handheld doc., sepia tones. 'Paula': macro close-ups, intensified colour. Poetry. Dream. Ellen wants to shoot at 1/25th. It will feel more like film. We'll use smoke to create atmosphere – except in 'Greta', where we want sharper lines.

Went on location-scout upstate. Jenny and Brian have been cruising all of the towns around where we're shooting and knocking on doors. They have an amazing selection of places. I love their approach; it's driven, generous. Finding locations for this film is like casting houses more than designing sets. Judy will certainly have a lot of work to do but the fundamental feeling of the places needs to be there. Delia's place is absolutely perfect. The people living in the house we'll use for her father, Pete Shunt's, place: an enormous woman from Brooklyn who never seems to get off her chair or take off her nightgown, and her ratty little snaggle-toothed husband, who enjoys Budweiser at any time of day. They live in a log house filled with guns. When I was out back looking for a place for Delia to hang up her breasts, I came across a severed deer head hanging from a tree. I guess we're as weird as each other, these people and me.

Parker Posey's manager read the script and loved it. Now, pray that she does.

James Legros pulled out. Got a money job. I can't blame him, though of course I do. He has recommended an actor named David Warshofsky.

Looked at the tape of David Warshofsky. He's very intense. Has a great face, big blue eyes, pock-marked skin. Really good. Will offer it to him.

Paul, the AD, got a better job, pulled out. Fuck him. Suddenly, I hate him and remember what a prig he was. Thank God I don't have to work with him now. The woman I preferred, Carrie Fix, is now available and wants to do it. What a relief. We interviewed Barry, a sound recordist known and recommended by Jenny and Brian. Barry has very dirty hair, terrible posture, seems deeply depressed and is extremely funny. The only problem is, his band will be on tour so he would have to miss the first few days. I guess we have to keep looking. Too bad; he seemed perfect for us.

Met a wonderful sound recordist with a ten-foot résumé. He is Indian, serene, quite regal. Hired him.

Met with Parker Posey. She felt like a friend in minutes. She arrived on roller skates, her hands dirty from pottery clay. I fell in love with her. It seems she wants to do it. Amazing luck. I can't believe it. Pulled out of the ashes again!

Costume fittings happening now. Got $10,000 from Liz Claiborne; we need to use their clothes for Greta and mention Liz in the dialogue. It was put to me this way: either I find a way of putting Claiborne in the script or we can't paint any walls. So I am doing it. Parker was so funny during her fitting that I almost peed in my pants. She is seeing Greta from the outside still – finding the physicality and the humour (all those ill-fitting suits), seeing her as funny, pathetic – and yet there are moments where I see her empathizing in a deeper way, letting herself be filled up by the character playfully, with such pleasure.

Thavi (Joel de la Fuente)'s fitting. Went through a few black suit or jacket and jeans ideas but he kept looking like an agent or like he was trying too hard. Ended up choosing jeans, a worn T-shirt and an old leather jacket. It will make him seem much more powerful this way – he's late, he's underdressed; she's early, she's dressed up. So it will mean more as she gradually shifts the power in the scene, taking the reigns and ultimately as the scene progresses moving from feeling vulnerable and ineffectual to powerful, sexy and competent.

Parker Posey: 'She felt like a friend in minutes.'
(photo by Pascal Perich)

Had a production meeting. Let everyone smoke around me during the meeting, instead of having a break outside, and I feel myself getting sick. Stupid girl.

Really getting sick. In my lungs. Coughing like a consumptive. Fucking cigarette smoke. Did location scout in Brooklyn. We'll shoot Mimi's party in Jenny's tiny apartment. I don't know how we'll all fit in there. The café where Greta meets Max is in Williamsburg as well. Great windows/light in there. I think I am going to have to ask my parents if I can use their apartment for Greta's. It would be perfect. Not too much character. Michael Rohatyn pointed that out – if her apartment is great and downtown and bohemian, it is less obviously a place to escape from. He probably just said that because I wanted to use his place, which is downtown and bohemian.

Met with a German editor today, Sabine Hoffmann. Have to look at her work, but from our conversation I think she's the one. Got chills at one point. She talked about triggers – I said I wanted the film to move like thought, and she was saying we need to find triggers within the fabric of the film to send us into flashbacks, time leaps and so on, and that the most important thing of all was going to be keeping the audience in tune with the emotion of the characters. So they don't get alienated by all the razzle-dazzle. I am in complete agreement. She clearly has a terrific mind and even likes the idea of coming to cut in Roxbury – as long as she can come into town for her women's group meetings.

Fairuza Balk: 'An unearthly quality.'
(photo by Inge Morath)

Met Fairuza Balk. She tottered into Gamin wearing spike heels, dressed entirely in Dolce and Gabanna (her sponsors), hair scraped back so tight, those uncanny cat eyes, raspy voice. An unearthly quality in moments. Her unhealthy-looking but chivalrous friend, Andrew, hovered outside while we spoke. He seems to be escorting her everywhere – she doesn't know New York so well. There's an old-fashioned movie-star helplessness blended in with her nearly punkish bravado, genuine vulnerability behind her tough little made-up child's face. She wants to do it, is interested in the idea that Paula is 'in a state of shock' for much of the film. I have a strong instinct that she's the one.

Offered Paula to Fairuza Balk. The movie is cast. The drawings are done. First day looms.

Costume fitting: Fairuza – one outfit throughout. Little fur on collar of jacket, vulnerable. Fairuza found the perfect jeans – on Sherri, the wardrobe supervisor, who was kind enough to take them off. Have yet to find the perfect T-shirt. She is so very tiny. We talked about her hair. A bob, I think. Reddish. She's doing a shoot for *Playboy* and they'll give her a free hair cut.

Am worried about Ellen; pushing the dates of her shooting means her commercial will conflict. She is trying to get them to push the commercial shoot. If they won't, I just hope she'll stick with me.

18 May 2001

Overcast. First day of shooting, Thompson Square Park. Our regal Indian sound recordist didn't show up!!! AND sent an *absolute moron* to take his place. He's fired, needless to say. Luckily Barry, the funny depressed guy in a band, was operating the boom for Ian, who is doing the documentary about us shooting the film. So we poached Barry off Ian – I guess he'll have to operate his own boom now.

Fairuza arrived slightly late with her friend Andrew. Apparently, something was wrong with her stomach and she had him running up and down First Avenue looking for some kind of herbal medication. But anyway – we shot in the park, when Paula meets Vincent. She didn't want to cry in that scene, which at first I was unsure of – I had my heart set on that one tear trickling down – but having seen it on the monitor I think it's good she just looks miserable, teary and exhausted, and we save the real crying for the motel. She looks amazing on the monitor, she has the look I was hoping for – sort of a cross between Louise Brooks and Chrissie Hynde. She's going to be terrific.

We also got some lovely impromptu shots of Seth Gilliam (Vincent) tossing the pear up and down – I had a flash of cutting that in before – somehow as if he were moving towards her, not knowing she was his fate. And the beautiful pear. Hope. His face seemed filled with goodness.

Next location was the club. Nearly got thrown out; owner suddenly wanted a lot of money – we somehow gave him the impression of being a big fancy film crew. We paid him off with money we don't have, then went downstairs and shot for three hours, got all the stuff for the club where Paula meets the guy. Nice red light on him; he worked all right, the Swede, though a bit stiff.

The two cameras will work. We have to be sure Martina (second camera operator) uses foreground as Ellen does. I loved the fact that sound didn't matter, so I was able to amble around in the crowd, talking to Ellen and Martina as they shot. I felt invisible. We got the whole scene done in two hours.

We had some kind of R&B dance music on. Carrie Fix picked it – I barely noticed – but one of the young punks we had at the bar said, 'Do they know we're punks?' It was a good point – though of course we won't use punk music in the film. Looking back, I should have used a faster beat. I'm so deaf.

As night fell, ran down to Varick Street to shoot the accident with Paula and the 'Norwegian man'. It went pretty well, though he kept getting calls from his girlfriend, and I felt I was interrupting him to shoot. Hard to light the street with our measly kit. Ellen ran after Fairuza for the running sequence and got great light smears, a sense of her desperation. You can see what an athlete Ellen used to be when she runs. A long night; Fairuza a great sport, very prepared. We made our twelve-hour day. Back at the production office I was walking into the ladies room when our Swede walked out followed by his girlfriend, who is about six two, looks like a transvestite, but apparently is not, Andrew, Fairuza's ubiquitous friend, assures me. He knew her 'back in the day'.

21 May 2001

Upstate. First of all, Lemore led the family and Vicki to our picturesque 'cabin on the lake': dirt driveway about a mile long; air grey with mosquitoes; lake ingrown and murky. Cabin looked like the perfect scene for a heinous crime: no curtains on windows; screens ripped; Vicki's mattress had a huge chunk clawed out of it by a large animal, possibly a bear. Decided on the hotel.

Arrived at Hudson River Valley Spa and Resort, a mammoth concrete hotel in the mountains. The design would have made Stalin proud. There is a Meter Readers Convention on at the moment, so the lobby is teaming with men in checked shirts and baseball caps.

Our company seems to be living in the condemned wing of the hotel. Even the staff look sorry for us when we tell them our room numbers. Drawers don't open. Can hear sneezes down the hall. Our son Ronan seems to like it all right. D. takes it with humour, thank God.

22 May 2001

Paula's mother's house. Perfect location. All actors terrific. Did a dry, emotion-free run-through so Ellen could light it. She came up with beautiful lighting, using one light outside the west window and the rest natural. As planned, we had A/B cameras each follow a character, keeping track of what coverage we had. Crossed the line deliberately a few times; I think it will work well for this scene, with all the intercutting.

INT. CAR, driving with kid (Lou Taylor Pucci) – very poetic images, the best of Ellen K. Little things – rain on the window, a close-up of an eye – are going to make this really sing. Ellen squashed behind actors in back seat, me with monitor in way-back, along with Barry the funny/depressed sound recordist. Thank God it's a station wagon. Blessed with overcast skies, drizzling rain.

Not to wake up D. and Ronan, I creep out of the darkened room carrying my shoes at 5 a.m., wash my face and brush teeth in public bathroom downstairs before call, dry face with paper towels. Was found by second AD. She thought it was pretty funny.

23 May 2001

Rained HARD, thank God – our measly rain machines more like shower heads. This 'macro-epiphany' aesthetic we're using for 'Paula' is strong. The kid, Lou Taylor Pucci, is a real talent. He's like a cat on-screen, can't put a foot wrong, has no falseness in him. He and Fairuza are perfect together, two lost souls. Andrew, Fairuza's friend, has come along upstate, gets her up in the morning and actually carried her into the van in her slippers today. I need a friend like that.

Outside Dunkin' Donuts: Lou Taylor Pucci and Fairuza Balk
(photo by Inge Morath)

Crew makes a remake of *The Shining* in the Hudson River Valley Spa and Resort half the night, after we shoot. Fairuza is playing one of the twins. Everyone loves her.

Ended up doing entire final scene in one shot with external simultaneous coverage from B camera. As we ran through it I realized there was no reason to cut till the very end.

For conversation outside Dunkin' Donuts in the car – about staying in Brooklyn – I suddenly thought we should just shoot the whole thing through the windshield, no internal coverage (though we did lots of coverage through the windshield), since we had shot all the other stuff from the inside of the car. It worked beautifully because the dribbles of rain accumulate like tears over the face of the boy as he watches her go into the shop and he makes his final decision.

Ate so many donuts I feel sick.

24 May 2001

Motel. Fairuza absolutely GREAT. I just kept rolling till she had it. Didn't always cut between takes so she could get the emotion going; sometimes I had to so we could get the smoke in there. Great shot in the mirror as kid undresses, Fairuza watching on left. Both cameras so ALIVE. I was outside the room with the monitor for the most part – motel room so small I couldn't fit my monitor in there. I watched the screen gripping John Nadeau (the gaffer) like we were on a life raft. The scene – tenderness. My favourite.

25 May 2001

A day from hell. This was the day we had to shoot sequences from all three stories. Began with 'Greta' in Lee's family home, saying grace. Improvised dialogue was so funny, had to hide behind a kitchen counter to laugh. Something about Parker. We then shot Lee's photos of the past, prom night, football stardom; then back to 'Paula', scene at the chemists – let that roll past where the scene ended so the actors found their own way out of the scene. *Première* magazine arrived to interview me and shoot photos of us all running around like mad people. Of all fucking days.

Then, Greta driving through Rosendale, New York – past the pharmacy.

Then, back to 'Paula': into some grungy student digs in New Paltz – which we are using for Vincent's apartment – very nice high shots of the two of them. She didn't want to get naked, but he more than made up for it. Did interview.

Shot fight between Paula and Vincent also – live action, though we will use stills from it.

Then, Greta's wedding. Huge costume job. Marie Abma (costume designer) seemed on the verge of nervous collapse. All will be in stills. I was barking out instructions so we could end the day within our twelve-hour limit (no money for overtime, ever) – AND WE MADE THE WHOLE DAY IN TWELVE HOURS!!!!!

'Paula' finished.

Returned to hotel to find about two hundred Hassidic Jews milling around in the lobby. Some taking naps on couches. Children running everywhere. Baby carriages. Thick stockings. Wigs. Wow.

26 May 2001 – day 6 of shooting, first day of 'Delia'

Today was a mess. The ADs concentrated so hard on getting yesterday planned, they seem to have allowed today to just form itself. When I arrived at Pete Shunt's house – the log cabin formerly filled with guns – it was pouring with rain, and one of our vans had two wheels over a ditch at the side of the road. I found a clutch of extras dressed as Adventists shivering in the open shed, rain sluicing down off the roof. That was bad enough, but in their midst stood Tim Hopper, a fine theatre actor who is playing Mr Brown! He was very polite about it, but I was so embarrassed. The worst of it was, he had brought his new wife along on the shoot, so she, too, had to huddle in the shed like a sheep waiting out the rain. Jesus. I managed to at least get them into the holding area, an inhospitable community centre (and the only available *toilet du jour*) a quarter of a mile up the road, where our Young Delia was having her hair blow-dried, clearly a little grumpy about being woken up so early from her adolescent summer sleep, her anxious parents hovering close by. The whole day I was cold, wet, teeth clenched. I somehow managed to offend Marie Abma; apparently I dismissed her from the set impatiently. I have absolutely no memory of this, which is a little scary. Nonetheless, I apologized profusely. I got a tight smile in return, so I guess she's not quitting – today.

The work itself – when we finally got to it – went very well. Young Delia has the still, sullen sexiness I was hoping for (her parents sat beside me by the monitor the whole day), and Brian Tarantina (Pete Shunt) is absolutely perfect. Great improvised dialogue between him and Tim Hopper (the Head Adventist). All the extras looked really good. The woman playing Marcia, Delia's mum, told me that she had been battered herself for years and stayed in the relationship for the drugs. Eventually she got clean, learned enough about law to represent herself, and got her ex-husband put in jail. She was perfect in the scene where she is getting a punch on the nose at the dinner table. She knew just what to do. Such a strange coincidence. There was one moment I couldn't get to work: after Delia's mother leaves, Delia puts her arm around her dad. I couldn't get it out of the melodrama department. Awkward and sentimental. I was getting discouraged. Ellen adamant we would keep at it till I was happy. In the end we worked out another shot: as mother leaves the house in the foreground, Delia watches her go through window of the door, with Pete Shunt in the background, smoking. I think I'll just cut out on that and forget the other moment inside. Cooler, yet more emotional because not manipulative.

29 May 2001

Kyra Sedgwick's first day. Kyra very internal, very real. She asked a few times, 'Do you want something else?' I didn't.

Later I did ask for more vulnerability and less stridency as alternative takes in the scene with Fay in the garage, so I can have the option when I cut and she doesn't seem too tough the whole time. Before we shot the exterior of her crying outside, Kyra happened to be standing in the garage waiting for us to shoot, silhouetted in the glass part of the door, and John Nadeau noticed this amazing golden light coming through, and we ran to shoot it. I had to ask her quickly to cry a little even though she had just been standing there waiting. Boy, can she cry. The poor woman had to sob uncontrollably on her very first day. I just let the tape roll for about fifteen minutes. I figure I'll jump-cut to shape the scene later. She told the entire story of the film that way – the loss, the sadness, and finally acceptance and a kind of hope. She has great emotional reserves which she can tap into very quickly. A pro in the best sense.

Kyra Sedgwick with Leo Fitzpatrick (photo by Inge Morath)

29 May 2001

Tough day today. Had to drop a scene – man checking Delia out in gas station – to make the day.

Leo Fitzpatrick very good, though I think he thought I didn't like what he was doing because I kept getting him to do it different ways. It was just so I could shape it later. I think he suffered a bit in the jerk-off scene, but it was fantastic. Ellen composed a killer CU of him with Kyra's hair in the foreground, very abstract. Some day I will write an ode to foreground.

31 May 2001

We went way over time today, but there was no other way. Make-up on Delia took three hours rather than one and a half, and I had to get him to take away a few of the prosthetics. I think we got a really good scene. Very real. Good improv from the kids. I hope the smack on the table works. Stills will be very beautiful – shot them in real time, will choose later. At the last minute, 11 p.m., as if everyone hadn't suffered enough, I thought of an extra scene: Delia imagining herself going back to Kurt, making out with him, then you see she is just standing there. The actors liked the idea and the crew went along, but they were grumpy. 'Delia' is done now.

Ellen really is leaving halfway through 'Greta' to do a commercial and taking John Nadeau with her. The client wouldn't push the dates; it's real money.

She has decided to go. Am very depressed, but I am not allowing myself to think about it. I have to keep going.

3 June 2001

'Greta' begun. Parker walked on in first take with funny flat-footed walk – she has Greta to a 'T'. Thavi created perfect accent. Not so happy with colours of walls, but that's life. Fun to work with Parker – it's like an extended conversation between friends.

Shooting at Grace Church for Harvard, Lemore smashed her cell phone to bits at lunch while having a conversation. My avenging angel. I dread to think of the disasters she is protecting me from.

Warren and Howe publishing a bit of a disaster. Security guard flipped out and tried to throw us all out of the municipal court building – he didn't think we had permission. He was armed and clearly psychotic (I would have cast Tom Sizemore to play him). I kept telling him not to be rude, which was probably not a good idea, but it was all I could think of at the time. Wally Shawn was chuckling in his 'dressing room' – an empty office. In the end we got hold of the man who gave us permission in the first place and kept shooting. End shoot. Second-unit day some time down the line.

6 June 2001

Ellen's last day. Avram's party. Worked well. Went with natural light through the windows for the beginning and lit some as the sun went down. When Avram comes out to Greta, at first he seemed too guilty. When I told him to smile as if nothing had happened, it worked. He wouldn't let himself feel guilty that way. Parker nailed it. Enjoying party and hating herself for enjoying it simultaneously.

7 June 2001

Moved slower; Toshi (new DP) is finding his sea legs. Finding myself much more authoritarian. Have to be – he's really good, but he doesn't have it under his skin the way Ellen does. Maybe this is good for me in some way (what was I thinking?). Scene in café where Greta meets Max and starts her affair went well, once it was finally lit. Ben Shenkman surprisingly photogenic. Good chemistry between them.

Mimi's apartment is so small and hot, almost unbearable. Oscar very good. Nice power shift in scene. Parker very, very good today. Can play several contradictory emotions at once so well.

15 June 2001

Shot love scene between Greta and Lee using the smear effect inside the camera. Had been thinking of Francis Bacon for the scene – bodies as meat; abstract; love-making as a fight.

Shoot over. Editing begins soon. Ronan's toilet-training in full swing.

Greta and Lee (Parker Posey and Tim Guinec)
(photo by Pascal Perich)

5 July 2001
Cutting at Sound One. Freezing in cutting room, boiling outside. Cutting going all right. 'Paula' came along fastest, partly because Sabine had that footage first and roughed it out. I think we are going to have to restructure 'Greta'. Flashbacks confusing. Need it to be more about the father; Gary and Lemore both agree. Father vs husband.

1 August 2001
Have decided to move 'Delia' to the opening, then 'Greta' in middle, then 'Paula'. 'Greta' in the middle is good because it's comic, breaks up the sadness. 'Delia' next to 'Paula' makes 'Paula' sad rather than lyrical. Also, I love the juxtaposition of class with 'Greta' coming after 'Delia'.

10 August 2001
Cutting in Roxbury now, in barn. Ronan happy. Will share cooking so Ingo not overwhelmed.

15 August 2001
I think the film might be pretty good. D. saw rough cut. Very positive. Spent afternoon with us in cutting room, helping select moments in 'Delia'. This is the fun part – shaping the reality, the moments. The structure is there.

30 August 2001
Have been shooting clouds myself. Will use them in-between the stories. Seems simplest, purest.

At this rate we should be ready to apply for Sundance.

Watched slow-down (to NTSC, American standard, which shoots twenty-four frames per second. We shot in PAL, European standard, which shoots twenty-five frames per second. So when the transfer occurs, there is a very slight slow-down. Incidentally, the sound must either be adjusted by hand on the computer or slowed down mechanically. I found this extremely frustrating.) Hardly noticed slow-down except in 'Paula'; must have been cumulative. Will trim bits.

Martin Scorsese watched it and said he 'liked it a lot'!!! Said, 'I really think you've got something here.' DV seems like a whole different medium than film to him. Thought the film was linked to early cinema verité. He was struck by how violent the scene in which Delia makes Mylert come was. I was proud to make him think a scene violent. He thought some of the stills might be too deliberate in pace. I am going to review them. Also, he thought there is something in 'Paula' before the breakdown that needs to be trimmed – didn't know where. Said it was the one place his attention wandered. I think he's right. Will investigate.

We got into Sundance!!!!

Met with credit designer. Has a very good reel. Friend of Ellen's. Will design the credits free. She liked the movie a lot. We talked about clouds, a woman falling.

Saw her storyboards for the credits. Of a naked woman, not falling. Shot in bits, where you can't see everything. Feels so odd to see another woman who is not one of the women characters at the beginning over the credits. I told her I had reservations, and she told me she 'really believed in' her idea. Hard to argue with someone who is working for free.

Credits design is a disaster. This designer thinks of herself as a director, wanted to shoot the credits off on her own in LA. I said no, she could come to NYC and be part of the shoot, but otherwise I would direct it, we would be shooting it. So we did, on a sound stage, but it wasn't under my skin. I felt wrong all day. I couldn't figure out how to make it mine. We were using a cloud backdrop and a rotating circular mount for the camera and a fan, but it looked fake and stylized and dead. Credit designer didn't like what we shot – we didn't either. So she insisted on reshooting her own stuff, at her expense, in LA. I agreed. Felt bulldozed. D. thought that was a mistake. He was right. We got her credit sequence back and it seems sort of slick, like a shampoo commercial – I mean, it's all right, but it doesn't seem right for the film. Plus, it's insulting to Ellen. Now, of course, it seems I owe this designer, but nonetheless, I think we have to shoot something else. But what? Out of money now, already had to go back to Gary Winick once. Moral of the story: there is no such thing as a free lunch.

D. had a great idea – three little girls on swings.

I called Lemore, told her we were going to reshoot. She's very happy. Hated the attitude of this woman too. Have to find three little girls who resemble the actresses.

Reshot credits. Great light. Took us an hour. Looks like it belongs in the film. Thank God. Perfect – motion, emotion, simplicity – and a great contrast to the violence of 'Delia'.

Sabine and I cut credits in with music (by Michael Rohatyn, the composer). Very moving. At first I thought it should all be piano. But now I think the synthesizer works well for much of it. The piano perfect for 'Greta'. Sounds like Chopin. So emotional. Michael is amazing.

Have the colour-correct just about right, thank God. Ellen and I worked out looks for all three; she has been working with the technician as I have been mixing at the same time. The colour is so beautiful now.

3 January 2002

Met with John Sloss (one of the heads of InDigEnt, sales rep at Sundance) in his office. He was, as always, magisterial and mysterious, but very pleasant and hugely confident – though not bubbling with optimism about our film. He feels that, eventually, we will have a buyer for it, even if it is months after Sundance. It felt like a relief to have someone taking care of us. I remember last time, with *Angela*, going to Sundance all alone with Lemore and Ron Kastner, and feeling so lost.

There were technical questions in the meeting; for example, should we have alternate formats as back-ups for the screenings – as it is there are just the high-definition video and a copy, which apparently they have good projectors for.

11 January 2002

Arrived at Sundance. Five months' pregnant. Ate muffin and fillet o' fish sandwich in airport. Feel huge. Olympics coming up here. Woman in plane actually asked me if I was an athlete! She must be legally blind.

Moved with Ronan and Adrian into the Lemores' chalet. Parker and Tom already there. Also J.T. and Melissa. It's very cosy. Ronan really likes the communal atmosphere. Everyone all excited.

12 January 2002

Drove with Gary Winick to Directors' Brunch, which was so different from last time. Then, I came up to the lodge with all the other film-makers in a van and there was some sense of solidarity with them; this time I know only Gary. I have even less possibility than last time to see films because the press is actually interested in talking to me now, and that takes up a lot of time. Robert Redford gave a speech about how prizes and being picked up for distribution mean nothing. Maybe not to him. But to those of us who struggled so hard to make our films, getting paid nothing or next to nothing, the idea that someone might actually see them is appealing. It doesn't make us corrupt. Does it? Of course, I love the purity of vision behind Sundance, which is precious.

Did press. All three girls are here. Fairuza, in vast silver fox (vintage), arrived with boyfriend in matching fur. They seem very much in love. Kyra is here with her team. Parker just has Tom and a ukulele.

First screening, library, 5.30 p.m.: went well, I think. Good laughter. Good attention. The film looks beautiful – absolutely could not tell it wasn't on film. The colour is so rich.

13 January 2002

Screening 9 p.m., the Sugar House in Salt Lake.

An offer – for nothing! From Fine Line. They would just put out the film. No advance. Basically, they are doing this because they want Gary's film *Tadpole*, and they are throwing mine in. I am saying no, of course. Are they insane?

Couldn't stay for the Q and A after the screening because John Sloss insisted we all show up for his party in a restaurant in town where I would meet 'distributors'. I did not meet any.

Ted Demme has died suddenly. Horrible, such a young man. Ellen was very close to him. She will go to the funeral.

14 January 2002

9.15 p.m. screening, Ekels cinema. 1,300-seat theatre. Image weaker because of distance thrown but very good response.

Press all day, walking up and down main street with the girls.

A little worried that John Sloss is not paying us much attention. *Tadpole* is taking him over totally; he clearly thinks it will be a huge sale and everyone wants it, which is great, but of course I'm a little worried. Sloss tells me not to worry, we will sell the film.

15 January 2002

An offer!!! From MGM/UA – for over four times the budget. Bingham Ray (used to run October Films) wants to meet. Wow.

Variety event. Squeezed into black knit dress which is way too small all of a sudden. This baby must have grown six inches in the past two days. Got a big laugh when I got up on the little stage to receive my framed *Variety* Director to Watch poster looking like I had a cantaloupe under my dress. So many photographers there, it was crazy. Ran into four sweet film-maker women (one of them had an actual beard) who adored *Angela*. I am always really touched when someone says they like that film. Also spoke to a crazy journalist from Finland who wanted to know how she could 'have everything', like me. I didn't know if she wanted to kiss me or stab me.

Getting steeled for meeting with Bingham Ray. If he wants to recut the film, I have to turn him down.

16 January 2002

Met with Bingham Ray from MGM/UA. He loves the film and doesn't want to change anything! Ours was the only film in Sundance he responded to. He just picked up Mike Leigh's new film as well. MGM is for sale right now, but no one seems to think his job is in jeopardy or that it's a problem for us. Apparently MGM is always for sale. I really liked Bingham; he is a bit of a character. Said he wanted to go to Cannes in May. I said the only problem is, I am having a baby during Cannes. He hadn't even noticed I was pregnant. Probably just thought I eat a lot of bagels. But he said it would be fine if we went to Toronto and maybe Telluride. Come out in autumn. We'll get half, other half to Independent Film Channel (the parent company of InDigEnt). An audience of absolute strangers will actually see this film!

17 January 2002

8.30 a.m. screening. A hundred people standing on line for stand-by tickets. A beautiful screening – the people love it – D. there! Very moved, so sweet. I was sitting behind Roger Ebert and was in agony every time he looked away to write something down. I wanted to say, 'Excuse me, sir, but you're missing something good here.' At the end, he said he thought it was very good, I am a real director, he was just sorry it was on video. Not sure exactly what he meant. A lot of crying, laughing, in audience.

Saw *Tadpole* at last. It's terrific, really sweet and funny, and it has a certain wistful, melancholy nostalgia about it that I found heartbreaking. The audience was so with it – lots of laughs. What has Gary been complaining about? It's true that visually it is less sophisticated than the direction and the acting. His DP wasn't up to Gary's talent. But I think there is a kind of naivety in the way it's shot that works for the film. If it was slickly shot, it might not be as strong, who knows? Anyway, my God, he just sold it for millions of dollars.

Award ceremony tomorrow. Ellen is convinced she'll never win best cinematography a third time (she won for *Swoon*, by Tom Kalein, and *Angela*, my first film). She can't come anyway because of Ted Demme's funeral.

Prizes don't matter, don't matter, don't matter, don't matter.

18 January 2002

WE WON THE GRAND JURY PRIZE!!!!

And Ellen won the Cinematography Award! (Gary won Best Director – what a night for InDigEnt, what a night for DV.) I had to get up and receive Ellen's prize first – just like last time with *Angela*. After that, when the prizes kept going by, and when Gary got Best Director, I thought, forget it. It never occurred to me that we would win the big prize. I was so shocked when they called out *Personal Velocity*, I forgot to thank the actresses. So, of course, I was consumed with remorse, Greta-style, for the rest of the night. But happy too. So happy.

Katia Lund

Katia Lund
interviewed by Isabella Weibrecht

Katia Lund and I grew up together from the age of seven in a small American Catholic school in São Paolo. We lost touch once we dispersed to go to colleges here, there and everywhere. Somehow she found me again in Ireland after fifteen years, and during our awkward, tentative conversations I found out about her involvement in the Brazilian hit film City of God.

Opportunistically, I asked her for an interview. This gave us a reason to stay in touch though, needless to say, we were sidetracked more often than not about who was married and who wasn't, who came back to live in Brazil, and whose childhood home had recently been demolished. The chit-chat has been edited out.

Isabella Weibrecht: So, how did you end up making movies in the favelas? That is the last place I thought I'd find you.
Katia Lund: I had been working in Brazil as a production person, mostly as an assistant director. I'd done twelve features as a first AD. When Michael Jackson came to Rio to do his music video (for 'They Forgot about Us'), I was hired by the 'favela locations expert', Tim Maia, to work on locations. Everyone thought he was mad, putting me, with bright red hair and blue eyes, into the favela. He, of course, said it was safer to put a woman in there, since no one would allow a Brazilian male to give orders on their patch. So, I got stuck in there, hiring kids to be runners, to work on construction, to help with the catering, etc. I had spoken with the drug dealers, and they had agreed to let the kids work for me. Because it was Michael Jackson, the media in Brazil went into overdrive. Within days, headlines started appearing in the papers: 'Drug dealers co-produce Michael Jackson video', and the like. Needless to say, the opposite was true. They did it all for free – the drug dealers were *honoured* to have Michael Jackson in their favela.

IW: Did Michael Jackson realize this? Did he do anything for them?
KL: The production company had $5,000 to donate to the community. $2,000 went to a child-care centre near the top of the hill, $2,000 went to a child-care centre near the bottom, and $1,000 went to the local Associação de Moradores [local government or administration].

Anyway, one day, I send this little kid across the favela to deliver a hammer to the construction crew. He runs off, turns a corner and smashes straight into a line of cops, who start roughing him up. I run over there and start explaining the situation, and they completely disregard me. They told me that I was doing my job and that this was theirs. I was outraged. I pay taxes for this! That incident was a catalyst for my work from then on.

IW: From Michael Jackson to *City of God* . . .
KL: I was first assistant director for Walter Salles on *Central Station*, and I spent an evening haranguing him about the situation in the favelas and what I'd seen there. He suggested that we do a documentary on the situation. We would show the points of view of all the parties – the victims, the dealers, the police. It was called *News from a Private War*. I was almost arrested for that documentary because we had given one of the dealers money to write his story so we could get it published – he was not in jail at the time.

IW: Did the author of *City of God*, Paulo Lins, have anything to do with this documentary? It seems right up his street.
KL: Yes, I interviewed him for it, when *City of God* was still in manuscript form. He claims it was his first interview ever. Later, because my films and his book discussed the same subjects, we participated in many conferences and debates together. We became close friends and then even directed a music video together. When the book *City of God* came out in 1997, all the directors around wanted it. There was a real tussle for it, but Fernando Meirelles bought it and hired Braulio Mantovani to write an adaptation.

IW: Can you explain the co-directing credit? I'm used to directors being very possessive of their work.
KL: A lot of work is co-directed in Brazil. It's just the way we do it. Fernando's previous two features, *Crazy Kid II* and *Maids*, are co-directed. Walter Salles has two features that are co-directed. Documentaries and music videos are also co-directed. This trend has emerged in my generation and in the wave of films that appeared since 1996, when tax laws helped Brazilian film come back from the ashes. Fernando Collor had destroyed the film industry in 1990 by closing Embrafilme and destroying the economy as a whole. When MTV started in the early nineties, music videos had insignificant budgets, but they offered a space for new film-makers to show their talent and experiment with visual styles. Directors, cinematographers, art directors, writers, etc. would give up their salaries and take a screen credit instead. MTV only gives credit to directors, so everyone took credit as a director. It was also great fun, because the creative process was a brainstorming session, where the best ideas were made better by all; the collective vision of the film was the film's real director. Since there is no money to be made in film here (except in advertising), anyone doing film is doing it because they are crazy and passionate about what they are doing. Co-directing became a way for friends to get together and work together for the

best possible outcome. Each director was also responsible for a different technical area.

The other reason is that producers don't really exist in Brazil due to the lack of profits. So directors are the ones who create the ideas, write the scripts, raise the money, hold the crews together, look after distribution, etc. It is very lonely to be a director. I was at a Brazilian film festival last year in London, organized by the Brazilian Embassy, where one third of the films were co-directed.

IW: You had problems with your credit once the film was released internationally, though. I remember reading Philip French's review, and he made a point of saying that this was Fernando's first film as sole director. And French is usually very accurate.

KL: All you have to do is look at the body of my work to see where this film fits in. It deals with the same subjects using the same tone, shooting style and acting techniques visible in my previous work. Even a lot of the same actors. If people look at my previous work and Fernando's previous work I believe it is easy to see how each contributed to the directing of this film.

My credit is protected on the screen by contract but not in the advertising, unfortunately. I hope to have a better agent and lawyer next time around. Fernando Meirelles had the rights to the book and acted as both producer and director in this film. I co-directed this film with him. Fernando was unfamiliar with the universe portrayed in the film and had never worked with this cast before. For this reason, he asked me to participate in the project, and I said I would, but only if I had co-directing credit. He agreed and we worked together on the script from the fourth draft to the twelfth draft; we developed the cast together from August 2000 to June 2001. When shooting began, we worked together on the set every day and discussed everything on the way to and from the set each day. Our thoughts were completely synchronized throughout the production process. The film was also being edited as we shot, so we could see the results of our work. Later, Fernando went on to finish the editing and music in São Paulo and I was only sporadically involved in the post-production process.

IW: Was it a case of machismo?

KL: Maybe machismo in general, but not Brazilian machismo. There are many female directors here, as there are mayors, governors, etc. I never felt any sexism working in film here until I worked for American films. I went for an interview for first AD on a film called *Anaconda*, which was shooting in the jungle, and I was told that the producer didn't want a woman because shooting in the jungle was difficult. I eventually did get the job and I remember a producer's wife coming on set one day and being shocked that there was a female first AD. I made an issue of wearing a dress to the set every day.

In Cannes, too, when I was doing press for *City of God*, I constantly felt that the people interviewing me assumed that, if you co-direct with a man, he does all the work.

IW: So, once Fernando had the rights, how did you become involved?
KL: We had never worked together before, but Fernando had already seen the documentary, music videos and short films I had shot in the favelas with local actors. He asked me to help him get into that universe, improve the script and find the actors. He was from São Paolo, a commercials director, as far removed from that world as anyone. We discussed the project and realized that we couldn't use professional actors for this piece. The way the people of the favela walk and talk and scratch their heads is completely different. It can't be faked.

We needed to find between fifty and sixty speaking parts. I came up with the idea of setting up an acting school so we could create a cohesive body of actors. Fernando agreed and the cost of the school was paid for by the production.

IW: Was the idea of the acting school similar to the great samba schools of the favelas – which are more than just organizations that put on shows for tourists forty days before Easter. The samba schools are for me one of the things that makes Brazil such a great place. Here you have the poorest of the poor, living in the most miserable conditions surrounded by violence, hunger and disease, and the one time they are given a world stage to express their discontent – *carnaval* – they make a scathing political attack through the most extravagant song and dance show in the world!
KL: Yes, the favelas all have various forms of local government. They've had to organize themselves because they were so abused. They needed to send emissaries out to campaign for electricity, water sources, sewage pipes and, most importantly, avoid their removal to distant places such as City of God, away from jobs, schools and transport. We sent the word out about the acting school – it would be a free acting course and we would provide transport and a snack. We did not tell them about the film until diplomas had been distributed. This way everyone enjoyed the collective experience, free of competitive tension and test anxiety. The course succeeded in creating great energy, and that energy is on the screen.

IW: How many people turned up?
KL: Two thousand.

IW: Oh my. Then what?
KL: We selected four hundred of them and started doing improvisations with them.

IW: What kind of improv?
KL: All stuff that they could relate to and which was pertinent to our subject:

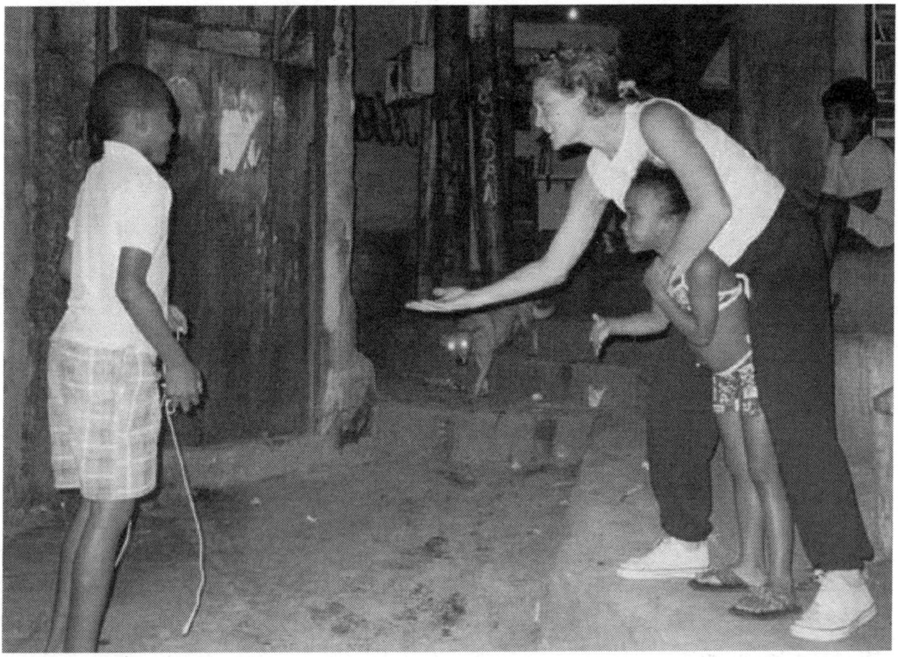

Top: Katia Lund at the acting school in the favela . . .
Bottom: . . . and with the eventual cast of *City of God*

life in the favela and gang warfare. We gave them the situation and the intention, and they worked from there. We incorporated language and lessons learned for the improvisations into the script. From these, we chose two hundred for interviews.

IW: How old were they?
KL: Between ten and twenty-five years old.

IW: Then you started casting the film from there.
KL: Before selecting actors for specific roles in *City of God*, Fernando Meirelles and I made a pilot for a TV series called *Golden Gate* in December 2000. We used children from the acting workshop, instead of the usual TV Globo actors. We used this short as a rehearsal for *City of God*. It is where Fernando and I developed and tested the visual language of the film, tested film stock, favouring the non-professional acting style with camera and editing techniques. The show was a huge success at the time and won numerous national and international awards. Thirty-five per cent of the Brazilian public watched it – that's an audience of 40 million people. We were able to talk about important and harrowing social issues in a humorous way.

IW: That presumably paved the way for *City of God* to be made.
KL: Yes. The budget was $3.3 million.

IW: How did you prepare the kids for these harrowing scenes?
KL: We had an acting coach, Fatima Toledo, who specializes in training kids with no previous acting experience. She worked on *Pixote*, *At Play in the Fields of the Lord*, *Central Station*, etc. She approaches it psychologically and prepares them over a long period of time, scene by scene.

IW: I'm thinking specifically about the scene in which Zé Pequeno shoots the little boy in the foot. I found this almost pornographic, given the fact that these kids live through this type of thing on a daily basis.
KL: That was actually the hardest scene to shoot. It came quite early on in the schedule. And the boy had not rehearsed with the actor playing Zé Pequeno, but had prepared for the scene intensely over the course of one week. The scene goes on even further. The author, Paulo Lins, really wanted the whole thing in the film because he witnessed it with his own eyes. Zé Pequeno lets the boy go, with his foot shot, and he hobbles away, turns a corner and gets shot in the forehead. As Paulo Lins says, the film is lighter than the book, which is lighter than reality.

IW: It's also one of the few scenes where the camera is quite still, as opposed to the very flash editing that goes on in the rest of the film.
KL: The editor is a twenty-four-year-old former DJ called Danny Boy. He worked as an intern for Fernando, then became an assistant director on

commercials and worked his way up from there. He also suggested much of the music, which is period and mentioned in the book. The only music that is missing are some songs by Jorge Ben, who didn't want to be associated with the film. He never even watched it. I think he would have changed his mind.

IW: Do you feel a sense of responsibility for the kids in the acting school? I'm thinking of the kid in *Pixote*, Hector Babenco's film, who ultimately returned to the streets and was killed in much the same way the film portrayed – by a police death squadron.
KL: That boy did have a career after that film came out, but did not have the discipline or drive to continue learning and growing to meet the new challenges without coaching. I think Hector has been unfairly blamed for the way things turned out. Hector gave him a house to live in with his family and a job in his production company. He robbed Hector, then went on to commit more crimes with his brothers. The police finally caught up with him and shot him while he was hiding under his bed.

That incident has made us all more cautious. Walter Salles took extra care of the little boy in *Central Station*. And we were worried about our kids. But there is no guarantee. There is only so much you can do. You can only help those who want to be helped. Some do. Some don't.

IW: What can you do?
KL: Fernando agreed to continue financing the school for another three months after we finished shooting the film. We hired teachers and tutors for the kids and we met every Saturday to give them a sense of belonging, of a community. But all that was four months before the film was released in Brazil. I continued financing it for a while and am now still trying to get funding elsewhere.

IW: Presumably Globo and Miramax could help? They must have made quite a bit of money on it.
KL: I have a call into Harvey Weinstein, but so far we are playing phone tag . . . In early 2002, Fernando said he would no longer be funding the group, so in order for it not to die until funding arrived, I invented a project for them to continue working on. The idea was to shoot two short films with borrowed equipment and help from friends in the business. Each participant would come up with an idea for a one-minute short film. We'd meet on Saturdays and work together to improve all the ideas, then vote on two to produce. With the experience they had gained on *City of God*, they had the responsibility to do it all – write it, produce it, hire actors, equipment, hussle for freebies. The first film they made was called *Cidadão Silva* (*Citizen Silva*) about an adolescent like themselves who is contemplating whether or not to commit suicide. The second was called *Bathroom*, a very funny conversation between the shower, the toilet and the mirror about the family that uses them.

IW: That's fantastic. So you oversaw these?

KL: At this point, they oversee me. The leadership and administration is mostly in their hands. I am very much involved, but in a collaborative and fund-raising role. At the end of 2002, I had to leave Brazil to participate in the launch of *City of God* overseas, so I opened a bank account for them and put 5,000 reais in it. They had complete responsibility for running it. About twenty of them took the lead and set up a type of talent agency that provides actors and crew, mainly for music videos and documentaries. They also organize educational debates in schools, so there is a social aspect to the whole enterprise as well. These activities partially support the school. The drive is for self-sufficiency.

IW: Lula's new Brazil. I remember him so well from when I was living there. He didn't give up. I read an article in the *Guardian* that said that Lula seems like he should be in the White House and Dubya seems more like the dictator of a banana republic.

KL: There is great optimism here at the moment. It's very exciting, the idea that change must happen at grass-roots level. I can't think of living anywhere else.

IW: What's next for you?

KL: We've been hired to continue the series we started with *Golden Gate*, using the same core actors, over five years – four half-hour episodes per year. Fernando and I each direct an episode each year and get in other directors to direct the rest. Also, I am editing a documentary I did on the role of hip-hop in Brazil, the United States and Cuba. In the Third World and communist countries, hip-hop is a form of social activism and education. In the States, commercial interests have taken over. I am also writing my next feature project.

Linda
by Allison Anders

A few years ago, living in London, I had renewed a girlhood fascination with a long dead and forgotten silent star named Olive Thomas. The internet has been both a godsend and curse at reuniting me with every former obsession of mine, be it an obscure rock or pop band, a favourite place, an obscure movie, record or frivolous object I was momentarily fixated on.

In my net surfing on Olive Thomas, I found tons of entries, most with the wildly inaccurate details of her tragic young death, which would become the first Hollywood scandal when the young Mrs Jack Pickford took bichloride of mercury in a suite at The Ritz in Paris on a second honeymoon with her charming young actor husband and brother to Mary. It took Olive days to die from the poison and, though it was ruled an accident, there was speculation about whether it was a suicide and why: Was Jack unfaithful? Was he a drug addict? Was she? Did he give her syphilis? Had they been partying wildly in Paris that night at the oh-so-punk-rock-sounding Montmartre cafe called The Dead Rat? Well, at least this much we know to be true: they were indeed imbibing and no doubt more at the cafe where Rimbaud had committed his passions to paper.

I don't know what happened to Olive that night, nor why she did it or made such a gruesome mistake, but I loved her – I couldn't explain why – and I had since I first saw a picture of her in a library book when I was seventeen years old and read the small bio underneath her gaze. She was regarded and billed as 'The Most Beautiful Girl in the World' at one point in her career and, though in 2003 most people have no idea who she was, her funeral in 1920 was so widely attended that fans were crushed trying to get to her casket. Her pall-bearers were Irving Berlin and the elder Selznick brothers. A decade plus later, Jack Pickford ironically died at the very same Paris hospital where he sat in vigil with his young beautiful wife.

In my intoxication for their story, I discovered a web site for silent films called Grapevine, which offered a partial film of Olive's. While ordering that, I also found a King Vidor early silent and, to my bemusement, a film by someone named Mrs Wallace Reid. Sounded like a matron from the Women's Temperance League. I had to laugh, but nonetheless was intrigued – this was a woman who directed a movie in the silent era. It was probably just an industrial movie directed at youth gone wild, but what the hell, worth looking at. The name of the film was *Linda*.

Mrs Wallace Reid and her children

The package arrived at my flat in Belsize Park and I went first to watch the Olive Thomas movie, *Love's Prisoner*. It was clearly not the finest movie she had ever made, but I hoped somehow to see more of her films if any were available (none are as of yet). Then on to the King Vidor movie, *Love Never Dies* (1921). A little dull, I was rather surprised to discover, but hey, he was learning. Yet nowhere was the spark of his genius we would later see in *The Champ*, *Northwest Passage* or *Ruby Gentry*. Lastly I let the videotape slide into the black mouth of the VCR for the offering from Mrs Wallace Reid, *Linda*.

From the very first frames, I was enthralled. Linda (played by the lovely, delicate but strong Helen Foster) is a young girl of about fourteen years of age who lives in a poor family. She longs desperately to be educated and loves to run

Olive Thomas

away from her alcoholic father and her beaten-down mother to read her books in her favourite tree. She also has a mentor: a modern woman from the city who is an educator and who takes a real big-sister interest in Linda. A kindly, much older man (Noah Berry) in the village sees Linda reading in the tree. He himself can't read and is impressed as she reads to him. He is also taken by her young, pure beauty and goes to her father and asks to marry her. The alcoholic father is all too happy to sell his daughter off for a little drinking cash and to have one less mouth to feed. Even her beaten-down mother wonders if Linda wouldn't be better off in his care.

The young girl's devastation to be sold off to this older man, with all it implies, is heart-wrenching. I have never seen the dread and betrayal and deep pain played to the core as superbly as this in any other silent movie. Mrs Wallace Reid even got her young actress to portray such fear during the dreaded wedding night that the empathy you feel for this character is almost unbearable.

But then, she surprises us. In time, Linda, while never giving her heart to this man and never resigning herself to her fate, becomes a very good wife and then a wonderful mother to their baby son. Her older husband loves her so dearly. And while Linda has never lost sight of her dreams, she is making a success of her life.

One of the most exquisitely directed scenes in the film is when Linda's ticket to freedom arrives in the form of a woman with a young boy in tow who appears on the doorstep claiming to be Linda's husband's real wife and this is his son. Linda now has her long-awaited way out from the marriage as she is ordered out of the house by this woman. Linda gathers her baby son up and a few belongings but, as she leaves, Reid again surprises us. Linda, having now grown compassionate towards her husband, has lingering worries over his well-being. She reminds the first wife of what things her husband will need: 'And Mr Decker likes his coffee in the morning,' continuing as she begins out the door, 'And don't forget to . . .' It's directed with such a delicate hand that it's not just a scene that moves the emotions, but also one that moves one to steal it!

Linda goes to the city to live with her mentor, and there she meets a young doctor who is a much more appropriate suitor, one who is her choice. Linda completes school and becomes a teacher but needs to get a divorce from her husband in order to marry the young doctor. When she arrives at his house she finds Mr Decker sick and dying, and in tears of joy to see his baby again. When she sees how much he has missed her and his son, she is devastated; she simply can't leave him.

The last scene in the movie is one of the most gorgeous moments in any film I have seen. When the old man dies, Linda takes her baby out and sets the house on fire. The camera is behind Linda, her baby and the young doctor. The cabin Mr Decker had loved is ablaze. The flames are oddly elegant and without menace. She and the young doctor watch as it burns, and as the fire lights the sky in the idyllic country setting . . . a tremendously beautiful unexpected ending.

It was time for me to find out more about this woman director who had skill far beyond the work of young Vidor. I went to the web and gathered books from Ebay by Anthony Slide (*The Silent Feminist*) and Ally Acker (*Reel Women*) and writings posted by various fans on the net. Mrs Wallace Reid's life was as dramatic, dignified and empowered as her young heroine's life had been. She was born Dorothy Davenport and reared in a theatrical family, the daughter of thespians Alice and Harry Davenport. The Davenports were Christian Scientists with very progressive social views. Dorothy grew up believing she would never marry because she could not imagine herself tied to the home. She was an actress on the stage and then, when movies came around, she appeared in those

Mr and Mrs Wallace Reid: 'She took to motherhood with complete commitment.'

too. She was working for Universal, which was where she met actor Wallace Reid. Reid did everything to court Dorothy, but she was uninterested. In order to be a worthy suitor Reid had to prove himself more than just a handsome, charming movie star. He had to prove he was educated, multi-talented and as progressive as the young object of his desire. He proved to be all of these. Wallace Reid was a musician, a painter and a thinker, and was beginning to be influenced by Dorothy's very liberal, Quaker-like anti-racist, anti-sexist, humanistic view of the world.

She finally agreed to marry him and, like her heroine Linda, took to marriage and motherhood with complete commitment. She was madly in love with her

Wallace Reid arrives in Los Angeles met by Mrs Wallace Reid and Billy

husband and he with her – they were tremendous partners, in spite of any infidelities Wallace was reported to have committed. They had a son Billy and later adopted a three-year-old girl who was rumoured to be Wallace Reid's love child. If this is true, it only emphasizes Mrs Wallace Reid's compassion.

The tragedy that unravelled their happiness came when Wallace Reid suffered an injury in an accident on set. He was given morphine to ease the tremendous pain he was in, and his addiction to the drug became his undoing. For the next three years Wallace Reid was in and out of rehab, becoming a well-known hazard on the set due to his addiction, which also erupted into full-blown alcoholism. He was targeted by William Hays as part of his mandate to clean up Hollywood. Instead of covering up for her husband, Dorothy did an incredible thing: she wrote a piece in the local paper on the disease of addiction. This was years before Bill W. and Dr Bob founded Alcoholics Anonymous, which would be based on the same premise. Dorothy urged the public not to judge her husband or any other drug addict or alcoholic for an illness over which they were powerless.

That powerlessness in the end took Wallace's life in 1923. Although he had finally managed to kick the morphine, he had done so much damage to himself in the process that he died after several months' stay at a rehab clinic with Dorothy by his side, holding his hand. After his death she made a national radio broadcast that began with the words, 'This is Mrs Wallace Reid.' There is no question in my mind that the dignity and pride in her voice was the inspiration for a similarly powerful ending in *A Star Is Born*: 'This is Mrs Norman Maine.' The girl who would be no man's property proudly took his name and referred to herself as his 'Mrs' to her death. Often, in a feminist attempt to show her in her own right, writers refer to her as Dorothy Davenport or Dorothy Davenport Reid. But I feel she was determined to be Mrs Wallace Reid (or just Dorothy), and that's how I prefer to call her.

After the death of her husband, Mrs Wallace Reid's first order of business was to establish a sanatorium called the Wallace Reid Foundation for drug and alcohol rehabilitation. With two children to care for and stories to tell, she began to take her talents behind the camera. Like her mentor, director/producer Lois Weber, she would begin by making 'message' films. In 1923, Thomas Ince gave her that opportunity. Moved and inspired by her work with addicts, Ince hired her to produce a film about the dangers of drug addiction called *Human Wreckage*, which was a huge box-office success. She produced one more film for Ince – *Broken Laws* – before his mysterious death. This time Dorothy hired her friend Adela Rogers St John to write the script. She would go on to collaborate with other women on several future pictures. Her commitment to working with women is best summed up in her own words, quoted by Anthony Slide in *The Silent Feminist*: 'I believe it takes a woman to believe in a woman's motives, and every story intended for the screen should have a woman working on it at some stage to convince the audience of women.'

After Ince's untimely death a year later, Dorothy was on her own and the first film she produced after forming her own production company was *The Red Kimono*. She was very hands-on with the direction under Walter Lang, who would go on to become a long-time collaborator with her. Dorothy appeared in the film in a supporting role and hired Dorothy Arzner – who would later become a legendary film director herself – to adapt the screenplay from an original story by Adela Rogers St John. The film is about a girl's struggle to overcome a desperate life in Storyville, New Orleans, as a young prostitute. This was based on a true story about one Gabrielle Darley. There was a huge lawsuit, the first of its kind, which overshadowed the film: apparently the young prostitute whose story was portrayed and whose actual name was used was, at the time of the film's release, living as a married woman in prominent St Louis society and did not appreciate being outed! Hence the maddening struggles we go through today in trying to name characters who bear no likeness to those likely to come out and sue. The very existence of what is known as Errors and Omissions Insurance on most film productions stems, in part, from this lawsuit long ago

The Red Kimono

surrounding Mrs Wallace Reid's film! By all accounts *The Red Kimono* was a very gritty and edgy portrayal of street life – without moralizing – which until then had not been seen in Hollywood. I haven't seen *The Red Kimono*, although I do own a beautiful hand-tinted colour lobby card from the film which credits all three legendary women: Adela, Dorothy and Dorothy.

By the time she came to make *Linda*, Mrs Wallace Reid was ready to try her hand at directing. She hired Maxine Alton to adapt the play for the screen. There is little information available on the production of the film, but it has been called a 'quickie'; as a woman indie film-maker I know the hell and the joys

A Woman Condemned

of 'quickie film-making'. But it's something to note when looking at *Linda*; all that you see was done on a small budget with very little time in the schedule. Knowing all too well what that means, to me it makes the film all the more masterful. The film also contains some synched sound effects and a synched soundtrack score, before sound in films came into being.

Dorothy continued to write for films up until 1955, including writing many of the Curly and His Gang movies for Hal Roach. But the last film she directed, *A Woman Condemned*, was in 1934, around the time when most women directors became unemployed. She managed to produce for another four years, but her personal work was behind her. Ally Acker's book quotes her saying, 'Women have a lot to give to motion pictures, but not in the capacity of producer. Men resent women in top executive positions in films as in any field of endeavor.'

Her masterpiece is without question *Linda*. When I first saw it, I was both awed, thrilled to have discovered her, and angry that I never knew about her before. She had lived in Woodland Hills – right here in the San Fernando Valley – through the seventies. I could have met her, but I simply didn't know she existed. Anthony Slide has said that women directors of today looked at him numbly when he informed them they were not the first women directors. I gathered he took this to mean that they were uninterested. My guess is that this numbness he encountered is utter disbelief and bewilderment that we never knew of them before; most of us went to film school, so why weren't we told about our foremothers? And also Slide may have encountered a frozen panic: if women directors had such power in Hollywood, before we even had the right to vote, and we have never heard of any of them nor their accomplishments, what fate awaits *us*? Will we be as forgotten?

Just yesterday, by pure chance during my research on short rock'n'roll films, I discovered another woman director I had never heard of before: Barbara Rubin. Aged seventeen (in 1963!) she made *Christmas on Earth*, which many agree may have been the first multi-screen presentation of a film ever. But this is hardly the most remarkable quality of the film, which is a wildly radical meditation on sexuality on two reels. The idea is to project both reels simultaneously, with the projectionist choosing a random AM radio station soundtrack (much harder to find a good soundtrack at random in this clear-channel age). Remember she was seventeen and this was 1963, and she was a girl! Barbara Rubin is noted for being not only an experimental film-maker of monumental importance but for being the girl who introduced Andy Warhol to Bob Dylan, Edie to Warhol, the Velvet Underground to Warhol, and Edie to puking up her food. She was also Allen Ginsberg's only girlfriend ever. Why do we not know about this woman? As far as I can tell, few of her films, with the exception of *Christmas on Earth*, remain. How I would love to get my hands on her Velvet Underground films or films of hers which they did live soundtracks to, or one obscure one credited to her called *The Day the Byrds Flew into the Factory and I Went Out*. Though I have seen none of these, I have made it a mission to keep looking and letting people know about her.

I saw a young woman walking in the mall last night wearing a T-shirt which said 'Andy Warhol Films'. I stopped her and asked where she got it, and she said at a conference on Warhol's movies. I asked if she knew of Barbara Rubin; she had never heard of her. I began to tell her all about what I had learned, as though it were my duty and my pleasure, and this young woman was enthralled to learn about this amazing film-maker. She said, in that frustration I know all too well, 'I even took a class on Warhol in college and they never mentioned her!' You'd think people would include the person who introduced Warhol to Edie at the very least, eh?

So, as a woman director, again the question comes to haunt me when I think about Mrs Wallace Reid and her magnificent work: Will we all be as forgotten as she is? Maybe so. But not necessarily for ever. Somehow, Reid's gem made its way to me . . . over seventy years since it was directed by this remarkable woman at a time when a woman's right to vote was in its tender infancy.

Susanne Bier

Susanne Bier
interviewed by Jason Wood

Susanne Bier studied at the Bezalet Academy of Arts and Design in Jerusalem and read architecture in London before enrolling for the film direction course at the National Film School of Denmark.

Her graduation film, De Saliges Ø *(1987), won first prize at the Munich film school festival and was distributed by Channel Four.*

Her work since then includes the award-winning features Freud Flytter Hjemmefra (Freud Leaving Home, *1990*), Det Bli'r i Familien (Family Matters, *1993*), Pensionat Oscar (Like It Was Never Before, *1995*), Sekten (Credo, *1997*) *and, last but not least,* Den Eneste Ene (The One and Only, *1999*), *which won numerous Roberts and Bodils (Danish film awards).* Hånden på Hjertet (Once in a Lifetime), *featuring Helena Bergström, was released on 25 December 2000.*

Also the maker of shorts, music videos and commercials, Bier's most recent film is the widely acclaimed, multi-prize-winning Open Hearts.

Jason Wood: Could you begin by talking about how you first became involved in film directing and some of your motivations for doing so?

Susanne Bier: I studied comparative religion for a while and then I studied architecture, and whilst I was studying architecture I became much more interested in movie-like elements such as set design. Then I became more interested in the people within the walls that I would design and began reading scripts. I applied to the National Film School in England to be a set designer. During the interview, I told them that I was undecided as to whether I wanted to be a set designer or a director, and they told me that I should go home and think about that. Very soon after, I applied to the National Film School of Denmark as a director. I am not like many of the male directors who have been film fanatics all their lives.

JW: Were there any particular directors or film figures at this time who did exert an influence over you?

SB: I was incredibly influenced at that time by directors such as Antonioni and others who used architecture very significantly. Eventually, as I progressed through film school, I became very interested in the American directors of the seventies. I think that if one is to talk about Dogme and that particular sensibility, then we are heavily indebted to the 'movie brats' and what those American directors did for cinema in the seventies. I think that what they were aiming for and what we are also aiming for is some kind of deeper sense of realism and a deeper sense of dealing with a character's truthful world.

JW: Were you also influenced by the tendency amongst many of the directors of that period to concentrate more on character than on adhering to formulaic narrative conventions?
SB: Very much. I was very interested in films such as *Dog Day Afternoon*. On its most simplistic level, this is a film about a bank robbery, but if you look at other films about bank robberies this is not classically what they look like. This was a movie where they were incredibly focused on character; I was very influenced by that. I was also very influenced by the notion of a character being beyond the narrative.

JW: *Open Hearts*, your most recent film, explores the notion of the fragility of life and the shifting sands on which modern life and relations are built. You have stated that this theme became even clearer to you when shooting the film in the post-11 September climate. The current situation in Iraq, I think, further emphasizes this.
SB: We wrote the script before the events of 11 September but shot it after them, so while we were working on the film this notion of fragility became very strong, especially for our actors. The screenwriter, Anders Thomas Jensen, and I actually met through my own very strong personal sense of potential catastrophe. I think that this has to do with being Jewish and having a sense of history where the impossible is a possibility. I think Anders also has this sense of potential catastrophe so this was very close to us. The events of 11 September have really altered most people's perception of fragility on a grand scale. On that day, if you happened to be late for your train you survived, whereas if you just happened to go into the office early you were dead.

JW: There are moments that are both emotionally and physically shocking. Joachim (Nikolaj Lie Kaas) being struck down by a car, Niels (Mads Mikkelsen) deciding that he is going to leave his wife. These moments frequently seem to come out of the blue, acting almost as a slap in the face for the audience. Was this intentional?
SB: I felt that the accident had to happen like that. As for Niels leaving his wife, I think that this is how these things actually happen. In these situations you do things that are not necessarily planned, and actions become more definite than you intended them when you actually started talking. It's the kind of situation where you realize, after you have taken a major action, the long-term implications of what you have actually done. Telling somebody that you love them is the same; the words often just fall out of your mouth. Telling a person that you are leaving them is often fake because there is this assumption that you have planned it and it is not always like that. In fact, the act of telling somebody that

Open Hearts: Sonja Richter with Nikolaj Lie Kaas (top) and Mads Mikkelsen (bottom)

you are leaving them is often more shocking for the person doing the leaving than it is for the receiver.

JW: To return to the accident sequence, how difficult was the accident to set up? It avoids histrionics, which makes it all the more harrowing.
SB: In terms of practicalities, Nikolaj obviously went through the scene with a stuntman so that he wouldn't hurt himself. That was basically it. There are no effects at all, and I was initially scared and anxious that it wouldn't be enough and would lack impact and simply not work. Actually, I feel that it is much harsher than if there had been lots of technical effects. From a technical perspective, I am perhaps most proud of this scene.

JW: In playing a paraplegic Nikolaj Lie Kaas has perhaps the most difficult acting task. How did you help him and what specific technical issues did the scenario present?
SB: We had a specialized nurse who deals with such injuries with us all the time in order for it to be right. This is why in some scenes he is on his back and in others he is on his side. The nurse also helped shape the way in which we show Joachim being encouraged to deal with the reality of his situation. It was then up to Nikolaj to administer the performance, obviously acting only with his face. I was keen that he avoided some of the usual histrionics that are common when actors play invalids.

JW: The film marks Sonja Richter's (Cecile) screen début. What convinced you that she would be right for the part and how did you help her find and develop her character?
SB: I had a casting agent audition thirty or so actors for the part and then, from this, I auditioned the best seven or so actors myself. As soon as she came into the audition I thought, 'I really hope she is good because she is the one I want.' She had a frailness and yet a kind of strength. She was very confident in herself in working with the more experienced actors and certainly wasn't timid. Sex scenes can be intimidating for an actor doing them for the first time, but Sonja handled them extremely well and threw herself into it with a lot of authority.

JW: You convey very economically the distinctions between the somewhat staid marriage between Niels and Marie (Paprika Steen) and the subsequent burgeoning relationship between Niels and Cecile.
SB: It was a very fine balance because I wanted the wife to be attractive and I wanted the marriage to be a good marriage. I didn't want it to be a dead marriage but, on the other hand, I did want it to be the kind of marriage where somehow you felt lonely. What often happens is that you fall into patterns with one another and that the gap between you can actually grow without anybody

noticing because everything seems to be fine. Marie seems to be in charge of everything, but I think Niels has been feeling increasingly lonely whilst still performing the functions of family life. With Cecile he is suddenly given a new chance to define himself and find out who he is after he has grown up. For Niels this offers an injection of life that proves irresistible.

JW: How deep was your involvement with Jesper Winge Leisner's score?
SB: I worked quite closely with him on this. The score was actually composed before shooting; because of the Dogme rules, the majority of the music comes out of Cecile's headphones, so all the songs were composed in advance. I was keen that the slower ballad – the one which is played the most and which is associated with Cecile – was slightly slower than Leisner's original concept. I wanted it to capture who she is, and as soon as I heard it I thought, yes, that's her.

JW: The film uses a very distinct palette. The sombre greens of the hospital, contrasted with the more sensual oranges and reds of Cecile's apartment.
SB: The natural lighting that was available to us dictated this. If you use a lot of candles, as Cecile does, you do get a very warm, reddish hue. It was also a way of offering a juxtaposition between the comforting interiors and the harsh exteriors that are a reality of a Scandinavian winter. We wanted to push this element. Also, we Danes simply use lots of candles; the days are so short so we have to have a way of making it cosy.

JW: How did the raw emotions with which *Open Hearts* deals contribute to the shoot?
SB: When you shoot a Dogme film you have a very small crew, so everybody is part of a scene and the mood of the scene is very much the mood of the set so, yes, certain days were very painful. The two or three days over which we shot the disintegration of the marriage – which features arguments and recriminations – were quite tough and there was a certain amount of relief when we had finished with this painful period. Also, as a director, if you want the honesty that you desire from a scene and from your actors, you do also have to live within the content of a specific scene.

JW: There seems to be a very natural bond between the actors. How did you encourage this?
SB: Well, Paprika and Mads are quite friendly off-screen, and I am on quite close terms with both of them. I often find that actors are far too polite to be really familiar with one another. Sonja and Nikolaj did not know each other, but I think this was an advantage because their on-screen characters have the crispness and spontaneity of a relatively new relationship. It was important that they weren't too familiar.

JW: With regards to the smaller crew, did you enjoy working within the more intimate Dogme parameters?

SB: I have never worked with huge crews, but I had certainly not worked with as minimal a crew as this before. The rule of working only with available lighting, of course, reduces the crew immediately, and there are other people that are not on set who normally would be, such as costume, make-up, etc. Everybody has such big responsibilities on a Dogme film that it often gives the movie an edginess that I find very satisfying. *Open Hearts* is the most exhausting film I have ever made but certainly the most exciting. There is no waiting around on a Dogme film, so you are able to shoot all the time. This makes it vivid and invigorating, but there is an explosion of energy that ultimately makes it exhausting.

JW: How does the actual process of making a Dogme film unfold? Are there various approvals that are required?

SB: There was a Dogme office that is now closed, but nothing has to be approved. You submit yourself to the vow of chastity and then you follow the rules. The question of obeying the rules is itself a question of interpretation. The Dogme rules are also very much open to interpretation, as is the whole political content. Making a Dogme film is a political act somehow because it is saying that movies – and then, in a broader sense, art – has to deal with your own world. I think that the most important rule is that of the director not assuming any sort of aesthetics, of not loading the movie with an aesthetic. I think that this is an impossible rule to adhere to because any artistic decision is an aesthetic decision; when you make a cut it is an aesthetic decision. Having said that, for me it is also the most important rule because psychology must be beyond anything else. In a traditional film there may be the temptation to dress the actors in certain colours in order to create a specific visual effect. For example, in many Bergman films the actors all wear very natural colours. You cannot do that here because the actors bring all of their own clothes themselves and choose whatever they find to be particularly suitable for their character. You can't put an aesthetic above psychology.

JW: *Open Hearts* has a realist aesthetic that can be attributed to the Dogme practice of production, particularly the use of hand-held cameras. This is particularly good for highlighting the moments of intimacy and awkwardness between characters. Was this one of the enticements for working within the Dogme format?

SB: I had been talking to Peter Aalbaek Jensen at Zentropa about making a Dogme film for a few years but didn't feel that I had the right story. It was after we had made the first version of the script that both Anders Thomas Jensen and I thought that it would be extremely suited to a Dogme film because we felt that the storyline would gain from being forced into reality. One of the Dogme rules, of course, is that the camera has to be hand-held, so this was a consideration. For me, it was very important to have elements in the film that did not adhere to rational aspects of storytelling but which did embody the psychological space between the characters.

JW: Did you find any of the Dogme rules prohibitive?
SB: I do find the rule that the sound has to be produced at the same time as the image prohibiting. I understand that it prevents the director from indulging in filmic stunts, but the problem is that while shooting it becomes very complicated. For example, if you have some extras talking in the background and you want real sounds from them, it has to be produced at the same time as the more important dialogue in the foreground. This makes the actual process of shooting in terms of sound incredibly inflexible and actually opposed to the realness of the Dogme credo.

JW: Are you contemplating working again under the Dogme regulations?
SB: Yes, I am, because I don't feel that I have investigated it all the way through. I feel that I want to take it further.

JW: Somewhat in contrast with the Dogme realist aesthetic are the inserts of daydream sequences where Cecile imagines Joachim's hand moving towards hers.
SB: We wanted some kind of medium for the characters to act upon impulses in a way that they were unable to actually do. For example, Cecile really wanted to touch Joachim and him to reach out and touch her, and so the Super 8 sequences were a means of allowing this to happen. In the original cut there were many more quite extreme instances of these fantasy sequences. I wanted them to be almost real, but not completely. I find these sequences offer a feeling of relief. I very much like the scene where Joachim moves his hand. There was a lot of discussion about this because it almost feels as if it is too much.

JW: The opening and closing images of the film use a heat-sensitive camera. What were your intentions here?
SB: I wanted an image that would have the characteristics of an X-ray, and this was the closest we could get. Because it was winter it worked extremely well because the area was so cold and the bodies were so hot. We had this camera with us throughout the shoot and used the technique quite a lot, but we realized during the editing process that it became disturbing within the actual narrative because you went continually in and out of the fiction. Therefore, we used it only at the opening and closing of the film. It also worked well there because there were lots of people, heightening the effect.

JW: And why was this X-ray effect so important to you?
SB: It was my way of saying that these people could be any one of us, that once

you take away the actual faces of people we are all alike on the inside; the events that occur within the film could happen to anyone.

JW: Was the film radically altered during editing?
SB: It did change a lot. Eventually, it did become the movie we wanted it to be whilst writing the script, but the first cut was three hours long and felt very monumental. The first cut was very arty and certainly very heavy; it didn't really capture the light that exists amongst the sadness. I invited eight or nine friends – who also work in the film industry and whose opinions I respect – and they kept saying, no, you mustn't cut it down, but I knew that this version was not the film I wanted. I wanted something that didn't impose the themes upon the audience; it contained them but did not overwhelm you with them.

JW: In Denmark you are probably best known for your comedies. *Open Hearts* treads a very fine balance between comedy and tragedy and has a humour that evolves from the reality of the situation – the recently paralysed Joachim having difficulties using the electronic page-turning device, for example.
SB: I do think that life is a balance between tragedy and comedy. My earlier work, including the comedies, does have a sadness to it. True, they are more funny than sad, but both elements are present. I could never make a purely 'sad' film because I do not believe that life is like that. I always have a hard time with certain Scandinavian movies where a lonely woman stands and cries silently by a window. I think that the scene with the book you mention is very truthful; life can be like that. For me, humour can be a way of understanding tragedy. I personally understand tragedy much better through dark humour than I do through the heavy movies I was subjected to all through my childhood.

JW: Your mention of the woman at the window crying reminds me of the refreshing way in which *Open Hearts* handles the theme of infidelity. You avoid the cliché of the vengeful spouse and that of the lust-addled husband.
SB: I don't approve in real life of the vindictive bitter woman. The only person you are actually harming is yourself. Also, to paint all men as bastards – life is not really like that. One of the things about growing up is realizing that people and situations are not black and white. These kinds of representations in cinema have nothing to do with life.

JW: Your work has been critically and commercially successful in Denmark. How much does this mean to you personally?
SB: Well, I had flu when they were giving out the Bodils and I thought about staying away. I want to be indifferent and cool about it but, as the evening approached, I started to put on my good clothes and began to get all excited. I was incredibly happy to receive my award and cannot really pretend that it doesn't matter. It doesn't, however, in any way influence what I will do next. It

is also important for me that the movies I make do have an audience. I believe that cinema is a mass medium. Obviously, I am not saying that I would not make a film that I knew was only going to draw a very small audience.

JW: Internationally, *Open Hearts* has been the most widely released of your films so far. Is it a natural desire for you as a director that as a measure of success your next project be released in a similarly expansive manner?
SB: Yes and no, because I also do think that as a Dane it is incredibly important for me to make movies that are for Danish people. I don't necessarily feel that a sign of development is to have my films released to increasing numbers in terms of a world audience. It would be fantastic to make a film that does appeal to people all across the world, but it is also important to remain true to one's roots. You do not necessarily have to remain rooted to them, but it is important not to lose them.

JW: Do you have ambitions to shoot outside of Denmark?
SB: It is not an ambition that I actively cultivate, but I would like to. I also think that my way of telling stories could and does apply to people outside of Denmark because the cocktail of sentiment and humour that you find in my work is not culturally and nationally specific.

JW: The theme of family and the imperfections of the family unit comes across very strongly in your most recent work and is, I think, a theme that recurs in many of the films of your compatriots – *Festen*, and *Minor Mishaps*, for example.
SB: I recognize this also. I think that what the Dogme films have done – and I recognize that *Minor Mishaps* is not a Dogme film – is to deal with families in a state of dysfunction. I guess that in the western world this is a very pertinent problem. In fact, the problem goes deeper and relates to our difficulty in defining our identity and reaching out for new identities. We are still living with eighteenth-century ideals of what relationships should capture and families should contain, and yet we are living such different lives. These movies reflect upon the new directions in which we are going.

JW: There is a high regard for the films and film-makers coming out of Denmark. Do you see this as a particularly fertile period?
SB: It's a fantastic time. We have been so incredibly lucky to have a combination of good reviews and strong audiences. Pretty much all of the directors you are referring to have emerged from the Danish Film School. We have a new approach to film, a new sense of the importance of the script, the story and a questioning of the stories the directors want to tell. This started at the film school at the beginning of the eighties and has now borne fruit. I also think that another important factor is that a lot of these directors, like myself, did not necessarily

begin as film fanatics but had other experiences in life. This, I believe, creates and contributes to diversity.

JW: How do you view this whole process of talking about your films as opposed to actually physically making them?

SB: There is a depressive element to it because you want to continue your creative investigation, but I also have a very pragmatic view because I do consider it as part of the wider process and, as much fun as the rest of it is, this is very much a part of it.

Jason Wood is the author of the forthcoming *Mexican Cinema*.

That Rushing Current
Pauline Kael on Jean Renoir

Introduction by Michael Almereyda

Pauline Kael supplied the following interview as potential narration for a kind of film essay I was intending to make about Jean Renoir – a film now stowed in a personal Pandora's box of unfinished projects. The idea was to showcase seminal aspects of Renoir's work and to track a continuity linking movies by Jean Vigo, Godard and certain American directors in the seventies. I figured Kael's voice would float alongside other commentary, running over stills and clips. But I got sidetracked, and it wasn't until after her death in September 2001 that I began transcribing the three hour-long tapes. It then became clear that Pauline's memories and observations were focused and far-reaching enough to stand on their own.

Renoir's reputation is routinely glazed over by a kind of perfunctory reverence. His 'humanism', his love for his characters, his eye-for-landscape-and-light-inherited-from-his-painter-father, his hopeful egalitarian politics, his eagerness to experiment, his heroic persistence in old age – all these qualities can make the man and his work seem merely virtuous. Better to be reminded how, in a run of movies directed and co-written in France in the thirties, Renoir managed to refine or reinvent distinct genres – the low-life crime thriller, the bustling social drama, the breezy social comedy – by recombining familiar elements, with apparent effortlessness, into something new. Watching a Renoir from this period, you can count on a heightened sense of immediacy and aliveness, a fluid complexity, aligned with Renoir's tendency to share his stories among multiple characters and to apply a moving camera to translate the restless impulses at the heart of the action. His famous declaration in *The Rules of the Game* – 'Everybody has his reasons' – is often trundled out to define Renoir's essential generosity of spirit, but that's just the point at which his films begin. It's more difficult to account for the dual perspectives unfolding in these movies, the cross-currents of emotion and meaning, the way the stories can seem at once improvised and fated. What other director has managed to explore everybody's 'reasons' with Renoir's amazing mix of irony and warmth, lightness and gravity, tenderness and violence?

If I'm running on a bit here it's because I've pretty thoroughly removed myself from the pages that follow. Initial interviewing duties, if they can be called that, were split between me, David Edelstein (who co-ordinated the event and did most

Pauline Kael in San Francisco, early sixties

Jean Renoir seated in front of the portrait of himself painted by his father

of the driving) and Elvis Mitchell (who supplied his tape recorder).* I've taken the liberty of juggling paragraphs here and there to keep a chronological flow, and our questions have been excised, as had always been the intention. So what follows is pretty much straight and unfiltered Pauline Kael, mid-morning in her house in Great Barrington, Massachusetts, 21 May 2000.

She was a month shy of eighty-one. David cautioned me that her health had been shaky, and Wes Anderson's account of his Kael pilgrimage, printed the previous year, provided a portrait of the esteemed critic on medication for Parkinson's, slightly addled, a lovable, self-absorbed monster – suspiciously like a character in a Wes Anderson movie. This same Pauline Kael, when I encountered her, was terrifically lucid, gracious, engaged. We had dinner out with a gang of her friends, then stayed up past 3 a.m. watching a tape I'd brought for the occasion, a copy of Renoir's *The Lower Depths*. David trudged off to bed before the movie was half through, Elvis was unusually quiet, and I was fighting sleep, but Pauline, from what I could tell, was riveted, then ready for a second feature.

Preparing for the interview the next morning (as if for a mountain-climbing trek, with equipment scattered across the breakfast table) I discovered that my borrowed DAT recorder had gone dead. Pauline allowed me to bring out my video camera, as back-up to Elvis's avowedly cheap cassette recorder. And so I can report with an illusion of complete recall that she sat opposite the three of us on a red couch, her face taking on a reflected high colour from the couch cushion. She was wearing a dark grey blouse and black slacks. Beside her were a couple of her books, passages on Renoir flagged with slips of paper. Beyond this locked-off view, I remember a feeling of summer light throughout the house, a glow lifting to the rafters, bright foliage visible through every window.

Her voice was light and quick, sentences running together with little hesitation. When she groped for a name or a date, she'd apologize and laugh, but we were seldom able to supply elusive information without journeying upstairs to consult her crowded bookshelves. She'd primed herself for this conversation, clearly enough. She cared deeply about Renoir; the decision to go on record was hardly a casual one. The wealth of stored, sprung insight gave her talk that quality of headlong alertness you get in her prose – which, of course, always aspired to the condition of heightened talk. Also, Kael on Renoir couldn't help but highlight the essential, unprogrammatic concerns (intuitions, recognitions, raptures) at the heart of her love of movies. And if you catch her, describing

*It may be appropriate to mention that Elvis, writing in the *New York Times* later that year, listed my version of *Hamlet* as the best movie of 2000. He and I have carefully avoided one another ever since. David, however, a durable friend, slotted *Hamlet* into his ten-best list for *Slate* but was more sensible in his appraisal, taking pains to allow we're pals. This is by way of admitting that movie directors are vain and hypersensitive, and that, as Pauline noted, friendships between film-makers and critics are inescapably awkward. (I'd met her just once before, twenty years earlier, but that's another story.)

Renoir, talking transparently about herself – well, that's what we tend to do when we talk about the dead.

I'm trying to resist that myself, but feel compelled to spill one shabby confession: I was never under her spell, couldn't be counted a full-out fan, and didn't even own one of her books until she gave me an inscribed copy of her final, career-spanning collection, *For Keeps*. As a woefully serious teenager, subscribing to *The New Yorker* from the wilderness of Orange County, CA, I had found myself questioning Kael's authority, her sassy assertiveness, her stridency. She'd written savage dismissals of Cassavetes and Kubrick, and ignored Fassbinder altogether, while indulging studio pictures that seemed merely fun. Her famous flirtatious tone had seemed aimed at someone far more provincial than myself. And, even recently, I harboured a lingering adolescent grudge against her for causing grief to Orson Welles, whose failure to make new movies was only inflamed, I imagined, by the credit scandal fired up in Kael's 'Raising Kane'. (A part of me still wishes Peter Bogdanovich's scrupulous defence of Welles, 'The Kane Mutiny', could be appended to every copy of Kael's book.) All the same, reading Kael in bulk, I became a late convert. 'Movies broke down barriers of all kinds, opened up the world, helped to make us aware,' she wrote in an early, expansive piece, 'Movies on Television'. The sentence happens to define the impact of her own work – the boundary-breaking candour, the construction of a style and voice reaching beyond consumer council, a mode of rarefied awareness. Her review of Altman's *The Long Goodbye*, for instance, is a great example of critical intelligence meeting a subject head-on and from multiple angles – a stirring case of a critic rescuing a movie that had been underestimated, even trashed, by its first reviewers and then dumped by the studio. She lovingly describes the picture's slouchy style, its 'self-mocking fairy tale poetry', and pinpoints the elaborate charm of Elliot Gould's incarnation of Marlowe – 'there's a skip and bounce in his shamble' – while placing Altman's movie within a larger historical context, a hard-eyed assessment of Raymond Chandler and pulp detectives at large. As ever, the thoroughness and precision of Kael's commentary are belied by her kicky energy, that conversational rush, touched off by a quality of wilful impertinence. And she arrives – in a review written thirty years ago – at a searing conclusion that continues to ring true: 'At the moment, the shared pop culture of the audience may be all that people feel they have left.'

After the interview, I sent her a thank you note with a tape of a short film, then skated into a year of travel and work, two movies back to back. News of her death was embedded within the vaster shock of the World Trade Center attacks. At the end of that week, late at night, I walked the emptied streets of 'the frozen zone' where I happen to live. I lingered at the Islamic mosque on Second Avenue with its neon sign burning and a squad car protectively parked outside. It had rained the day before but the air still seemed scorched. I went home, rescued the tapes from a folded plastic bag and began listening to Pauline's voice.

'Lightning in a bottle,' David Edelstein said, reviewing the transcript. He also worried whether Pauline, with our encouragement, had perhaps revealed herself too much. No way to know how she'd have wanted her words edited or revised, but it's my impression that she had always willingly, willfully revealed herself – that's what she showed up for. I have a vivid memory of her near the end of that morning, looking childlike and owl-like behind thick-lensed glasses. She was, finally, tired, practically lying down, her head sunk well below the horizon of the couch cushion, her eyes meeting mine with a mix of speculation and trust. If it's lightning she was dispensing, I'm grateful for the chance, at this late date, in her resounding absence, to pass the bottle.

Pauline Kael on Jean Renoir

I was working at the drafting table at home when the doorbell rang; I went to the door, and Jean Renoir was standing there with several relatives and friends behind him. I'd never seen him before except in photographs, but I leaned forward and embraced him, and he embraced me. It turned out that he had been sent some pieces that I'd written about him when he was in France, and he was in Berkeley to see his son, who was teaching there, and he looked me up. He'd gone to the theatre [the repertory movie theatre that Kael ran from 1955–60] and found out where I lived, and he came to the house to meet me. No advance warning. I showed him around the house, because by a fluke that's not really just a fluke, a friend of mine, Jess, had painted scenes from Renoir's movies on the walls of the house. The entrance had the patterns – the sand paintings – from *The River*, and my daughter's bedroom had the designs from Anna Magnani's skirts in *The Golden Coach* patterned on the walls. There were various other Renoir movies given tribute in the house, and he was enchanted.

We hit it off, though we couldn't talk very much because he had all these other people with him – so I felt like a tour guide showing him around the house. But he stayed in touch with me. He worked in Berkeley for a year, writing a play and then staging it. The play was *Carola*. I think he wanted to be close to his son. And during that time we saw each other quite often. He would come over in the afternoon, and we'd talk into the evening. He was quite heavy in those years, and he broke a chair just sitting in it. His heft was too much for the rattan chair, and it went kerplooey. I was delighted because I had it as a memento of his bulk sitting in that chair, but he kept fussing with it, trying to fix it whenever he came to visit.

He liked to talk to me holding my daughter, who was then four or five. He liked to hold her on his lap while we talked. He was very close to her. He wrote to me whenever he wasn't in town to find out how she was doing. He loved looking at pictures of her. I have one picture of her that he claimed was 'the perfect picture'. There was nothing the matter with it in any terms. We spent a lot of time together for several years, and then when he no longer came to Berkeley, when he was in really poor health, I visited him in Beverly Hills.

He had a beautiful house with an open-hearth fireplace. He'd built the house and designed it with an architect, and he had his father's portrait of him as a young hunter behind where he sat often. There were other pieces of his father's – there was some of his father's statuary in the garden, and it seemed amazing to see these beautiful Renoir statues in a Los Angeles-area garden sitting there freely without any worry about their being stolen or carted off.

Renoir didn't talk that much about his father. He talked a lot about young film-makers and about what he'd wanted to do as a young man. There was one thing about him that always bewildered me in a man of his stature and ability: he wanted so badly to be beloved by the young that he praised the films of the young even though he often hadn't seen them. Sometimes people would drop in and he would talk in a very avuncular mode about new work that they had brought him to see, and after they left he'd say to me, 'It was all right, wasn't it?' He hadn't looked at it. But in general his interest in the young was one of the greatest things I'd ever seen in a movie director, because most movie directors are so competitive. They won't go to see other people's work and all they want is to hear bad things about it. They want the others to fail; they know they shouldn't but they can't help it. There are very few directors I've ever met who are really open-hearted about other people's work or who like it in any way – they find reasons not to like it.

The play he wrote, *Carola*, was set during the Resistance, and it was later staged commercially with Leslie Caron. It was not a good play. It was done at Berkeley with, oddly, Denise Peckinpah playing the lead. I can't remember whether she was a daughter of Sam's or a niece. I don't think there was any way it could've been made into a good play, but she did her damnedest, and so did the other student actors. He directed it, and I think they learned a lot from working with him as a director. But he did a number of things that were not good in that period. Some of his movie work was quite poor.

Dido, Mrs Renoir, became quite defensive when certain works were brought up, and it was difficult – you had to sort of waltz around them. There were movies of his that had been made earlier that I was not crazy about. There was one big movie called *Marseillaise* [1938] – he had made that before he left France – and she became very defensive when I indicated that I didn't think that it was one of his greatest movies. But we struck a balance. She accepted what I said later on. She became extremely cordial and kind to me. At first, I thought there was a little hostility. I mean, a critic is hard to accept as a friend sometimes, and I had unfortunately given certain people who

Renoir with his wife Dido

wanted to write about Renoir introductions to him, and she had hated what had been written. In one case, a college professor, using an introduction from me, got to know them and wrote a book about them, and Mrs Renoir said to me, 'But he's got everything wrong!' And I said, 'Well, I learned one thing from it that I didn't know before: that you were Cavalcanti's niece.' And she said, 'I'm not!' It's amazing how much misinformation gets into print. They were very angry about it. And they blamed me also for not writing a book about him. They felt I should.

I didn't know how to approach it, because I'm best dealing with something I've just seen and can really react to, and the only other work I'd done was *The Citizen Kane Book*, and that was fun because it was part of history and it related to so much of what had involved me in movies as a kid. I love the early talkies that were part of the 'Kane' story, and that was really great fun to write. I paused many times during writing it to laugh out loud – it struck me as such a funny history. But it would have been very difficult to do Renoir's life, because they didn't want someone to strike a balance; they wanted something altogether laudatory, and I couldn't do it that way.

I thought about how to do it a number of times, because I do think, all in all, Renoir is probably the greatest director of them all. I realize that he's the direc-

Renoir with Truffaut

tor that I use as a point of reference when I compare other directors, when I raise what their failures and their successes are. He's the one I say they've almost made it to, or they've been affected by, and I tend to like people who have some relationship to him. I mean, Satyajit Ray, Godard, Truffaut.

I ran into Truffaut at Renoir's house on one occasion, and it was a little awkward because, although I'd loved a lot of Truffaut's movies, I hadn't liked his most recent one, and it was very difficult. Also I suddenly felt an outsider because I felt very close to the Renoirs, but when Truffaut came in they spoke French, and I realized that I was displaced linguistically, because I don't speak anything but English. I was excluded by the situation and also by the fact that I had given Truffaut a bum review!

I hadn't seen Renoir's films in sequence, partly because some of the ones that mean the most to us now didn't play in this country immediately. *Boudu Saved from Drowning* [1932], which I love, didn't show for several decades. The first Renoir picture I ever saw was *Grand Illusion* [1938], which was probably the greatest picture I'd ever seen. I was in San Francisco and it didn't play in art houses; it played in regular theatres and got a huge response. It is a movie that people don't have to be movie specialists to enjoy. I think that *Rules of the Game* [1939], which is certainly a great film, could never reach the wide

Renoir as Octave in *Rules of the Game*: 'He saw himself as a bear.'

audience that *Grand Illusion* did in the thirties when I first saw it. It has an immediacy, and you understand everything in it, whereas *Rules of the Game* has a kind of mad capriciousness; the pulse of *Rules of the Game* is different – it isn't as naturalistic – and *Grand Illusion* was simply a heavenly experience for people who hadn't seen much in the way of European films. But even if we had, there was nothing comparable to it.

He brought over the French versions – he didn't have subtitled versions – of *La Chienne* [1931] and *The Crime of Monsieur Lange* [1935], and he knew I hadn't seen them. I had projectors in my house, in the same room I worked in, because I looked at films all the time to see what was worth running. Japanese films, for example, were subtitled for the Buddhist temples, but you couldn't tell which were the interesting ones till you looked at them, so I would keep them running while I made posters and displays and answered the theatre phones, which were in my house, not in the theatre. I had eight lines going at the time. It was quite frantic.

I had at home the first showing, in that part of the world, of the enlarged, restored *Rules of the Game*. There must have been thirty or forty people whom I invited, and we were just wowed. It was incredible. I fell off my chair, which I think I've done two or three times in my life. It was amazing.

Renoir was an actor himself – perhaps not a great actor, but a very easy actor. He figures in *A Day in the Country* [1936] and in *Rules of the Game*. It's interesting that he saw himself as a bear and played a bear in *Rules of the Game*; he was bear-like, it was part of his embrace of life and of experience and the fact that he couldn't reject anything. His arms always seemed outstretched to me. I never think of bears as walking on four feet – I always see them as upright, and he was that upright kind of bear. His embrace perhaps explains why I love his movies so much. I can't get a grip on this. It was more like: 'I accept!'

I don't think he was big on moral judgements, and that's partly what was great about him. His embrace was what you get in the play of light in his movies, in the openness to the air, what you feel in *Boudu Saved from Drowning*, the France of the time that you see on the screen, the inside and outside settings of *The Lower Depths* [1936], the way in *Rules of the Game* you're out on the hunt and you see what's going on in the chase outside and the chase inside. You almost never get a feeling of being locked in. You have a feeling that you can breathe and the movie can breathe – it's open-air film-making.

Renoir never tells you how to feel, and that's maybe the basic difference between a hack and a great film-maker.

He really thought Cocteau was the cat's pyjamas, as I did too. I adore *Orphée* and *Les Parents Terribles* [written by Cocteau, directed by Melville], and *Beauty and the Beast* isn't bad. They're a great pair – Cocteau having the sets and costumes and all, while with Renoir you feel they just dug out whatever was in the closet, even his bear suit.

The Lower Depths: 'So much like his father's paintings.'

I love what Cocteau said – 'You never know what is enough until you know what is more than enough.' And that's what Renoir really knew. He always knew what was more than enough. Except in a few of the wartime movies and the later ones, you never saw that empty poshness, that over-dressed and over-set feeling you got from Hollywood and from a lot of French movies. Christian-Jaque and a lot of the French directors gave you nothing but furnishings.

There's a sense of freedom in Renoir's films, which directors rarely achieve. There are some good directors who've been influenced by him, whose work is probably not as well-known as it should be. I think Irvin Kershner was quite influenced by him. *The Luck of Ginger Coffey*, *A Fine Madness*, with Sean Connery as a painter, *Loving*, with George Segal and Eva Marie Saint – that's a wonderful movie that never gets shown. And there were some marvellous sequences in *The Return of a Man Called Horse*.

Some of what Kershner did in *Star Wars II: The Empire Strikes Back* was really first-rate. The sequence when Harrison Ford turns into a bas-relief was a first-rate piece of work and it came right in the middle of George Lucas's sandwich. And what was it doing there, with all that sensibility and sensitivity? It's difficult for people who have that. It's amazing how many people do good work that's lost or buried in cheese.

Jonathan Demme is also influenced by Renoir. He has that crazy freedom that's so remarkable in *Melvin and Howard* and *Citizen's Band* and in parts of *Something Wild*. When he's good, he's so good he doesn't make any money. It's bizarre that his best films have been box-office duds.

Movies have become pretty pushy in the nineties. It's the terrible failure of nineties movies. Everything is shaped. But in the seventies, things seemed more open. That was when Altman seemed to be carrying on the Renoir tradition.

Altman doesn't talk about loving people. But it's implicit in Renoir's conversations and when he says, 'Everyone has his reasons.' Altman never really justifies himself. It's an interesting thing. Altman is a son of a bitch, but he doesn't try to be something else. Renoir wasn't a son a bitch. But he was much more old-fashioned in his personal vanities. Dido said he was waiting for a divorce before they could get married; everyone assumed that they were having an affair, and they were written about as if they were having an affair, but he wouldn't touch her until he could marry her. He was really a gentleman of the old school.

Some of the scenes in *The Lower Depths* were so much like his father's paintings, it's quite amazing. And the fact that his father let him get by without going to school – Jean just hung around and only picked up what he wanted to pick up, a great education for an artist.

The Golden Coach is explicitly theatrical. When Anna Magnani is on stage and the curtain comes down at a certain point in the film, you're told that it's theatre that you're watching, or her life is theatre. It's an amazing movie. I saw it the day it opened in San Francisco. It was a large, handsome theatre, and I was there with my daughter and one other person. It was just heartbreaking, because it was a glorious movie and it had its full colour then – it hadn't faded, nothing was there to diminish it – and nobody came. And I've had this experience with several other movies that have lasted which people now scrounge around to find videos of, and the videos are just like souvenirs of the original movie. Renoir had that experience often in his life, and he had his terrible ups and downs at having his movies chopped up. He had the experience of not being able to raise money to finance movies when he was in his mature years and didn't have that long to go as a director. He had all the ups and downs that we hear of in the directors whose ups and downs are more celebrated, like Von Stroheim and Peckinpah. A great many directors go through hell, and he went through that hell, and somehow it didn't cling to him because when he was working he

Renoir in the golden coach

worked in terms of . . . I can't say of love, but of acceptance. You don't really control a production and make a work keep going out of love. I think you have to be hard-headed. And he must have had a hard-headed side. He had his father's paintings that he could sell off to finance his movies in the silent period, but it took him a long time to get commercial financing, and then he had his terrible struggles in Hollywood, with the people chewing up what he had done.

But his work is not great in the Hollywood years. And his approach is not one that they could sell. It was probably a giant mistake on his part to think he could make American movies. I know *The Southerner* [1945] is well regarded, but there's something not quite right in the emotions. *Diary of a Chambermaid* [1946] is fun, but it's not a great movie. He never really connected with the culture – he connected with people. Movie-making takes something extraordinary in the intimacy with which a director works with his players, and you never get

Strangers on a Train: 'Robert Walker is inescapably American.'

anything in his American movies like the feeling you get between Louis Jouvet and Jean Gabin in *The Lower Depths* where the two of them are bumming together. He just didn't feel for Americans in that way. I think we want to believe that movies are an international art, but it's only our crap that travels. And it travels best to sub-literate cultures. It's easy for action movies to travel, but a good American movie has a hell of a time travelling – and a hell of a time at home.

Some of Renoir's American films are great fun, but they're not American. The American characters don't feel American. Hitchcock's American movies come closer – *Strangers on a Train* is closer to having an American feel. That may be because Robert Walker is just so damn good. He is inescapably American; Farley Granger could be anything. He's just a ham actor and any culture could've produced him. And *Notorious* is closer to being American, even though it's an English hero and a Swedish heroine. It's a very American movie.

Renoir never made a strict romance. He made a lot of movies about adultery and hell and men being betrayed – *La Chienne*, parts of *The Lower Depths*. He used women as betrayers often, and men as fools and weaklings, but he did it very delicately. On the women's side, even though they were often bitches, you felt for them too. He did take an open point of view towards his characters.

Grand Illusion: 'The way he uses Marcel Dalio is quite marvellous.'

I'll use an example: de Sica, I think, made a mistake when he had the landlady in *Umberto D.* being deliberately cruel. I don't think Renoir ever would have made that mistake. He would have let us see her having her reasons too. And the old man that she threw out or had no feeling for, or the young girl that she mistreated – they were probably a pain and we could have seen that they were a pain to her, but instead she was turned into a wicked villain. But de Sica rarely made that mistake. He didn't make it in *The Children Are Watching Us* through *Shoe-Shine* or his other great films, but he did in *Umberto D.* and it's a real flaw.

There's a lot of yearning in Renoir, and we identify with it immediately. But his films are partly so French to us because of the theatrical tradition that they come out of. The acting is very definitely from French theatre, and he used people who were famous in the theatre. He used them so easily and naturalistically on film, which, particularly considering the period, is amazing, because in American films people who came from the stage were given speeches to deliver and acted as if they had just stepped off the train. You felt that awful non-movie acting in stage people's acting; I'm thinking of the early movies of people like Ann Hardy and Irene Dunne and almost everyone who came up in movies in the forties and had their beginnings in the thirties. They were stage figures and they took pride in their diction; they enunciated to within an inch of their lives, they talked stage English, and they couldn't adapt.

His characters were theatrical, and we love them for that; they saw themselves as theatrical figures, and he understood that we all have that bit of theatre in us. We all want to be viewed as dramatic and picturesque, and the women all want to be divas. The people aren't just naturalistic, they're also theatrical – and acting theatrical naturalistically. This also has to do with what we love movies for. We don't want just to look at the girl next door. We want to look at the girl next door who imagines herself a countess. There's a complexity in why we respond to people in movies. We want something more from them than naturalism, and he always gives us that.

The way he uses Marcel Dalio in *Grand Illusion* and in *Rules of the Game* is quite marvellous. Dalio becomes a real figure; by the time he's got a title and is having a big house party, he sees himself as so important. He sees himself as a collector of objects that move. (Any director is a collector of objects that move.)

Renoir used the same actors in several movies. He had his own stock company. And, of course, he lost that when he came to this country – except for some of them who had fled the Nazis and were over here too, but he didn't get a chance to use them; they didn't fit into *The Southerner*.

He had very bad luck with his material in Hollywood. He really wasn't as interested in what was going on in American movies as he was earlier in what went on in French movies. He had started practically with the beginning of movies, making movies that starred his then wife, Catherine Hessling, and he made some extraordinary short films that were all feeling. They didn't need dialogue, they didn't need sound; the feeling in them was so strong that you were simply carried along visually. And he was able to keep that visual openness for a long time. He lost it, somewhat, when he started working in colour. *The River* is stiffer than his black-and-white movies.

[*Reading from notes*] 'Renoir put us in unquestioning and total contact with his people. And everything seemed fluid and easy and open in form, but his technique was invisible.'

I was interested in the fact that they're such egalitarian films, that he related to each character in turn. You never felt that the stars got more attention than the other characters. That's particularly true in *Rules of the Game*, but it's true in some of the others too. You feel he wants each of his characters to come through to you. But there's less visible technique than in any director I can think of except for Satyajit Ray.

I remember being astounded at the New York Film Festival. Press people always inevitably asked the director what camera he had used, what film stock he had used, all technical questions. And I remember somebody asking Renoir that in his home once, and he said, 'I have no idea. I left that to the cameraman.' Of course. Claude Renoir was pretty damn good, and having a nephew who's a great cameraman is a blessing.

I never thought of asking him any technical questions, and he never talked in those terms. He never asked how anybody else had achieved any effect. You got the feeling that when the need arose he would devise the solution, or the technicians would do it for him. But he did amazing things. I still don't know how he did *Boudu Saved from Drowning* with the feeble sound equipment of that period, how he got as much movement as he did.

The look of those films is amazing. The fact that you got outdoors and indoors within the shot, that there was something going on in the background, which was never just the background – it was part of the action. I love that passionately, and I don't know if I can explain why. There's something about seeing children playing in the same shot where lovers are having a quarrel that expands your whole vision of what a movie can do. It's part of separating it from live theatre. It just gives you more.

A Day in the Country has moments that are absolutely unforgettable, when you get the rushing current that tells you about the passage of years – and the passage of years in this case, in the lives of these characters, has such incredible poignancy because you know the beauty you saw in the beginning is going to be lost, and the central girl's life is going to go down the drain. That rushing current is like . . . well, it's the most potent metaphor for loss that I can remember in a movie. And since we've seen this girl earlier – her frightened face when she has her first sexual experience is like the eye of a hare who's shot – it's as if she's never going to come back to what she was before that awful moment of deflowering. It's awful for her, and we're never going to go back over that rushing current.

There was no one encouraging him to go back to France that I know of. In the sixties, there was some government grant that was given to films if the films were approved by the French critics, but the film he wanted to do was not approved by the critics, so he couldn't get the grant that he was counting on and that project fell apart. So he didn't feel at home in France. They may have felt he left them at a crucial time – I don't know. But he left very definitely. His father's model, Gabrielle, also left – he brought her over on the same ship he came over on. She lived next door to him in Los Angeles, and her son took care of him when he got too old for his wife to handle him. So he had a part of France with him in this country, and I don't think he had it when he was back in France. He lived surrounded by mementos of his father and his childhood. Even the fact that the house had been designed so that it looked like a French farmhouse – it was a part of France to him, and I think the real France had disappeared for him.

[Reviewing the later filmography in *Renoir on Renoir*] *Swamp Water* [1941] I can live without – his first American one. *This Land Is Mine* [1943], with Charles Laughton, is a stinker, a real war-effort movie. Maureen O'Hara, George Saunders – that's the worst one I know of. Then he made one called *Salute to France* [1944] which I'd rather not think about. Then *The Southerner* [1945]. *Diary of a Chambermaid* [1946] was fun. *The Woman on the Beach* [1946] – what do you think of that? *French Cancan* [1954] is pretty lousy. *Elena and Her Men* [1956] is a dog. And I didn't go see *The Testament of Doctor Cordelier* [1959]. That's a period in which he was making such lousy movies, I didn't really want to see it. *Picnic on the Grass* [1959] is pretty bad too. *The Golden Coach* was in 1952, and that does have some spectacularly good stuff. That's the last of the good stuff. It's wonderful, the bullfight on her face. It's a great way to show a bullfight. Although Francesco Rosi did a pretty good job with the real thing in *The Moment of Truth*. Your feeling for the bull is just overwhelming.

We showed *The River* [1950] in his print, which he brought himself, and it hadn't shown around commercially. It's not his greatest movie by any means, but it has some beautiful things in it. It was a beautiful colour print. He introduced it himself, and there was such a crowd that he agreed to come back that night for a later scheduled-on-the-instant show so people wouldn't go home disappointed, so that everyone would get to see it and to see him, of course.

The River was very beautiful visually, and very stiff; it had a very stiff story. But I don't think that audience cared, because it was before Louis Malle had made his *Phantom India* series. It was the first look we got in full colour of a real film artist looking at India, and it was wonderful enough.

He swept up the audience. They were absolutely mad for him. He didn't talk too much about the problems he had with the financier, who had confiscated the prints, or the hell of a time he had even getting hold of the print.

He had a touch of plainness. I think it's that plainness which is so great in his movies. He understood its virtues. And he had that in his presence too. In the way he communicated. There was nothing of a fancy Hollywood director about him. It was a wonderful combination of masterful control of the medium and the plainness of a man who doesn't exaggerate what he's doing.

I cooked for him between the two showings. I made a rabbit dish [*laughs*]. It was awfully good. I still have the big red Belgian pots. I did a lot of cooking while running the theatre, because I could do it at home while answering the phones, and the kids who worked at the theatre – the projectionists and the cashiers – would come down to the house after the showings and eat the remnants from dinner, which was a pretty large group too. It was a lot of fun.

Because he knew himself so well, Orson Welles appreciated what Renoir could do that he couldn't. Welles could not have made those simple movies. He didn't have the soul for it. It wasn't soul exactly – it was more like braggadocio;

he knew he was a braggart and, great as he was, he also knew he was a bit of a phoney. Renoir didn't have to contend with those forces in himself. Welles had terrific conflicts within himself to contend with, and that's what makes his good movies really good.

It's rare that directors show that they know themselves, that it comes through. Only the great ones come through with a strong personality. I loved what Welles did in that English picture, [*after much searching*] *Lord Mondrago*. He gave a performance that was right up there with the performances in his best movies.

This is new for me. I've only lost my memory – for names and names of objects particularly – within the last year. It's gotten very bad.

You'll enjoy *The Notebooks of Captain Georges* [Renoir's first novel, 1966] because you'll see that he could write. I thought his autobiography [*My Life in Films*, 1974] was a total fraud, and told him so. He had told me a lot of the stories that are in it, and he left out all of the bitterness and all of the facts in order to make it all sort of triumphant and wonderful and sweet to not offend anyone. He had told me hair-raising stories about how he'd been treated by different people, people he worked with and worked for, and he converted them all into sweet tales. He was so afraid of offending people. It's part of what's sweet about him, but it wasn't so sweet really.

It's the awful thing about having made a name for yourself: so many people are eager to tell you everything you do is a work of genius. And the people who don't, you tend to avoid, or they have to have compensatory qualities.

Renoir wasn't making great films when I knew him. I found it easier not to talk about the recent work. He knew. It's hard not to know. When the *Village Voice* ran an item saying, 'Pauline Kael is the critic who used to be Pauline Kael,' I couldn't get it out of my mind. It was one of the things that led to my retiring. If you think that you're just a shell of what you were and that nobody's telling you the truth, it's very hard to go on.

He talked about these [later] things as 'little movies' for television. It was as if someone said, 'I'm keeping my hand in.' He didn't talk about them in ambitious terms. They were sort of playthings he did with his friends of an afternoon.

It's tough if you've done great work as a young man to face getting older. And your work, even if it's good, doesn't have the shock value of your earlier work. I mean, people were stunned by his earlier work. He had done those great movies. And they're enough. But how do you live out the rest of your life?

I remember seeing Marcel Carné [1909–96; director of *Children of Paradise*, among many others] at Cannes when I was there in the seventies, and he would go up and down in the elevator and nobody spoke to him; they didn't seem to notice or care that that was Marcel Carné. The New Wave had destroyed the reputation of a lot of the older directors, and he was one of the ones who was shot down.

Renoir was so afraid of that happening to him, and he was lucky because Bazin and Truffaut, and others, held him up. It's very easy to be shot down by youth, and that may have been one of the reasons that he was so cautious about praising youth all the time. It doesn't take much for a director to be forgotten, because if his movies aren't revived periodically, nobody knows about them. There are so many great movies that are just lost.

He was very pleased that Warren Beatty often came to visit him. Renoir was living right there in the movie colony, making appearances at colleges where they had movie programmes. He was at ease most of the time. He lived a very comfortable life; he had a wife who was adoring, and whom he adored. And that's a great part of the struggle. They were very happy together. She was as involved in movies as he was. She was a continuity girl on *A Day in the Country* or one of those early films. They hit it off right away and they always hit it off so far as I know. I never saw anything between them that wasn't loving. If people that he liked were coming, she would prepare champagne, caviar and treats. She aimed to please and at the same time she was an independent woman.

Renoir was blessed by that plainness and simplicity – which we should all be blessed with, but aren't. It's very tricky. So many people in the theatre and in movies face so many pressures that often the worst pressures take over.

[*Referring to her books*] I marked something, a few little passages . . .

[*Reads*] 'In Renoir's movies, the light seemed natural. You looked at a scene and the drama that you saw going on in it was just part of that scene. And so you had the sense of discovering it for yourself, of seeing drama in the midst of life. This was a tremendous relief from the usual studio lighting, which forced your attention to the dramatic action in the frame, blurred the rest, and rarely gave you a chance to feel the action was part of anything larger or anything continuous.'

[*Another passage*] 'It seems right that Renoir himself should be one of the characters in *Rules of the Game*. He has never, even in his lesser movies, saved himself from total immersion in the work. Here, his role, that of Octave, the friendly observer, the friend of the family who is suddenly caught up in the game, suggests a parody of the artist as observer. No one in the film, not even its creator, remains aloof from the frenzy. Renoir dresses as a bear for the masquerade, and can't quite shed his animal skin.'

There was something here. Oh yeah –

[*Reads*] 'Film artists have the capacity to give us more than they consciously know. More than they could commit to paper. They can reach out beyond themselves. That is what the greatest film masters – high-rollers all of them – have tried to do.'

Let's see, what else . . .

[*Reads*] 'In the seventies, directors were trying to go all the way with movies, as they had earlier, in the way that Griffith and Renoir and other directors had. In the seventies there were expansionist personalities, such as Robert Altman, Coppola and Martin Scorsese. They allowed for the surprises an actor might come up with. They seized whatever delighted them and put it to fresh uses. They didn't simplify for a mass audience. They worked in movies for the same reason we go to movies. Because movies could give us almost anything.'

Supplementary reading:

Readers surprised by Kael's personal investment in Renoir might appreciate one of her last, uncollected interviews, a fairly contentious back-and-forth with Leonard Quart in *Cineaste* (vol. 25, issue 2, 2000).

Quart: Some critics have asserted that your real genius is sociological, and that you are antagonistic to the European art film.

Kael: That's a hostile question, especially with the sly 'your real genius'. Have you read me on Gillo Pontecorvo or Francesco Rosi? Have you read me on Bertolucci's *1900* or Truffaut's *Story of Adele H.* or Visconti's *The Leopard* or Tanner's *Jonah Who Will Be 25 in the Year 2000* or Bellocchio's *China Is Near* and *Leap Into the Void*? Or do you think I should have written more about the draggy ones?

And anyone interested in further reading on Renoir might profit from my initial research, which favored assessments by other filmmakers. Andre Bazin's book, *Jean Renoir*, is in fact a posthumous patchwork of commentary and notes organized by François Truffaut and filled out, in an engaging filmography, with reviews by the old Cahier crowd, most notably Godard, Truffaut, Rohmer and Rivette. Inconspicuous writing on Renoir by other directors includes Orson Welles's tribute in the *LA Times*, February 18, 1979, delivered on the occasion of Renoir's death (and excerpted in the Bogdanovich/Rosenbaum book, *This is Orson Welles*); Satyagit Ray's account of Renoir during the production of *The River* provides another unexpected angle (collected in Ray's *Our Films Their Films*); and Paul Schrader, interviewed by Gavin Smith for *Sight and Sound* (July, 1997) served up a rigorous appraisal of Renoir's virtuosity in shooting *The Rules of the Game.*

Misc. Crew
Libby Savill, Lawyer, interviewed by Rosa Bosch

In the beginning there were no lawyers. There were studios, there was a star system, and then there were agents. But things changed. The political darkness of the fifties led to the revolutionary and experimental sixties. Then the outrageous seventies rolled in and eventually folded into an age of stock-exchange excess. Now living in the hangover of those times – the age of 'creative' financing – a producer is faced with a never-ending list of intermediaries and a never-ending legal minefield before a film finally gets to an audience.

Do a search for 'lawyer' in IMDB.com and you will find them categorized under 'miscellaneous crew'. Surprised? The complexities of financing and distribution have given the figure of the lawyer a key role in the design of a successful film, but one whose creative potential is not always taken fully into account. They are a crucial element both financially and in terms of the artistic well-being and management of a film-making venture. These 'miscellaneous crew' have thus become a unique driving force in the viability of a project, but their importance and impact goes well beyond that.

Perhaps producers need to see beyond the artistic elements (how much more can you be obsessed by one line of a script?) and realize there are other equally important elements potentially rocking the boat. If as an industry we concentrated more on the long-term business side, perhaps we would achieve a healthier and more stable creative community and not just a seasonal group of fee producers subject to the latest financing gimmick or political lottery.

Eventually, I was fortunate enough to come across such brilliant 'miscellaneous crew'. Surely I'm not alone in thinking that as an independent producer and agent the single most important element that would have changed the quality of my life (good luck aside) would have been a creatively-minded lawyer who would have acted as safety net, safeguard and, not least, as a sounding board for ideas.

What follows is an interview with Libby Savill, head of the media group at the London-based law firm Olswang. It's a candid interview, not about the latest tax offering or recoupment schedules, but about the ethics and potential of her craft and profession. Libby – as she is widely known – is still a rare example: a natural-born lateral thinker with an extraordinary range of experience but, most crucially, with great intellectual weight and understanding of the film-making process. In short, a creative legal mind, someone who, over a four-

teen-year career, has commanded respect and fear (very useful!) from both sides of the financing fence . . . and praise from just about everyone she has worked with.

So when you are thinking crew, think again!

Rosa Bosch: Lawyers seem to have appeared on the scene quite late in film history, going back to the forties . . .
Libby Savill: I'm sure that's right. I mean, it was the studio system, wasn't it? There were lawyers but they were hidden in the backroom.

RB: Well, we still live in the studio system, and quite a lot of the studio heads are either lawyers or have a legal background. That was not the case then . . .
LS: It was when the studio system started to break down, with actors having more say. People like Lou Wasserman were probably a huge influence on the way business was done. He had a lawyer's brain even if he wasn't one. He was an agent who made a huge difference in the way the system operated. You suddenly had actors who had agents, and then lawyers. Their power, their salary was increasing – as was their influence.

RB: But lawyers became more prominent in the sixties and seventies . . .
LS: That's right. Certainly, it's been a lot longer coming to continental Europe, for instance, where it is still not accepted as the norm, whereas in England and America a lawyer has lots of influence over anything to do with film-making. I suppose the other thing in the States is that the companies became public and therefore had shareholders to please.

RB: Do you think the power of lawyers today is actually excessive?
LS: It may well be excessive, but the last thing one wants to do is make the financing arrangements complicated. I would love to streamline, but film-making today does not allow it. That role of the lawyer today is not particularly understood.

RB: Have we got to this point because the process is so complex?
LS: I think we have. And I'm not saying I applaud it. I have realized over the years that it's kind of an inverse effect – the more complicated the deals to put the financing together are, the less likely (though not always) that the film is going to be a huge success. It seems to be usually inverse to the commerciality of the project, and I guess that makes sense. The less commercial a project – the more you have to scrabble to put your financing together and therefore the more deals, the more people, the more vested interests have to be sorted out – and the more potential crooks there are likely to be.

RB: More and more, some of the big star lawyers are taking producer credits. Are you going that way too?

Libby Savill and Rosa Bosch (photo Jenny Lewis)

LS: I've never had a credit as a producer, nor as an executive producer. I have performed that function at times, but I have never even asked for a credit. I've been given credits – Legal Services and Special Thanks To. The credit trend is happening now. We act for a producer, who gets a bank loan, and the bank's lawyers put in the loan agreement 'and you will give a credit to banking legal services . . .'

RB: But like it or not, that's the way it's going. What are you going to do if everyone else is doing it?
LS: I disagree with you. I think it's a trend at the edges, and for the main providers of these services – not just me – that it will never be the norm. But moving on to that question of where we sit in the pantheon of the crew, you're right: I don't think we could be considered along the same lines as a gaffer or a grip. They are brought on to do a job and they get paid for it. Ours is a more executive function than that. More structural and creative than doing a job. We're not technicians.

RB: Although you're technical.
LS: True! But in terms of risk, well, if we don't get the film to principal photography with finance attached, I hate to think what the consequences are for our fees, because the independent producer can't afford to pay us. So 99 per cent of the time we'll bloody make sure that we get there, that the film is made and that we get paid.

RB: Is this to do with lawyers having an image problem?
LS: Yes, I think we do. During development, the fees that are paid are pretty tiny; they're tiny for the producer, they're not particularly great for the director, and they're very bad for the lawyer too. I mean, we're actually all in the same boat.

RB: Are you saying you do take a risk?
LS: We do. If I showed you the statistics, you would see that – against the costs of running an office, the costs of paying salaries, all our overheads. A director working out of his front room is in a different position to us. On the development work, again we have never covered costs out of the fees that we are paid.

RB: But how did this happen? Lawyers have a bad name or the reputation of being better paid than any others in the chain – except for Nicole Kidman!
LS: [*Laughs*] Yes, we do have a bad reputation, though perhaps this is just in the film world where deals have a tendency to unravel or change dramatically. It is a creative industry so therefore it's easy to go after red herrings, and people do. So lawyers maybe suffer from other people's malpractice or their client's naivety. Perhaps more than in other areas. If you are buying and selling houses there's only so much you can do.

RB: On the one hand, you should be an integral part of the process of putting a film together but, on the other, producers fear the fees and actually want to keep you at arm's length.
LS: In my experience, yes, there are many people who appreciate what people of my ilk can do, that we can be part of the process and that we are going to be sensible about when to get involved and when not to. Because, ultimately, we're running a business as well as advising. I think that is where a problem can arise, particularly with less experienced producers. There are a lot of producers around who think that all they have to do is hang out their shingle and then they are a producer. Then they think, 'I'll get the lawyer.' They'll get us to effect the introductions, do the deals – package their movie, basically. And I suppose there is some resentment there – actually that's your job, you're the producer and we work alongside you and help you do that.

RB: If producers came out of film schools, which not many of them do, what would you say to them?
LS: You already know we sponsor the European Film Business School (in Ronda, Spain, twice a year), and we help with the Producer's course at the National Film and Television School (in London). We run a business week for producers where we take them from the contractual side all the way through to the bank and other types of financing. I am told that that is the only training they get in that area of producing over the whole of the two-year course. They are, in essence, being trained to be line producers but not producers with any

business skills or any financial savvy. They come out saying, 'Help!' I don't think producers put themselves through the process that they should. In a way, they should be working at the feet of the Jeremy Thomas's of this world for a number of years before they are actually allowed to call themselves a producer. I think that contributes to the bad image of lawyers. To a certain extent, producers beg and plead for you to work with them. When we say we've got to run a business, these will be the fees, etc., that is when resentment arises.

RB: Do you think that perhaps this is a problem because you charge by the hour?
LS: We don't, not always. This is a misconception because, on productions, we know we can't. What we do is agree a fee with the producer and that fee is fixed. Some producers then want you to do a lot more than you've agreed to do and so that becomes a discussion – well, we're doing part of your job so shouldn't that be coming out of part of your fee?

RB: What about getting involved in a project as producer by investing your time?
LS: As I say, I think we do invest our time and services.

RB: Investment against success?
LS: No, I have no desire to do it. It just doesn't sit with our business model.

RB: You say you run a business.
LS: But that's not our business. It's like saying, 'Well, why don't you invest in property?' Well, it's not our business.

RB: Not necessarily, because this is what you do: you structure films, you put together finance deals – you said it yourself, you often do an executive producer's role for which you are paid a fee.
LS: Often. For which we are paid a legal fee, not an executive producer's fee.

RB: Wouldn't it be an interesting avenue of business?
LS: Maybe. Our internal economy is that we sell our time and we sell our services, so that in terms of investing time . . . I suppose what I'm trying to say is that the internal pressures we are subject to mean that even doing the production work is a major justification to my partners. Over the years we have worked alongside producers and said we won't charge you anything until the film is financed. But to really work on a project from day one – meeting potential financiers, pitching the project, doing the deals from square one – at the end of the day, to spend that kind of time and try and run a business where we are paying huge overheads – the two economies just do not fit.

RB: Was it a success?
LS: No. It's a bit like you say: everyone's a script editor. Isn't it good to have someone saying, 'I don't want to be on the creative side'? I don't think it is my strength to assess a project to decide whether or not this is going to be something

that will work. And pitching is not one of my strengths. I think one of the problems is that there are, quite often, too many cooks on the creative side. It's better to have a clear lead producer than have all these people chipping in with ideas.

RB: You have a bit of a reputation for being a lateral thinker.
LS: I think I probably am, which has to do with the history that we've talked about. It is about seeing it from all sides; maturity also plays a part. Not being flustered when someone from Miramax rings me up; actually being able to step back and say, 'Ah, but have you thought about it in this way?' And that's partly to do with the fact that I've been doing this for a long time and partly the beauty of not being someone's employee. I am an independent voice, and whether my clients are a small guy around the corner or a major studio, I think they want to hear an independent voice. There's no point in my being a 'yes' woman.

RB: What do you think are the key elements that make a good film lawyer?
LS: Lateral thinking. Lots of experience in the industry: having seen deals from most sides and having seen many different deals. Maturity certainly helps, and that simply means having 'been around the block' a few times. So it's not just simply seeing the deals, but seeing them in a context; it probably goes back to lateral thinking.

RB: What about on the paper-mongering side?
LS: I think you have got to have the right mixture of big thinking and little thinking. Big picture thinking – and detail, because the devil is often in the detail.

RB: Isn't it very difficult to be passionate and be able to do that in a producer's culture like the UK? Ninety per cent of all producers are what you might describe as fee producers . . .
LS: Yes, absolutely. Very few have the ability to think long-term, about not just being fee producers. It's very hard for them.

RB: Don't you think that however many lottery subsidies and other different schemes are implemented through the years, we are never going to have a proper solid producer's base if everyone is still a fee producer?
LS: I think you're right. It comes back to what we were talking about before, which is we have a culture that allows anyone to put out their shingle who says they want to be a producer, and you end up having lots of people who each have one project only running around trying to figure out how to put it together. Having said that, I have tested this with a number of clients, and I have some clients who do think about it; they are perfectly intelligent, they've made films, but they have no desire to have an infrastructure or build a business.

RB: So what do you think would actually change if you didn't have so much subsidising of development and you subsidised more solid business structures for production companies?

LS: I think it's a question of picking the right horse, actually being there and backing people who we believe have a good business sense and a vision for what they want to do – and there aren't many of them around. Coming back to Jeremy Thomas, who's been a client of the firm for twenty years, we helped him in some complex and expensive deals on splitting the rights on films like *The Last Emperor*, and that has stood him in good stead. It's given him a solid rights base. He's one of the few producers around now that knows those rights are coming back to him after a number of years. Sadly not everyone takes that long-term view.

RB: Might you say that one of the problems with the UK is that it is based on the same model as the US, but without the high fees for producers?
LS: I would. The US is such a big market, and for local companies like Pathé to say that on a £3-million film the producer fee should be a million pounds is not realistic. We should have a different system. Whether I or other lawyers can have an influence on that, I don't know. There's no doubt that the big thing now is lobbying for the retention of section 48, the tax incentive that we've got here, or something similar. We need some stability in our system. We have not had stability in any kind of financing systems such as Spain, France and Italy have enjoyed. Especially France – they've had the same system of incentives since the Second World War.

RB: Instead, in the UK they change every few years.
LS: And there's also been the nothing-to-something syndrome in this country. We're currently in the throes of having had something that has certainly attracted a lot of inward investment and probably helped to make films that would probably not have been made otherwise, though you could say some of them should not have been made. The film business is governed by the laws of probability.

RB: Are you involved in advising on this issue?
LS: Yes. I sit on two bodies: the British Screen Advisory Council and the British Film Commission Advisory Group, which has now become the Film Council UK International Advisory Group, which obviously supports the Film Council. It comes back to the details – you talk in generalities but you need to get down to the nitty-gritty. Generalities won't change anything.

RB: What would you change if you could?
LS: It's a very cluttered system. I suppose if you could start with a blank system, you would come up with something like a studio. You would have vertical integration and economies of scale; you would cut out so many middlemen. If you think about it – describing the process of putting together an independent film and distributing it – an outsider would say this is no business. You've got agents

taking a percentage of the deal, you've got producers working on their own who have to give fees to a distributor, fees to a financier, fees to a completion bond. So you are cluttering up the system with all these levels of fees and vested interests. It's suicidal. It's a wonder that a film gets made and distributed, let alone anyone making any money out of it. If you went back to a blank page you would come up with a studio-type system. I'm not saying that one would emulate the current way that the studios are set up. I did believe when the lottery franchises came out in the UK in 1997 that if the Arts Council had outlined the brief correctly it could have made a difference. We are seeing the results of that a few years later – they didn't get the brief right and didn't necessarily think through what it was that they were trying to achieve.

RB: How about paperwork? The endless piles . . .

LS: I'd love to streamline it more, but I think at the moment it is necessary. You have to react to your clients. It's often not the producer – mostly they want to make financing as simple as possible. But I also act for studios, and they want to cross every 't' and dot every 'i'. If you are going to make the process simpler, everyone has to step back and say, 'What do we want to achieve here,' and we could just do it with a set of standard terms and conditions. Rather than 'I'll do it this way' and 'You do it this way' and 'I'll draft my document this way'.

RB: We all like to think we've come up with a way of beating the system.

LS: Well, I don't know about that. If you are an end-user as opposed to an equity financier, you are going to have a different set of drivers in a deal. So it's a question of trying to figure out which drivers prevail. A financier is reliant on a distributor to get its money back. The distributor is simply keen to make sure the money is recouped and it gets an appropriate set of fees. It's interesting – I said before if you had a blank sheet of paper you probably would go back to the studio system. I'm currently doing more work for them than ever before, bringing in soft money into their budgets; they are under the same pressures the rest of the world is under.

RB: Do you see yourself as a matchmaker?

LS: I have personally performed that function. I certainly would introduce people that I thought would work well together. There's no point in making the deal aspect more unpleasant than it needs to be. My ultimate goal when doing a deal is to make sure that all sides end up feeling, relatively, that that was a pleasant experience. At the end of the day, if they can say that was done in a friendly, efficient manner, that's going to reflect well on my client and, hopefully, me for the next time around. That means that the financier might want to deal with my client again because it wasn't a nightmare, inefficient or unprofessional.

RB: And you might find yourself acting for the other side?

LS: You might. You never say never. You don't know who's going to be coming on to your radar next time around – and why make enemies? Many lawyers are very short-sighted about how they do deals. They can be really unpleasant. It is the ego thing. I believe a lawyer should sublimate their ego, because it's not ultimately his or her film. It's someone else's film and someone else's deal. Too many lawyers forget they are 'just' providing a service.

RB: If the film flops, it's none of your business.
LS: Now that's a very cynical way of looking at it. Of course, I make it my business but maybe there is a detachment and that is what we are trained as lawyers to be: dispassionate, disinterested – not uninterested – i.e. objective rather than subjective.

RB: Is that possible?
LS: I think you can be passionate about your client's passion and want to achieve your client's goal, but in the end it's not life and death. I don't think it's unhealthy to be disinterested. I'm not saying I haven't shed my share of tears in the middle of the night, when I've been working three days – morning, noon and night – on something. I have sweated blood.

RB: Dispassionate, but not heartless?
LS: Exactly.

RB: The perception is that most women in our industry work in organizational, time-consuming areas, such as line producers, sales agents, distribution and marketing. How about lawyers?
LS: I think the entertainment industry in Los Angeles is a very male environment – I can count with the fingers of my hand the women in senior positions there. At a senior level here in Britain it is much the same. Most of the senior lawyers in the UK doing what I do – the commercial side of the film business – are men. There are many women also who do this kind of work but have not risen through the ranks. Whether that's because they are simply doing it more as a job . . . You can't go to the next stage unless you are really interested in the industry and the way people operate. It is a demanding business to be in.

RB: Are you really the only woman at a senior level in film?
LS: I think I am. If you look at the rest of the law firms here, none of them have a senior woman in this field – apart from Jackie Hurt [also at Olswang], who is definitely on the rise.

RB: Is it lack of opportunitics?
LS: I don't think so. I think it might be the culture, it might be the work – it is sacrifices and commitment, when you have to be prepared to be working until God knows what time of night.

RB: So, if you want to have both career and family, you have to pay for it?
LS: Yes, you have to – and it is an absolute conundrum. I can tell you, as a full-time practising lawyer and mother of two boys, in my law firm I am very much in the minority of women who had babies and come back to work full-time. Women are entitled to say that they want to have more of a balance in their lives, but from a business side it is difficult when you are providing a service to people if you cannot provide at the level and timing that your clients want. You have to make personal sacrifices.

RB: Any role models?
LS: I think it's a generational thing. Women over forty have come from a time where we didn't expect to be able to have it all without being superwomen. Women who are ten years younger than me do think they can have it all. They are very much clearer about where the boundaries are – where they will stop and where they will start. Those half a generation older than us were hitting against glass ceilings left, right and centre, while we were able to go through those glass ceilings; we are each other's role models to a certain extent. In terms of my professional approach, I think that it has a lot to do with the law firms from which I came. Mark Devereux has certainly been an influence; he believes in quality, not doing what a lot of our competitors do, which is cut corners. They do it in a different way. I don't think they are unethical but they have cut corners because the pressures on fees and speed of producing the work are huge. Many firms have decided to be very passive – just churning out the paper, not having an influence on the process, not necessarily driving the process like we do and not trying to think of all the angles.

RB: Any advice for future lawyers?
LS: Sheer determination. I absolutely loved it when I came into the industry; at last, after all those years, I found something where I was interested in the end result. It's become a cliché now – I can't tell you how many lawyers I have interviewed from City firms over the years, who are four, five, six years qualified, who say, 'I am sick of churning out work in an industry that I have no interest in. I want to be a film lawyer because I'm interested in the end product.' That's what I said fourteen years ago . . .

RB: What gives you the most satisfaction?
LS: It has to be being in the role of trusted advisor, to have that rapport with a client, set a goal and help them achieve it.

RB: Which is the biggest personal challenge?
LS: To keep up the level of enthusiasm and to continue to bring the same drive to get the best deal each time. In the end that is what it is about.

Ramona Sanchez
interviewed by Matthew Sweet

Ramona Sanchez is a production supervisor. Her decade or so in her field has seen her name appear on the credit rolls of, among others, The Shawshank Redemption (*1994*), Jade (*1995*), Beyond Rangoon (*1995*), In and Out (*1997*), The Out-of-Towners (*1999*), Sleepy Hollow (*1999*), Shaft (*2000*) *and* Zoolander (*2001*). *If you want to exasperate her, simply tell her how the online Kodak Glossary of Motion Picture Terms defines her job: 'an assistant to the producer, in charge of routine administrative duties'. It's symptomatic, perhaps, of the low esteem in which her branch of the film-making business is held. Ray-Banned, cigar-sucking producers who declare that the kid stays in the picture radiate Hollywood glamour and power like a green light. The people who prime them to make the decision – totting up the comparative cost of sacking or retaining the kid, and how that will affect the shooting schedule and the overall budget – are generally regarded with suspicion and contempt. But before we decide that Ramona and her kind are the enemies of creativity, wouldn't it be a good idea to get some idea of what she actually does?*

I meet Ramona in her office in the Stanley Kubrick Building at Pinewood studios, where she is working on Tomb Raider 2: The Cradle of Life *with the action director Jan de Bont. To give some idea of the scale of her responsibilities, she takes me on a tour of the production. Our first stop is the 007 stage – originally built to accommodate the submarine base of* The Spy Who Loved Me (*1977*) *– which de Bont's crew has split down the middle. The north end is occupied by a small mountain range: rugged outcrops, vertiginous gullies, spindly trees sprouting from the rock. Walking around the perimeter of the set reveals how it was constructed: underneath is a web of wooden splints, like something from a Gold Rush mineshaft, forming a base upon which layer after layer of plaster has been moulded.* (*It's a particular delight to Ramona: a redressed set from another production will shave a few thousand dollars from the budget.*)

Beyond this space is a Greek temple with Ionic columns stretching up towards the rafters, a huge sacrificial altar and a statue of Alexander the Great. As the floor is tilted at a steep angle, it's quite difficult to walk across this space. Ramona explains that the set was constructed on the level, then adjusted to meet de Bont's requirements. In a few days' time, it will be flooded with seven feet of water, half submerging the structure and rendering it plausibly Atlantean. She also draws attention to the roughness of the finish on the temple walls: plaster and wood caked in a layer of friable sawdust. There's no need to spend extra money adding a detailed finish to the set if, on screen, something simpler is equally convincing.

In a suite of offices on the ground floor of the Kubrick Building, Michael Redding, the construction co-ordinator on the production – a veteran of the Pinewood art department since 1973 – is poring over the models and blueprints of a set that has yet to be constructed: the inner sanctum which houses the film's principal McGuffin – a crenellated cricket ball that holds some mysterious primal energy. Dramatic adjustments to these plans, it seems, can be made at a surprisingly late stage. Several have been scaled down to suit de Bont's needs: a gulag set lost its mess hall and its rocket launchers when it was decided that they were superfluous to requirements. Lara's Retreat – a territory somewhere between Tracy Island and a Japanese meditation centre – has been dropped altogether. Others – and the room seems to be filled with them – have been built and struck, or are awaiting construction: an underwater ice cave; a petrified forest; the villain's hideout – christened 'Bin Laden's lair' by the design team. Not all are built from scratch: rural China was reconstructed in the Welsh valleys; a mountain village menaced by an erupting volcano was realized by adding collapsible extra walls to buildings on the Greek island of Santorini. Ramona, however, has saved the production's most impressive set until the end of the tour.

Steam issues from vents in the street; billboards peel from the bricks; the shops are well-stocked; lanterns swing from weathered awnings. Even the teacups abandoned outside one household look suitably battered. You have to tap the wall and listen to the hollow clunk of the fibreglass, or scuttle around the back to see the bare boards and the scaffolding, to convince yourself that you're actually standing in a field in Buckinghamshire and not on the backstreets of Shanghai. On a stretch of backlot once occupied by Billy Wilder's Baker Street *and the volcano from* You Only Live Twice *(1967), a small chunk of Asia has been transplanted. In a few hours, Angelina Jolie will roll up, ready to strap her holsters on to her thighs and scutter up and down the walls of this unreal city. Before that, however, there's time for Ramona to sit down and explain herself.*

Matthew Sweet: The accountants are regarded as the villains. They're the people who say no.

Ramona Sanchez: It's not my job to say no. It's only my job to put up a red flag or give a warning. You don't really control anything; you just monitor and advise. Sometimes I bring doom and gloom, but sometimes I'm the bringer of good news. Because I'm looking at the fiscal realities all day, I know that there might be other areas of the budget where we've spent less than we anticipated, so I can go to the director and say, 'We have this in the pot. Present your argument for spending more here, and I'll see if I can make it work.'

MS: So you warn directors about impending difficulties?
RS: You shouldn't be like Chicken Little, saying that the sky is going to fall in, because it just creates confusion. You have to be very careful about the kind of things you point out, so you're not just one more hysterical person trying to make a movie. There are a lot of people in this business who tend to try and create problems in order to solve them and make a point and justify their existence. This business is full of those types, and you've got to deal with them.

MS: How many sets of people are you dealing with?
RS: Every day, I'm dealing with the studio, the producers, the production team, the director, the department heads, the cast. Do they need anything? Are they happy? If the unit is happy, then the director gets a good movie. The trick is being able to keep the lines of communication open. A lot of it comes from years of experience. You just learn how to deal with people. I always try to have a good rapport with the entire production. I can go to them and ask what's going on, how the schedule is moving. And I have to have a better relationship with the producers, so that they'll feed me what I need in order to do my job.

MS: So whose side are you really on?
RS: You're really working for both sides. For the production, you want them to think you're on their side. And for a big part of your job, you are. You're there to help the director make the best film they can make. To realize their vision. And you have to do it very gracefully. Sometimes it's like walking through a minefield, and you don't know where the bombs are planted. There seem to be so many people involved with the decision-making process that you're sometimes not sure who you're supposed to be reporting to.

MS: But, ultimately, the studio wants to keep a director under control.
RS: Big studios are not *auteur* film-makers. They're about making a profit. I don't mean any disrespect to the people whom I work for. They pay me well to do what I do. But it's a money-making business. The people in the studios are all about dollars and cents. They don't want to know about the blah blah blah. The bottom line is – what's it going to cost us? They just want to know the numbers. And I have to sift through the blah blah blah to get the numbers. I see the world in black and red. Directors don't always see it that way.

MS: And some are more profligate than others?
RS: From the first or second day's shooting, I know what kind of director I'm dealing with. And let me tell you, there are not many producer–directors left. Directors who thrive on being under budget. It's a lost art. Look at how smart James Cameron was with *Titanic*. Fox was freaked out by the escalating costs, and Paramount came in and they made a co-production deal. James Cameron knew that the picture was going to be financially successful, break box-office

records. Tim Burton, however, is a little boy in a man's body. He doesn't do dollars and cents. And many creative minds don't. You've got to have a good solid production behind Tim because he doesn't know these things. You can put a mediocre team behind John Boorman, say, or Jan de Bont, and they'll be OK because they have the sense and the knowledge.

MS: What about Scott Rudin? You worked for him for several years, and then suddenly stopped.
RS: I never worked for him; I worked for the studio, on Scott's pictures. I needed a break. I worked on five of his pictures, back to back, with no holidays. I was tired. Three years without a holiday! But from where I stand on a picture, next to John Boorman he's the most responsible producer I've ever worked with. Scott is a brilliant producer who proves himself over and over again. Most of his films open at number one, and if they don't make a lot of money, they get critical acclaim. He's a smart guy. He optioned *The Corrections*, and Stephen Daldry was attached to the project.

MS: You worked with William Friedkin and Bob Evans on *Jade*.
RS: Yeah, we even shot a scene in Bob Evans's house. Well, I'd read his book. I got to sit in the projection room in his famous leather chairs. I got to see the bedroom with all the silver boxes with all the initials with the pubic hair inside them. His collection. Many of those initials had changed over the years and become very famous women.

MS: So how do you go about budgeting a film?
RS: You can write a script and give that script to somebody to cost who might simply observe the basic mechanics of the piece: how many days, how many nights it will take to shoot. But the cost depends on how you choose to shoot it. Will you have visual effects? Will there be big sets? Is it a period piece? Then you can take that budget and hire a director who has a vision, an appetite. Then you have to figure out a compromise between appetite and profit. You can shoot it in Canada rather than New York. Or, like *Titanic*, you can go and build a studio in Mexico if you think that will increase profits. You schedule a movie based on your best-case scenario. You never really budget for worst-case scenarios. You try to, but the studio rarely lets you get away with it.

MS: And the studio is always desperate to keep the film on schedule?
RS: At any given moment the director may decide to swap the schedule, at which point my job is to figure out what the financial impact of that might be. So you're constantly preparing for scenarios that may never occur. Working in London, I have the advantage of having eight hours to prepare before the studio wakes up in LA and the phone starts ringing. I know that if we're not making

The set for *Sleepy Hollow*: 'The craftmanship in England is like no other country.'

our schedule the studio's going to pick up the phone and ask what yesterday cost and what tomorrow will cost. You're constantly trying to put together information because you know the phone's going to ring at 5 p.m. London time. But your day doesn't end at 7 p.m. London time because over there they haven't even had lunch yet. They can harass you until 1 a.m. You can be out to dinner or at a movie, but they don't really care about that. They just want answers. So I give them answers.

MS: Are there financial benefits to using studios in the UK?
RS: All the big built sets are done here. *Star Wars*, James Bond, *Tomb Raider*, *The Mummy*, the Harry Potters. The craftsmanship in England is like no other country. When we did *Sleepy Hollow*, those sets were so well constructed that we were actually able to shoot the interiors of those sets, even though we hadn't planned to. There are big tax advantages for US studios to shoot here, and we can work without the union problems that we have at home. There's an element of diplomacy in this too. We're taking work away from people in our own country who pay union dues. Most studios constantly review the production slate and sound out the producers' guilds to avoid getting a lot of heat from the unions.

MS: Is it always possible to stick to the budget?
RS: You start a movie with a budget. And you either proceed without any hiccups and everything gets done to schedule, or you come across a period of time when shooting slows down. Sometimes a picture starts shooting and takes on its own personality. It grows. And that's OK, so long as the powers that be agree to the changes, so that when we get to the end of the day the cost is not some huge surprise. *Waterworld*, for instance, took on a life of its own. It's not a precise science. It's more like going on a blind date. But, in the end, you always go back to the agreed budget. No matter what happens during the course of the film-making, the studio is always going to go back to the agreed game plan and will want to know about the benefit of any changes.

MS: Does a long location shoot make sticking to the budget more difficult? You were out in Kenya for *Tomb Raider 2* . . .
RS: Yes. Kenya! Africa! South Africa has an infrastructure for filming, but Kenya has nothing. Half the time we were completely out of communication with the studio. When a studio picture goes out on location to a foreign country, we hire a production service company who are responsible for all local expenditure. So we look to them to be a mini-production team within our group. And there are always surprises when you turn up. If there are a lot of questions being asked and not a lot of answers being given, that's when you have to worry.

MS: What makes a film go over its budget?
RS: You can go over budget for a number of reasons. It can be due to the weather, or some sort of disaster. An actor or director can become ill, but that's covered by insurance. When we did *Sleepy Hollow* the director of photography got very ill from all the smoke we were using, and we had to shut down for a week. So then it was my job to figure out what that week would cost, in order to present the figures to the studio. In America we're stricter about health issues than you are over here.

MS: And changes to the script must also have an effect.
RS: You may have a particular set that's scheduled to take three days, but after script revisions you get to that point and see you've got motion control work, complicated movements and tremendous amounts of dialogue. Most of the changes that are creative, and don't relate to dialogue, have a cost attached. They sometimes add it, they sometimes take it away. I have to keep up with new pages, fix the schedule, look at what will happen if we go down a day. There are so many variables. A good production team always has a plan A and a plan B. For instance, it's useful if there's a weather cover set – somewhere you can go if you get rained or stormed out. But the director hasn't time to think about these things; he's got to take care of his vision. So a good producer will work at the

plan and cost the vision, and allow him to keep within the schedule – because for every day you don't make your schedule there's a financial impact. There's always a knock-on effect. And that's what I try to do all day and every day. It's a wonder I don't try to commit suicide.

Matthew Sweet is the author of *Inventing the Victorians* and the forthcoming *Sheperton Babylon.*

Denise Breton (photo by Philippe Quaisse)

Denise Breton
interviewed by David Thompson

Regarded with something close to awe within the film publicist community, Denise Breton has proved that there is far more to her profession than just organizing screenings and handing out brochures. For her, films could be nurtured and more effectively promoted by individual campaigns reflecting her own enthusiasm for them, and not by slavishly following what Hollywood might dictate. Based in Paris, at first working for Fox (1962–81) and then as an independent, she showed that European sensibilities often responded more positively to American directors than their compatriots. In the words of one fellow highly regarded publicist, she possesses 'intelligence, integrity, style and class'. To another, she has demonstrated that 'the most rewarding aspect of the business is to have good relationships with film-makers, and that's enormously precious'. She now insists she is easing into semi-retirement, and at the time of this interview (June 2003) was busy dispatching the contents of her office to the film archives in Lyons and Toulouse. But she continues to honour her special long-term commitments to Robert Altman and Woody Allen, whose latest film, Anything Else, *she had just signed to promote.*

David Thompson: Did you always plan a career in the cinema?
Denise Breton: No, it happened by accident. When I was eighteen, I started to work in Paris at the American Embassy, in the legal department. I was just starting out, and I knew nothing, I had shorthand but I couldn't type, and I had come back from England after spending two years in a convent in Bromley run by French nuns. My aunt, who was a teacher, had persuaded my father to send me to England after I failed my exams, but for me it was not punishment, it was a wonderful time. Some of the girls from the convent had rented an apartment in Soho, and we all had an enormous amount of fun. When I came back to France during the Christmas holidays, I met Claude, my husband, at an Ella Fitzgerald concert in the Salle Pleyel, and we wanted to get married, but both our parents were adamant: I had to complete my studies, while Claude was starting a new job. I got the job at the Embassy through an American soldier I knew. They said I needed my father's signature, which he refused, so I signed for him and left home. I took a small maid's room in Montparnasse. At the Embassy I worked with a girl whose sister was a film editor, and then one day she said her sister had found her a job as secretary to Darryl F. Zanuck. She said to me, 'He's starting on

The Longest Day, he's hiring people left and right, do you want to come?' I said, 'Why not, it sounds fun!'

DT: What did you do for Zanuck?
DB: I became his secretary, number five; he had one English, one American, one Australian, one French and me. He was an independent producer at the time, finishing *The Big Gamble* with Juliette Greco; he was also in post-production on *Roots of Heaven*, which was written by Romain Gary. Looking at these films, I thought if that's what the movie business is about it's not going to be fun, but then *The Longest Day* started and that was a whole different ball game.

When Zanuck was head of production at Fox, they were making fifty-five or sixty films a year, and he knew every script and every director, and he would watch all the rushes. He would always change things for the better; he was a great editor.

DT: What was your contribution to the film?
DB: On *The Longest Day*, he hired Romain Gary for an incredible amount of money, and Gary kept postponing the writing. Since I was Zanuck's French secretary No. 2, I was assigned to Romain Gary. Zanuck was already in Normandy shooting, and he was waiting for the French scenes. And he kept calling and saying, 'What's the matter?' And I said, 'Nothing, I've been here since ten o'clock this morning. I've been playing cards and chess with Jean Seberg, but he hasn't given me anything.' So one day, finally, Gary wrote five pages, and as I was typing those pages I thought, 'My God, this is terrible.' I could just see those French actors struggling to say those lines! When they arrived in Normandy by helicopter, Zanuck was furious with me because on the phone I'd said I didn't think the lines were very good. 'What? Who are you to judge the work of a Nobel prize-winner? Did you change anything?' 'No, I didn't.' Then he got his English secretary to call me to say the French actors like Jean-Louis Barrault had refused to say the lines, and they were rewriting the scenes on the spot.

DT: Zanuck respected you?
DB: Yes, because I stood up to him. If you did, and you were right – and you'd better be right! – then you gained his respect. I thought the incident with Gary was the end of my career. I remember one day he fired one of his American secretaries, because she'd done something wrong, without giving her another chance. Zanuck had a great gift: he had a fantastic memory and a talent with people – he knew exactly what they were capable of achieving. I learnt so much from him. He would say, 'Call me so-and-so,' as he never had a telephone book, and you had to second-guess him, but most of the time I was right.

DT: So *The Longest Day* was your introduction to dealing with movie people?
DB: Yes. It was on *The Longest Day* that I first met Sean Connery. I also met

Robert Mitchum, John Wayne and many of the fifty-two actors who were in the film. With Mitchum, the first day he came to the location in the Ile de Ré, all the English technicians were having a party in one of the nightclubs in La Rochelle. A fight broke out, the police came in, and he said, 'Watch, they're going to look for me.' And they did! 'It's always like that. Whenever I get into a ruck, it's always me.' We stayed in touch until his death, and I saw him in the last film he made in France. You'd say to him, 'How are you?' And he'd reply, 'Worse.'

DT: How long did you work with Zanuck?
DB: I worked with Zanuck until he decided to take over Fox. He was the major shareholder at Fox and the company, under Spyros P. Skouras – with all that was happening with *Cleopatra* – was not doing well, and his stock was falling. At the end of *The Longest Day*, he asked me to come to America with him and open his office, spending three months in New York, while my mother-in-law looked after my two-year-old daughter. Then I said I was going to look for another job, and he said, 'No, I want you to stay at Fox.' He asked me what I wanted to do, and I said, 'Work in publicity.' This was the wrong thing to say, as he immediately pushed a button, and there was a company called Diener, Hauser, Greenthal who were the advertising agency for Fox. And so the last month and a half I was in New York I worked at this agency with Mr Herbert Hauser, who became my mentor, to learn what publicity was all about. I found this fascinating, because in Europe publicity was as yet unknown. I realized later that Europe was, in fact, ten years behind.

When I came back to Paris, Fox was undergoing a complete reorganization and I was assigned to the European Advertising/Publicity department for Europe. When Zanuck offered me the job, I said, 'I'm new and young, I don't know anything.' But he said, 'Just do it, hire the right people, get the older ones out. That's what I want. It's the way to ensure the kind of publicity campaigns and the release I want for *The Longest Day*.' And I did. After three years, we had the best advertising, promotion and publicity team in Europe, which everybody envied – except in Italy, where I had a lot of problems. They had people there who had been around for too long. They did not want a woman in publicity, but I insisted and hired Tilde Corsi, Fellini's publicist, who today is an important and successful film producer in Italy.

DT: Was it unusual then for a woman to be given such a high position?
DB: Yes. In fact, I was the only one. On the annual report of Fox, they had this famous line: '20th Century Fox is a company that gives equal rights to women and to blacks.' So I was one of them! It was very unusual. In fact, I didn't think it would work, because I was so young, and there were so many people who were much older and would look at me wondering, 'Is she Zanuck's mistress or something?' Which I wasn't, but I never denied it; if that's what they wanted to

believe, that was fine. It was a way to make the changes that were needed because they were afraid of upsetting Zanuck!

DT: As Head of European Publicity for Fox, what films were you dealing with?
DB: We would get all the films the studio made and, because of the high volume of production, we would choose the twenty or thirty films we thought had the best chance of working in Europe. The managing directors of the French company would look at them, and I would do so from the point of view of European publicity. Since the films had already either opened well or flopped in America, if I thought something was interesting, we could just take it, design a new campaign and release it.

DT: What was your main method for publicizing films?
DB: Because the European Sales and Publicity headquarters was then based in Paris, I was very close to the French office, where I wanted to recreate the MacMahonian concept by finding young journalists or cinephiles who wanted to work with me. In the sixties, there was a group of cinephiles who were using the Cinema MacMahon as a theatre for releasing American films, and they had a little restaurant called L'Etolie Verte next to the rue Troyon, where they met all the time. In those days telephone calls were very expensive, so they used to come to my office to use the telephone and call America. Pierre Rissient was a regular. They wanted to bring over directors like Arthur Penn to help promote their films. And they started a monster which has become impossible – numerous screenings before a release. In England, when you release a film, you usually have one big magazine screening and one big press screening; here, we now have seven, eight, ten press screenings and our press list has 700 names! They started that and it became an institution, and no one knows how to stop it.

I was always aligned to the attitude of the MacMahonians as opposed to the people at Fox, who saw film as a product. They'd say, 'This film does not have a chance,' and I'd say, 'How do you know? If a particular press loves it and if we, through what they write, can create a desire for people to see it, the film can work.' But they didn't believe in that. I remember when I became the head of publicity, the one big film I started to work on was *The Sound of Music*. I knew instinctively when it was being made in Austria that this was going to be a big film, and we brought Robert Wise to Paris, where *West Side Story* had been playing in a cinema on the Champs Elysées for five or six years. But I could not convince them that you had to create an interest in a film while it was in production. Later on I was working with Nicolas Roeg on another film that Fox had, *Walkabout*; the film was selected for Cannes, but Fox never released it. It went straight to television. That's when I met Jeremy Thomas, who was still a student at the time but who impressed me as a possible MacMahonian. He was already a great cinephile.

Going back to the MacMahonians: the director was very important. I think that's more true in France than in England and most of Europe. I went everywhere with directors like Mel Brooks, Paul Mazursky and Robert Altman. I brought them to Europe; the MacMahonian system was the great inspiration. I wanted to do that in every country, but England was always separate, Ascanio Branca was the Sales Manager, and the Director of Publicity was John Fairbairn, and they had their own way because they were directly related to what was happening in America.

DT: How much of Europe were you responsible for?
DB: I had seventeen countries. France, Germany, Italy, Spain, Holland, Belgium, the four Scandanavian countries, the Middle East, Greece, Turkey, Israel and Iran. And I had them all working together as a big family; we had conventions where they saw all the films, and what I really wanted to do was stimulate them, have them exchange their ideas, which was one thing that Alan Ladd Jr, who ran Fox in the seventies, was impressed by. Because what worked in France could very well work in Germany or somewhere else, we had a weekly activity report in which everybody wrote about what they were doing, and it circulated throughout Europe. And then we got together every three or four months in one location where ideas were interchanged. In fact, I'm going at the end of this week to Denmark because my ex-publicity directors and I continue to meet. Nobody really lost their jobs in all the various mergers, and I think they were able to carry through that camaraderie into their new jobs.

DT: Did these other countries ever feel dictated to by Paris?
DB: No, because they were never dictated to by anybody. It's not my way; I just wanted them to talk to one another. I wanted the person in Sweden to talk to the people in Denmark and Norway and Finland. And they didn't have to come through me. What I was interested in were the results. We had a lot of films with Mel Brooks, and Mel Brooks is not an easy person. Not easy to sell and also not easy to deal with! I wanted them to be autonomous, to call the director directly if they had something interesting to suggest, perhaps getting the local correspondents to meet him; they didn't have to come through me for approval. What I was interested in was that when the films were released – and we had a general pattern all over Europe – that they were doing well. With Mel Brooks, they wanted to have a one-hour show in Denmark for him and advertise it throughout Scandanavia. We managed to get him a contract so that he would get paid by television to do the show, which would be broadcast when the film was released, so everyone was happy. He made a lot of money because it was tax-free – and he made me sign the papers!

American directors loved to come to Paris. Usually they made a stop in London because it made sense in terms of the overall budget. Then came the era of press junkets, which are just a nightmare. What I did was take a director and go around Europe. We would normally go to one place in Scandanavia, often Sweden. We would then invite the journalists from the surrounding territories. The interviews would never be less than forty or fifty minutes with one person. I did that with Fred Zinnemann. Can you imagine him participating in one of these junkets today? He would never have accepted.

DT: How did you deal with Zinnemann?
DB: I admired him greatly and first met him during the shooting of *Julia* in Paris. It took time for him to accept me as he hated publicity and considered publicists a nuisance on set. So I went quietly every day until he finally decided that we could discuss what we could do to publicize the film.

He was a man who did not want to go on television; he wanted to remain behind the camera, not in front. He did not like the idea of being interviewed. We did something special on *Julia*, a 16mm documentary lasting ten minutes, with Vanessa Redgrave and Jane Fonda at the station in Strasbourg at 5 a.m. Zinnemann didn't talk to the camera, but you could follow him working, and it was a difficult task for Michel Parbot, the cameraman, to get what he needed without interfering with Zinnemann's direction. When he saw the finished film he was pleased and asked Michel to direct second-unit sequences for *Julia*.

My whole life at the time was centred on him and the film. When it came to dubbing *Julia*, I realized that my involvement with films should extend into dubbing and subtitling, since the dubbing is so important. I said, 'Fred, you have to come here because your films are being redirected by someone who doesn't know much about them and is only concerned with lip-sync.' So he decided to come, and we had Jane Fonda do her own voice because she spoke good French. Fred spoke French and German fluently, and Italian and Spanish fairly well. I told him he had to get involved in the text, choose voice tests and direct the actors on the dubbing stage so that the film kept his vision. And he said, 'How come I have lived so many years without knowing that my films were being redirected in the dubbing?' But, of course, Fox disliked that, because when he was on the set, he was so particular that what usually took one day took three with him as a director! Fortunately, in those days Alan Ladd Jr was very supportive, and what I thought was needed to make the film work, we were able to do.

DT: When did this business of press junkets begin?
DB: After I had left Fox, it really became a working tool. The directors didn't come; they had junkets in America. Some would insist on coming to Europe, so they decided on London or Paris, and did the same thing as they would do in America; it works but it takes away the pleasure of good interviews. I would say it probably began in the eighties, and then it just mushroomed. The stars hate it. I was always saying to Alan Ladd Jr, 'Why can't you put it in the contract, if they

do a film, they have to do promotion?' But the agents don't want to do that. Previously, you just had the lawyers doing the contract. You didn't have the agent, the personal manager, the personal publicist and all the peripheral personnel. I had a big confrontation over Meg Ryan. Pathé bought a film with her and Russell Crowe, and she wanted to come to Paris. In exchange for certain considerations her agent offered two hours of interview time. I told Pathé it was going to cost so much, so why not just buy good advertising for the film and tell her to stay home? And they were furious, her agent particularly.

DT: But most directors and stars enjoyed coming to Europe for you?
DB: They did because we gave them time to enjoy it. If they came to Denmark, they would go to the Tivoli gardens; in other cities, they were offered visits to museums and so they could come with their wife or girlfriend or whatever. We had so many interviews in the morning, so many in the afternoon, and we also organized a première where a lot of celebrities were invited. Paul Mazursky loved coming to Europe; Peter Yates and Robert Altman too.

DT: Did television become part of your promotion?
DB: It started in Germany, where national publicity is hard to get. It's a little like ten different small countries – eleven if you count Austria. You had to do something locally in Munich, something locally in Frankfurt, but you cannot have a real national campaign in Germany. So when they realized that television was a unifying concept, they decided to use it to promote films. It started earlier in America with TV spots, which, of course, we didn't know how to make at the time. It turned out to be cheaper to advertise on television in Germany than in the big national newspapers. So we started there, and then I realized that while the studio could do it for big films, the small independent films would never be able to afford it. I was really pleased when the French government decided not to allow television in France – and it's still not allowed – to advertise films. Recently, it's been changed for video and records, but for years you could not advertise any cultural event. Which was good, because you had many programmes, with interviews and the 'Making of', which would cover films; everybody had access if you had the right contacts and could make a 'tie-in' with the film.

DT: Why did you leave Fox?
DB: Alan Ladd Jr, with whom I had a very good relationship – we called him Laddie – left Fox when he was making more money for them than they had ever made. I left Fox in the year of *Omen II* and *Omen III*. My boss in the USA gave me the whole line-up for that year, and I just said, 'No, I can't work with these films.' I told the new president of Fox that none of their slate of films excited me, there was really nothing. I felt that they were not interesting, and it would have been difficult for me to generate the publicity machine around them. I was sim-

ply being honest. I said I would continue to work part-time, and the other half of the time I would work for other companies, because I felt that I needed to be interested in the things that I was doing, like *Popeye* with Robert Altman. I also had directors who wanted me to work for them, and at the time Mel Brooks was leaving Fox, Gene Wilder was leaving, Paul Mazursky was leaving, Peter Yates had already left; they were all disappearing because of the new management. Fox said no to my proposal, so I stayed for a year and left at the end of December 1980, and just before I went I was pivotal in getting *Chariots of Fire* selected for Cannes, which, in an unprecedented gesture, was announced in January. But David Puttnam still insisted I take *Chariots of Fire* to Cannes, which was a mistake, because once you have left a company you have to let the new people take over, and the film did not do well in Cannes. Fox put a great deal of pressure on me to stay, but Laddie was opening his own independent company at Warners and wanted me to work with him, so I said yes to Laddie. I don't think that Fox believed my reason for leaving was because I didn't like the films!

DT: So you continued your relationship with Alan Ladd Jr?
DB: Laddie's first film at Warners was *Divine Madness* with Bette Midler. He told me to go to Warners in Paris, but on seeing the office they offered me, I said I could not work in those conditions. I took that film on about three weeks before it opened, and I knew that it would be terrible for me if the film flopped. Well, it didn't flop; Bette Midler came over, we did all the usual things, we had a big première. Then I opened my own office and started to work with The Ladd Company as producer's representative to Warner Brothers. We did *Outland* with Sean Connery, *Star 80* and *Blade Runner*.

For my PR company, I had the kind of contract that allowed me to work for other people, and that was a deduction from the flat fee The Ladd Company paid me. They had first priority, but Laddie understood that, in order to accomplish the very best for his films, I had to broaden my horizons and work for other people, like Jeremy Thomas, who was then involved in Julien Temple's *The Great Rock'n'Roll Swindle* and went on to produce his own films. David Puttnam was very much the golden boy at the time. I introduced Jeremy to the Cannes Film Festival and worked on all of his productions – *Insignificance, The Hit* and the Bertolucci films.

DT: Were you keen to work on French films as well?
DB: At Fox, the one thing I had never promoted was a French film. So I decided to take on what seemed to me the most difficult project, a film by Michel Lang, who had made *A nous les petites Anglaises*, on which I had met him. He had a script called *Le Cadeau* which I read. I said to myself, 'Well, this is a true French film; the script is so-so but it has good actors, Pierre Mondy, Claudia Cardinale and the young Clio Goldsmith, who is so beautiful.' From my perspective, I

thought if I can make this film work then it will open up new doors for me. I realized that by taking on something particularly difficult everyone would be looking at me saying, 'Ah, now we'll see what she can do.' I thought that was fine and I welcomed the challenge. It was a way of opening up new avenues for me, and it did. In fact, I think the film still enjoys the record of having nineteen cover stories. With Gilbert de Goldschmidt, the producer, we had this idea, which we shared with the director: we have the beautiful Claudia Cardinale, who at the time was forty, twenty years older than young Clio, why not have them both photographed for the cover stories? Before production started we did a photo session, and I said to Claudia, whom I knew from having worked with her on the promotion of *The Leopard* at Fox, 'Clio's so young, you can be like her mentor.' These photos made practically every magazine cover in France, and it's one of the achievements I am most proud of. I started promoting *Le Cadeau* with a very supportive producer and a willing director, both open to all sorts of ideas, including having Clio photographed with the French football team outside a cinema on the Champs Elysées. So there was a lot of coverage for the film and it worked, but not just because of my ideas; it was a good movie.

DT: Did you now deal with more European films?

DB: When I was at Fox I did not know any European directors. I started to look for those I admired, and the ones I liked most were the British directors. I loved working with Ken Loach on *Hidden Agenda*, and more recently with Julien Temple on *The Filth and the Fury*, with Mike Figgis on *Hotel*, and with Mike Hodges on *I'll Sleep When I'm Dead*. I guess I have a natural affinity for their films; I know what they're expressing. I've also worked with Wim Wenders after his *Buena Vista Social Club* on *Ten Minutes Older*. I have followed the career of Emir Kusturica with the two films that won the Palme d'Or at Cannes, *Father Is Away on Business* and *Underground*, and another Serbian director, Goran Paskaljevic, whose film *Powder Keg* was shown in Venice. Of all the European directors, Bernardo Bertolucci is the most important, as I worked with him first at The Ladd Company on *La Luna* and *Tragedy of a Ridiculous Man*, and then with Jeremy Thomas on *The Last Emperor* and *The Sheltering Sky*. I also worked with Kurosawa, and with Oshima on *Merry Christmas Mr Lawrence*, which Jeremy produced.

When I established my company, three other publicists joined me. At some point I realized that we had been handling some 140 films. And I said, 'This is too much, it has to stop.' So I told them to go on their own, taking some of my clients. I am happy to say I was in a position where I was able to nurture many talented individuals. One is at Warners now, one at Disney, and two others are successful independent publicists.

DT: Does the Cannes Film Festival continue to be important?

DB: Yes, but it has become very big and the competition is kind of an alibi for the market aspect, which overshadows the films in competition. When you look at the press list for Cannes, there are some three thousand journalists! I knew Cannes when there were just 120 journalists from all over the world, including print and radio press. With the advent of television at the beginning of the seventies, it grew enormously. In those days television could make their own programmes at Cannes as there were not too many people. Now it's impossible. We wanted to have free television publicity, so we dealt with them, but at first journalists wanted to do more in-depth interviews and take their time. Now the whole process of conducting interviews has become much more hectic and frenetic.

DT: I believe you had to look after Cannon Films in their heyday at Cannes in 1986.

DB: Yes, that year they had four films in Cannes – *Fool for Love* by Altman, *Runaway Train* by Andrei Konchalovsky, *Othello* and one other. In those days, the president of the Cannes Festival was Robert Favre le Bret, and the two cousins, Golan and Globus, wanted the world to know how great they were, so they invited Monsieur Favre Le Bret to Israel for a week, where he was treated like a king. They came the following year with four films in competition and nineteen bodyguards. This was the time when they announced one project after another, including the famous deal with Jean-Luc Godard, who signed his contract on a napkin on the Carlton terrace. That signing was a major coup and made headlines around the world. Although none of the films won any awards, Cannon got an incredible amount of publicity worldwide.

DT: Weren't you very instrumental in the discovery of *M*A*S*H* at Cannes?

DB: I first met Bob Altman in 1970 when he came to Cannes for *M*A*S*H*. I went to pick him up at the airport before the festival. I looked at him, and he said, 'Is there something the matter with me?' And I said, 'No, but I thought you were younger!' And he said, 'Right, we're starting well, you and me.' He was so full of life and bubbling with enthusiasm. For me *M*A*S*H* was a film made by a twenty-five-year-old.

I had watched it with the head of French publicity, Marc Bernard, and we laughed and laughed. I had Bertrand Tavernier and other cinephiles see the film with us, and I thought if they felt like we did, then it was something worth fighting for. So Marc and I went to the French managing director and we said, 'You should release this film.'

DT: This was before its success in the USA?

DB: Yes, and they were regarding it as a loss. I called Alan Ladd Jr and said, 'Laddie, this film is great. We had such fun watching it.' He said, 'Well, I agree, see what you can do with it.' Then we decided to show it to Gilles Jacob. He saw it and liked it, so I called Laddie again and said, 'Let's go with this film in

Cannes.' At the time, Fox was making *Those Magnificent Men in Their Flying Machines*, and there was a big royal première to which I was supposed to go, and I said, 'No, I'm working on *M*A*S*H!*' We took the film to Cannes with Ingo Preminger and Bob and Sally Kellerman, and the film won the Palme d'Or.

That was the beginning of my relationship with Bob. I remember that when we showed the film to the French managing director, he said, 'People won't understand American football, no one will want to see this film.' I said, 'Let's release it and see.' Once we got the Palme d'Or, naturally they were anxious to release it. Laddie told me the Palme d'Or, which at the time was worth something, was going to add five million dollars to the box office. Then they opened the film in America, and it was a huge success. So from that moment on, Bob liked working with me.

DT: You've been involved with practically all his films since *Three Women*.
DB: Yes, but when I was with Fox I could work only on the Fox films. *A Perfect Couple* is my favourite of his films. I don't know why, except I was in Los Angeles when he was making it. I really liked it and I think we did not handle it properly. Of course, Bob loves all his own films, even *Pret à Porter*.

He really controls everything and he's got his own vision of what he does. Actors love him and he is a genius in every way. His casting is brilliant, and when he claims he just has the actors do it, it's only partly true. At the same time he's like a sponge, stealing ideas from everybody. When he was shooting *The Company* in Chicago, I was in England working with Mike Hodges on *I'll Sleep When I'm Dead*, and Malcolm MacDowell came over from acting in Chicago. I asked him, 'How is the film?' And he said, 'I don't know. I went on the set and Bob said, "Come on, go ahead and surprise me!"'

DT: How would you deal with Altman and the press?
DB: With journalists he always says, 'No, I don't want to see anyone, I don't want to do this interview.' But once you get people on the set, then he's very nice. The best time to get him is when he's shooting, because he moves quickly on to his next project.

Gosford Park was a real job of 'marketing', which was done by Bob with Julian Fellowes. Some of it involved preparing a family tree of the nobility upstairs and the servants downstairs, as well as creating a board game. The game was Bob's idea, as he loves to gamble, but then he lost interest. He decided it wasn't that good. It's now a collector's item.

DT: How did your relationship with Woody Allen begin?
DB: It was when I saw *Take the Money and Run* at Fox, at a time when no one was interested in the film and no one knew who Woody was. Catherine Laporte was a friend of Gilles Jacob at the time, and I had the resources to send her to New York to do an interview with Woody. After *Take the Money and Run*, he

worked mainly with United Artists, and then I started again with him in 1994 with *Bullets Over Broadway.*

DT: Isn't he a notoriously reluctant interviewee?
DB: He did not want to do many interviews, and he never did press conferences either, except when he had his problems with Mia Farrow. I said to him at the time, 'Woody, maybe you should do one press conference; if they ask questions, are you ready to answer them?' And he said, 'Yes.' It was the first time he did such a thing in Paris, and it was very well attended. We did do a kind of a press junket with him, but a very limited one, with only a few interviews. And he speaks to the same journalists all the time. There's a journalist at *Le Monde*, Jean-Michel Frodon, who wrote a book on him, and he always gets an hour. The one thing he likes about the French is that they really don't care about scandals; they respect him as a film-maker. They never ask him anything about his private life.

DT: His films have lost their popularity in Britain. Do they still do well in France?
DB: Yes. Last year Gilles Jacob invited him to come to Cannes and said he would open the festival with *Hollywood Ending*. The film got great reviews and we had lots of coverage. It got over 800,000 admissions. I remember when we had the musical, *Everyone Says I Love You*, I made him do a television show, which I'm still ashamed about. I said to him, 'You have to work for the film, because the way the French distributor bought it, in order to break even we need over one million admissions.' I sent him a cassette of the show hoping he would refuse, but he didn't even look at it. It is normally a live show with an audience. For Woody they agreed to tape it and there was a letter of agreement that if he didn't like it they wouldn't show it. During the show they had a guy bring in a clarinet for him to play, and of course he wouldn't. Afterwards, I was livid, and so was he, and I said, 'I'm so embarrassed.' When we were in the car, the first thing he said to me was, 'Would Fellini have done such a show?' And I said, 'No, Fellini hated television.' I said he didn't have to worry because part of the deal was that if he didn't like it, we could forget about it. And he looked at me and said, 'Are you trying to tell me that you convinced me to do that show and now we can forget all about it?' He said, 'No way.' Then the driver, who had been in the audience, said, 'But it was wonderful. I had such a good time.' I could have kissed him! He said, 'No, no, let it go.' But the French love him and his films, year after year.

DT: So, for you, the director remains the most important element in promoting a film?
DB: Again, it's something I learnt from the MacMahonians, that it was best to use the director first – who could tell you about the film – and then the actors. But for me the captain of the ship is always the director. Especially Bob Altman; I felt he was the best person to promote his films.

There's one word I really hate and that's 'marketing'. What does it mean? It means nothing. Suddenly there are experts telling you how to do things. They want to merge advertising, publicity and promotion. But each film is a separate entity; there is one thing in each film you can use to publicize it. You have to find out what it is and use it. So that means thinking, designing the right campaign, finding the right 'catchlines' and doing the right promotions.

DT: What do you think of the way in which marketing has become so important to the success of companies like Miramax?
DB: If it works for a film it works; if not, then they drop it. In a way that's not the wrong way of doing things, because if you've done everything to promote a film and the film doesn't click, you can do anything you want afterwards and it won't make any difference. But they drop things very quickly, whereas in the old days, if a film didn't work, you gave it time for word of mouth to really penetrate, and films would last for more than the four or five weeks they do now.

There was one film that Serge Silberman produced, *Diva*, which I thought was very good. I remember going to press screenings, and Serge would start apologizing for the film, saying, 'It's a little film, we need your help.' The film did not work, but when they re-released it after it got a prize at the Cesars, then it did well.

DT: So awards are still valuable?
DB: Having a prize in Cannes used to be more meaningful. The only advantage of having a film in a festival is that at one point you get the whole world to see your film. If the film is worth it, then it works. If it's not that good, then it can hurt the film seriously.

What's difficult is explaining to directors why festivals do not want films. I had an experience with Chen Kaige last year. He had a jewel of a film called *Together*, and he wanted very much for it to go to Cannes. But he wasn't ready in time for Cannes, so then we tried for Venice. I had it subtitled into French, and we invited the president of the Venice Film Festival, Moritz de Hadeln, to see it. And it was the most embarrassing moment. Moritz did not like it and, at lunch with Chen Kaige, he sort of explained why, and I didn't know what to say. Afterwards I told Kaige, 'The man has no children, so if the little boy who plays the violin didn't work for him, that's understandable but does not reflect on the film.' I believed in it and we got the film selected for Toronto, where it was screened one night and bought by United Artists the next day for US domestic release, with Etchie Stroh's Moonstone Entertaiment handling international sales. It's opening everywhere now. But the fact that Venice refused the film was a blow for Chen Kaige. I try to avoid that – when festivals see films I don't want the directors to be around!

DT: What was your experience as a producer?
DB: *Le Voleur d'Enfants*, by Jules Supervielle, was a book I read when I was

fourteen years old, and I thought it would make a wonderful film. I was in Avoriaz with Freddie Francis at the time of the writers' strike, and I said, 'Why do we have to go to writers when we have such books in the public domain?' And I mentioned this wonderful book called *Le Voleur d'Enfants*. Freddie said, 'Yes, let's do it,' as he knew the book. So I came back to Paris and I called Gallimard, and they told me that the book was available and we could option it. Stupidly, instead of optioning it for myself, I optioned it for Freddie Francis, and a writer was engaged, and they started writing a script. We were looking for someone to play the lead role, and my instinct told me that Michel Simon – if he was still alive – would have been perfect, but I said, 'What about Marcello Mastroianni?' Freddie said, 'Yes, that's a very good idea.' So I sent a note and the book to Marcello, and instead of sending it directly I gave it to a publicist who was working with him, Simon Mizrahi. He called me back to say Marcello was interested. I called Freddie, saying Marcello wanted to see his films. Freddie had just done *The Doctor and the Devils*. Unfortunately, I showed this film to Marcello, and he said, 'No, not this director.' So my associate producer suggested Christian de Chalonge, who had just done *Dr Petiot*, and Marcello said, 'That's the man.'

So I went to London to renegotiate the rights. Christian de Chalonge and his wife Dominique wrote a new screenplay, and the shooting went well. Then, when it came to the editing, I don't know what happened, but I could see it went wrong. In France, the director has complete artistic control and my associate producer could not have his way. I made all sorts of mistakes, like asking Marcello to do a thing he didn't want to do, because I thought if the director wanted it, then the actors had to do it. Marcello said it wouldn't work, and I said, 'Well, let's give it a try.' I didn't realize how much an extra day of shooting cost in those days. Of course, when we saw it, we all agreed it didn't work, so it ended up on the cutting-room floor.

The film was released and did nothing, but Robert Wise saw it, and he said, 'Give me all the rushes and I will re-edit it.' But it was too late; it had already been sold to Italy. My associate producer claimed it was not sold, but a friend of mine saw it in Cairo, where they had taken out the name of the director and recut the film. It was an experience that convinced me I could never be a producer, because I don't know how to say no, especially to a director. I enjoyed being involved in the writing of the script very much, though I have no credit for it. The whole process of production through to distribution was a valuable and useful experience for me. I wanted to try producing once, and if I hadn't done it, today it would be one of my regrets.

(With thanks to Wren Arthur, Mike Kaplan and Charles McDonald)

David Thompson is the author of *Scorsese on Scorsese*, *Levinson on Levinson* and the forthcoming *Altman on Altman*.

Clare Binns, Film Programmer interviewed by Jason Wood

Clare Binns has over twenty-five years' experience in the film industry. With her encyclopaedic knowledge of film and cinema, she is well-known and respected throughout the industry and has excellent working relationships with distributors, producers, directors and other industry bodies. Having run and booked some of the most successful independent cinemas in the country (including the Ritzy Brixton, The Gate Notting Hill, The Phoenix East Finchley, The Everyman Hampstead, The Electric and The Cameo Edinburgh), Clare is now regularly invited to speak about film and cinema exhibition and sits on the Industry Panel for the London Film Festival and Film London. She is also the Director of Contract Cinemas at City Screen Virtual.

Jason Wood: Could you begin by explaining how you originally became involved in film programming and what drew you to it?
Clare Binns: I worked as an usher for about six years, and one of the things that ushers do is stand around and criticize the person that's putting on the films in the cinema. It's a long tradition that will always continue; the person working in the cinema obviously knows better than the person who is booking it. The Ritzy Brixton at the time was a cinema that had been started off by Pat Foster; the management was very loose and it was all a bit of a scramble in the days when repertory cinemas were very alternative and not the structured businesses they are now. There were opportunities to do things outside of the box that you were put in – that could include being the cleaner, which I also was for a time, so you had to take the good and the bad. Liz Wrenn, who went on to run Electric Pictures, was booking the site, and I just kept pushing and pushing to take on the late-night film booking whilst carrying out all my other on-site duties. They didn't want to lose me because I was a mainstay of the front-of-house team and so I was given the chance to book the late nights. Those opportunities are still there, especially in a company like City Screen and, I suppose, in companies such as Odeon as well, but I think there was more flexibility when I was starting out.

JW: Can you remember what your first late-night double bill was?
CB: No, but I'm sure it was a near disaster because in film booking people always think that their personal taste is going to make lots of money, and so I'm sure that I thought that some ridiculous double bill would fill the cinema. You learn by your mistakes. The Ritzy also learned by my mistakes.

Clare Binns at the Ritzy

JW: Prior to working as an usher, did you study film at all? This seems to be the route now taken by most people coming into the industry.

CB: I left school very early because I was a bit of a rebel, and the only education certificate I have is a swimming certificate. This has helped enormously with Esther Williams seasons. I had no film-related qualifications whatsoever but what I did have was a really strong interest in foreign-language films and that was mainly through watching films at peak time on BBC2 and going to the Tyneside Cinema in Newcastle. There was also a cinema that showed double features slightly off first-run within fifty yards of my house. This was the Jesmond Picture House, which is, sadly, now closed. I was going to the cinema maybe two or three times a week; cinema was my thing.

JW: Television today is very different and BBC2 does not have the same remit.
CB: It's certainly changing. There are more channels now on television and they are going to have to fill them. BBC4 shows more interesting films now and has essentially become what BBC2 was. There are more avenues opening up, but the real problem for cinema now is that there are more choices open to people regarding what they do with their free time. Cinema is one of a hundred things that people can do. There are still lots of films out there for people to see, and companies like City Screen are the ones that will increase the numbers that are there; it's just a problem of getting people to actually go into the cinema. In my day, if there was a new film from Truffaut you would just go; you wouldn't think twice about it.

JW: Is it no longer an *auteur*-led environment?
CB: No, I think people are led by marketing, essentially. They are driven by what is hip and the way that films are sold. The other difference is that I was prepared to be disappointed; I was prepared to not come out of the cinema feeling good. I went because I was interested in what a director was trying to do or say and to then discuss it with people afterwards. These days people are stressed in a way they weren't previously and so they want to come out of the cinema happy. Faced with a choice of *Bridget Jones* and *Lilya 4-Ever* they'll invariably choose *Bridget Jones* because they know they will come out feeling OK.

JW: Was there a specific point where this change occurred? Escapism has always been one of the pleasures of cinema, but you indicate that this is now totally dominant.
CB: No, I think there has been a gradual shift towards this, linked to the way that films are released in the US, the rise of the multiplex and the need to fill so many screens with product. I've always liked a full range of films, including Hollywood blockbusters, but I was always more interested in the film-makers and what they were trying to say. I think mass cinema-going is not about that and, in a way, why should it be? There is nothing wrong with the multiplexes; it's just that they are delivering a different kind of film and a different kind of experience in a different kind of environment than people like myself want anything more than only occasionally.

JW: But the multiplexes are also copying the independent circuits and dedicating a number of their screens to specialist product. Is this a cultural decision or a purely financial one?
CB: Multiplexes aren't there to make cultural decisions; they're there to make financial ones. Any business is there to make financial decisions, but I think that the spirit in which most of the people that I am involved with came into the business was through a love of a broad range of cinema. The multiplexes may well have people working there who are interested in cinema – in fact, they

absolutely do, there is no question about it – but I think the endgame is very different to that of an independent company such as City Screen. Here the endgame is not just a hard, cynical 'We want to make a buck at the expense of anything we put on screen.' If tomorrow the fashion became cinema from the Ukraine, then providing it was in their commercial interests, the multiplexes would no doubt fill their screens with that. We would too, but we would also want to have other things going on as well. Multiplexes are in it for the money; there's nothing cultural going on at all.

JW: What about the challenges faced by independent distributors in this country? Studios distributing specialist titles is not anything new but companies such as Artificial Eye, Metro-Tartan and Optimum now face very stiff opposition from these companies because they simply cannot compete in financial terms with regards to marketing. Could the increased distribution of specialist titles signal the demise of such companies?

CB: It could do, but it's the same for specialized cinemas. What specialized cinemas and specialist distributors have to do is play the game, and in order to play the game these distributors have to adjust the way they do the marketing and the way they release films. If City Screen can build up a chain of cinemas that are successful and deliver to a specialized audience, then those independent distributors can do exactly the same. What they cannot do, and what some of them are in a danger of doing, is assume that the climate is as it was ten years ago. You have to move with the times. Ten years ago the majority of specialized cinemas were uncomfortable, had bad sound and bad picture quality, and unless you invest in the sort of comfort that the multiplexes now deliver you will lose your business. It is the same for distributors; they have got to wake up about how they put their product on to the screens.

JW: Are they doing this and how can they be more opportunistic in terms of getting people in to see their films?

CB: In the past, the relationship between exhibitors and distributors was very combative, but that has changed and is changing and people now work together far more closely in terms of scheduling pictures and commitment to length of run. This also extends to the actual films that distributors buy so that they do not commit themselves to picking up a title that nobody is going to want to play. I think that the way in which the independent distributors spend their money has to be looked at more closely; I also think that they have to look at how they can further develop their relationship with their potential audience – it's not all about ad spend.

JW: For independent cinemas the direct relationship with the audience is essential. Look at the popularity of director talks and Q&A events.

CB: The way you develop an audience's understanding is essential. If an audience goes to see a Q&A with a director, then they are perhaps twice as likely to want to see that director's next film. In a sense there is too much information around for people, but you should give them a choice about learning more. I'm a great believer in programme notes actually – even better than lots of material produced in a brochure. If they choose to go and see a certain film, they may then wish to pick up material that tells them more about it.

JW: To return to the discourse you mentioned between exhibitors and distributors, what kind of personal relationship do you have, and do you advise on the films you feel would be worthy of UK distribution?
CB: I go to most of the major festivals, and it's a fact that if you go to Cannes or Berlin you will be in a constant dialogue with the independent distributors. There have been occasions where I do think I have had a direct influence on somebody buying a film.

JW: For example?
CB: Funnily enough, the one that sticks out was not bought by an independent. *The Ice Storm* was a film that almost everyone at Buena Vista International had seen but had thought was not very good. Daniel Battsek, the managing director, then saw it in Cannes, where I also saw it, and I was very vocal about telling him he should buy it. There have been other films that I have talked to the distributors about, and the independents obviously talk to both Tony Jones and myself about whether film titles should be bought because, without the cinemas that we are involved with, those films will not get a decent release. Distributors are being lured into the belief that they can get good dates at multiplexes for specialized films, but at this point multiplexes are not delivering the kind of money for these films that specialized sites do.

JW: Back to the nuts and bolts of programming – how would you attempt to describe the role of the programmer and some of the decisions that have to be made?
CB: If you are a good programmer, it's trying to use the cinema to maximize its potential so that you're not just playing it safe but constantly trying to understand your local clientele and how you can reach them. Every cinema is different, every area is different, and every place has its own character, so you have to play to the strengths because that is what is going to bring in your box office. For example, at the David Lean in Croydon it is better to play films that appeal to a slightly older audience. However, that should not then stop you from trying to encourage the audience to go and see something exciting and new. It's very satisfying that over the last week the David Lean has been playing *Russian Ark* and it has sold out every show. I believe very strongly that if the audience trusts the films going in, then they are more likely to try something a bit different because they think, 'Well, generally I like what's on at this cinema.' I think a good pro-

grammer doesn't just do things by numbers. The bottom line is that you have to make the revenue and hit your targets – which also involves weighing up the viability of paying the terms that the distributor is requesting – but it is also about broadening the opportunities of your audience to see something different.

JW: Have there been examples of where you have really gone out on a limb and taken a chance on a film that in your heart of hearts you knew was probably not going to work in a commercial sense?
CB: Godard's *Eloge de l'amour* is one. Von Trier's *Dancer in the Dark* is another. As the day of release loomed ever nearer everybody knew that it was going to be a bloody disaster. All the critics loathed it, and I just knew I was on a hiding to nothing. To me it was one of the great films of that year and Von Trier is one of the greatest directors working today. Sometimes you do have to go out on a limb, but you can't afford to do it too often. If you have a cinema with more than one screen it allows you to be a little bit more adventurous, but you can't use the cinema to indulge your own personal favourites.

JW: On the subject of personal favourites, what specific directors would you count as perennials?
CB: Of the Europeans, I greatly admire Buñuel, Pasolini, Ozon, Melville, Tavernier, Godard, Truffaut, Almodóvar. From Japan, Ozu and Kurosawa are major sources of inspiration. From Britain, I would cite Alfred Hitchcock and Ken Loach; from America, John Ford and Martin Scorsese. One thing the Ritzy did, and was very good at, was showing first films by directors, such as Quentin Tarantino's *Reservoir Dogs* and Danny Boyle's *Shallow Grave*. When you see a director's first film the adrenalin rush of seeing somebody's new view on the world is so exciting. I also have to say that I go into the cinema every time wanting to like a picture, and when the lights go down I still get the same thrill that I may be about to see something, independent or otherwise, that may blow me away. There is a wealth of wonderful films out there, and if you were to ask me this same question tomorrow it is conceivable that I would come up with a different list of names.

JW: Similarly, are there specific genres or historical movements that interest you?
CB: When I first started watching films, the first genre that exerted a powerful fascination for me was film noir. I remain passionate about it. I also adore musicals and I'm never happier than when sat in front of Fred Astaire or Ginger Rogers, particularly *Top Hat*. I also very much admire the films and directors of the French New Wave. In fact, I generally go for French cinema, though some of their comedies leave something to be desired. Something gets lost in the translation. Italian cinema has obviously gone through great periods, though sadly it appears to be in the doldrums at the moment. There's also a lot of interesting stuff happening in Latin American cinema, especially the exciting new crop of

Mexican films, including *Amores Perros* and *Y Tu Mamá También*. Sadly, for one reason or another, African cinema seems to have waned, which is a great pity. I think Africa has many great tales to tell.

JW: To return to the business aspect of your profession, could you also explain what happens after you have booked a film into one of your sites for an extended run?
CB: The cut and thrust of it all is known as the 'holdover'. Holdovers work on how much a film has taken, and on a Monday morning, if a film has performed well, then the distributor argues that it should stay in the same size screen. If it hasn't done well, then the exhibitor will be looking to move it to a smaller screen, perhaps take shows out or even take the film off. The distributor, of course, wants the film to stay in the biggest screen possible, to play as many shows as possible and to remain in the cinema for as long as possible. The exhibitor is concerned with maximizing each screen, so they make a judgement about how the film has done for them. The Monday morning holdover process is the negotiation between the two parties.

JW: If it comes down to cold, hard figures, then what about the independent title which traditionally may take longer to find its audience through word of mouth?
CB: The shelf life of a film can be very short. In our domain we tend to be kinder to independent or specialist films than to major studio pictures. There was an example a few years ago where I took off a Harrison Ford picture that had taken a few hundred pounds more than an independent film. At the time the studio didn't notice, but they found out later and as a result I had trouble in getting product from them. As far as they're concerned it is based purely on figures, but for us there is a slightly different view. If a specialist picture doesn't open big for whatever reason – bad date, sunny weather, etc. – it will never recover. But there is some truth in that an independent film can tick along quite nicely over a prolonged period of time in a small screen, but there is very little room for that these days. If a film doesn't perform on its opening weekend, it is screwed.

JW: Is there a particularly good calendar period for independent titles to open?
CB: Everyone wants to open them during the BAFTA and Oscar corridors but, because of the amount of product, we are trying to persuade distributors that there are advantages and money to be made – though perhaps not so much – by releasing in June, July and August, as opposed to the most competitive times – September and January.

JW: This counterprogramming is a relatively recent trend. I remember Optimum re-releasing *The Third Man* in the summer when the only other film on that date was *Star Wars: The Phantom Menace*. Consequently, *The Third Man* did rather well.
CB: This is an important route to go down and it's a sign of savvy to put out a

quality film against a blockbuster. Not everyone will want to see the blockbuster; the quality film gives these people an alternative.

JW: Do you welcome the trend, led by the British Film Institute, of reissues?
CB: I think it's incredibly important. I took my eleven-year-old daughter to see *Sunset Boulevard* on Saturday, which she thoroughly enjoyed after initially complaining about having to see a black-and-white film. With the current choices people question why they would want to see a fifty-year-old movie, which is why I would like to see these films more smartly marketed. But the actual process of reissues and restorations is a fantastic trend.

JW: In terms of sustaining an interest in cinema and in film culture, education obviously has an important role to play.
CB: Most certainly. One of the best things that funding bodies could do is to pay the schools to get people into cinemas to see a diverse range of films. At the Ritzy we had an education officer who would put on films such as David Gordon Green's *George Washington*, which the kids in Lambeth would ordinarily not have gone to see. However, we got local schools in, the kids saw it and they absolutely loved it – they could identify with it. We had to work to make them go but it is important to do so – and not just for young people; for older people, as well. We have to keep this culture alive.

JW: One of the other obstacles to keeping film culture alive is the lack of available prints of older titles. These films are gradually being lost to us.
CB: Absolutely; distributors have to take responsibility for this. They are the ones that are junking the prints; their idea of dealing with it is to give a clapped-out print to the BFI. They have to bear some responsibility for keeping these prints in circulation. They are very happy to put on five hundred prints of *Jungle Book 2*, but they also have to look six months down the line and some kind of preservation policy. In terms of repertory titles, it is always alarming to learn about the prints that are no longer available.

JW: Prints seem to be available in other countries in Europe, so why not Britain?
CB: It is certainly something that needs to be addressed and it doesn't seem to have been thus far, at least as far as I know, by the Film Council.

JW: Mention of the Film Council brings me to talk of their plans for a digital circuit. Could this provide an answer in terms of preservation?
CB: The desire for a digital virtual circuit is still to be confirmed and is largely dependent on the production of a standard digital projector. We are in a similar position, I suppose, to that faced by exhibitors when talking pictures looked set to replace silent ones. I think the digital age for film is very exciting, but it is not quite as close as people think it is. We are all beginning to experiment with digital projectors, and that's going to allow cinemas to be able to show all sorts of

different things that they were not able to show before. It means that you will be able to show films in places such as village halls and swimming pools.

JW: Perfect for your Esther Williams . . .
CB: I can do another season! It does open the door, but it is also very important that it is not just the majors that are involved in what happens and how the digital age moves forward. To be quite honest, having all the big studio pictures sent over by satellite is a very nice concept but is perhaps not as important as being able to show, for example, Sokurov's *Russian Ark* in Hartlepool or the latest documentary produced locally.

JW: You've returned to *Russian Ark* a number of times. Is it a film that you greatly admire, and did this influence your decision to widely support it?
CB: *Russian Ark* will without doubt be one of my top ten films of the year, and I do think that there are certain upcoming titles, such as *Etre et avoir*, Von Trier's *Dogville*, Gus Van Sant's *Elephant* – both of which I recently saw in Cannes – that I feel passionately enough about to commit to playing. These are also titles that do stand some chance at the box office, but there are others that I may enjoy which I know haven't got a cat in hell's chance, so these have to be fitted in when and where the opportunity arises. It is very heartening that people are going to see *Russian Ark*; it almost makes the struggle all worthwhile. It is a truly great film, and technically and visually breathtaking.

JW: Is Sokurov someone whose career you have followed closely?
CB: Absolutely, from *Mother and Son* through to *Moloch* and *Taurus*. It may well be, however, that *Russian Ark* is his pinnacle, both commercially and critically. Jean Renoir famously said that each director simply makes the same film over and over again with minor variations, and there is certainly truth in this. However, if they manage to make at least one great film, no matter where it appears in terms of their career trajectory, then this doesn't matter.

JW: I have a similar feeling about Claire Denis and *Beau Travail*.
CB: I think Claire Denis will certainly make another great film, whatever you say about her work. I know that people were disappointed by *Trouble Every Day*, but it is never less than interesting. I was tremendously impressed in Cannes by Clint Eastwood's *Mystic River*, and the wider perception is that he has had a very poor patch recently but has returned with a very strong Hollywood genre picture. The film is intelligent, ambiguous and has the power to make you think. Eastwood also wrote the score, which is simply fantastic. Never write people off.

JW: Your earlier mention of Hartlepool and your point about the need for cultural diversity in the regions is made all the more prescient by the BFI's plans to dissolve their regional programme unit.

CB: If you'd have asked me this question regarding the dissolution of this strand of the BFI I would probably have said fine, but I have changed my opinion over the years. I used to think that subsidised cinema was not necessary; I now realise that in some areas it is very important. What has happened with the BFI is similar to what happened at the BBC. John Birt went into an organization totally lacking in focus and cut out some of the flab and some of the waste, but also cut out some of the good bits. The BFI needs someone who cares about it and I hope that the new appointment, Amanda Nevill, will nurture it. What the BFI should do is sustain film culture in areas where it is difficult for the cinemas to have a varied and interesting programme of events. In terms of education and representing all that is good in film culture going right back to the beginning of cinema, we cannot underestimate how important the BFI is and has been, and so I think it is a great shame what has been happening with it.

JW: To conclude on a more personal note, what would be your dream rep double bill?
CB: I think . . . *Eraserhead* and *Day for Night*. *Eraserhead* because it's simply amazing; *Day for Night* because it's about cinema and is the first film I saw with my husband.

JW: And finally, you find yourself marooned on a desert island that happens to have a screen and a projector. What one film would you like to be marooned with?
CB: I'd probably have to go for something sentimental. I would say: *The Philadelphia Story*.

DIVERSE OTHERS ON FILM-MAKING

Ingmar Bergman (far left) in the early 1950s

Carrying Out a Good Piece of Craftsmanship: Ingmar Bergman interviewed by Jan Aghed, translated by Charles Drazin

Ingmar Bergman will be eighty-four years old this summer, but there is no perceptible let-up in his energy or creativity. After the success of Ibsen's *Ghosts*, which he directed for the Royal Dramatic Theatre of Stockholm, he has turned his attention to another giant of Scandinavian drama, August Strindberg. Bergman has done an experimental radio adaptation of the playwright's 'chamber play', *The Pelican*, which includes fragments from an unfinished play that Strindberg was inspired to write by the Arnold Böcklin picture *Der Toteninsel*. Next there follows an important TV project, with Bergman, as writer and director, returning to the couple who featured in his celebrated TV series of thirty years ago, *Scenes from a Marriage*: Erland Josephson and Liv Ullmann will once again take up their roles as Johan and Marianne. As he agrees on the telephone to meet me for an interview for *Positif*, Bergman speaks with infectious enthusiasm about the opportunities this sequel offers him, in particular the use of a new kind of digital video camera. Scheduled for September 2002, the filming is expected to take eight weeks.

He meets me in the foyer of the 'Dramaten', as the Royal Dramatic Theatre is familiarly known. He ran this respected institution between 1963 and 1966, and has returned there many times to direct acclaimed productions. As he guides me along the corridors and stairs towards the rehearsal room and the office he still has on the third floor of this impressive building, he asks me if I've read *Doktor Romand*, the Swedish translation of the short novel by Emmanuel Carrère, *The Adversary*. When I tell him that it was one of the most unpleasant reading experiences I've ever had, he laughs and says, 'Sure, it gets under your skin in a very unpleasant way, but it's terribly well written!'

During the preparation of the Ibsen play, Bergman gave each member of the cast a copy of the Carrère book, and they discussed it during the rehearsals. Bergman felt that the story of the criminal doctor, Romand, had an important point in common with *Ghosts* in that Ibsen's characters also live a destructive lie. 'It's about a deceit that takes over an entire life; the façade, the disguise, the lie which eats up a human being from the inside. In this respect Romand's story really helped us. A fantastic, intriguing book, but at the same time awful and unpleasant to read. When I read it, I thought it was crying out to be made into a film.' Bergman was not familiar with the films based on the Romand tragedy that Laurent Cantet and Nicole Garcia had directed; when I mentioned them, he showed enormous interest and said that he couldn't wait to see them. What impresses one talking to Bergman, even now, is the way he still finds the cinema so exciting to talk about. He mentions films with a boyish enthusiasm; old films, new films, old and young directors, his favourite directors and, not least, his own collection of videos and 35mm prints. It's the mark of a curiosity and love for the cinema that seems to have continued unbroken ever since he first started going to the cinema as a young boy. I have never met a director, particularly one as old as Bergman, with such a keen appetite to see films.

He tells me that every spring, in accordance with a special decision taken by the governing body of the Swedish Film Institute, he sends a list of 150 films which he would like to see held by the institute's film archive, the Swedish equivalent of the Cinémathèque Française. At the beginning of June each year, these films are delivered by lorry to his house on the island of Fårö, so he can view them in his own fully equipped viewing theatre. There, Bergman has established an unbreakable ritual: he sees a film at three o'clock every weekday through the summer, often in the company of his children and grandchildren on their holidays. On the Monday he gives them a list of the week's films.

Besides these 150 titles, there is another list made up of the most interesting or most talked about films to have been released in the last months, which the various distributors kindly make available to him. In this way, albeit with a small time lag, he keeps up with current production, both Swedish and international. If you mention to him François Ozon's *Sous le sable*, he'll tell you that it's a fantastic work which made such an impression on him that he's seen it several times.

More than that, Bergman has lovingly looked after a private collection of 400 prints and a video library of some 4,500 titles supplied to him by a London company that has had a first-class stock list ever since films began to appear on video; these films are projected on to a giant television screen. No surprise then quickly to discover when talking to Bergman that he has an encyclopaedic knowledge of cinema history, both artistic and technical. Little matter if his opinions on various film-makers and their work seems unorthodox and rather contrary to conventional opinion. For example, his attitude to Orson Welles: 'For me, Welles is a phoney,' says Bergman. 'He is greatly overrated. He is shallow, not interesting. *Citizen Kane*, which by the way I have in my collection, is, of course, the favourite of all the critics, always put at the top of the best films of all time lists. But I don't understand why at all. Take the performances: they're terrible. Welles walks about in a mask, as he plays a tycoon who's supposed to be William Randolph Hearst, but all the time you can see the joins between the mask and his own skin. Terrible! No, it's a bad film which bores me to death. *The Magnificent Ambersons*? No! Equally annoying. And I don't like Welles any more as an actor. In Hollywood, there are two types:

Charlotte Rampling in *Sous le sable*: it made such an impression on Bergman he's seen it several times

actors and personalities. It's a very useful distinction. Welles was beyond compare as a personality. But in the part of *Othello* . . . I won't even bother to tell you what I think – it's unprintable.' With only two exceptions, Bergman has nothing good to say about Michelangelo Antonioni: 'I've never much liked his films, except for two which are totally different from the others: *La Notte* and *Blow Up*. I have *Il Grido* on video; my God, it's dull! It bores you stiff. You see, Antonioni has never properly learnt his craft. He's an aesthete. If, for example, he needs a certain kind of road for *The Red Desert*, then he gets the houses repainted on the damned street. That is the attitude of an aesthete. He took great care over a single shot, but didn't understand that a film is a rhythmic stream of images, a living, moving process; for him, on the contrary, it was such a shot, then another shot, then yet another. So, sure, there are some brilliant bits in his films. But *Blow Up* is marvellously well put together. The same is true of *La Notte*, which I also have and look at every now and then with great admiration and pleasure; a marvellous film in which the young Jeanne Moreau has something to contribute. But the much praised *L'Avventura*! No, thank you! I have no regard for it at all. Only indifference. I can't understand why Antonioni is held in such high esteem. And as for Monica Vitti! I've always thought she was a lousy actress.

La Notte: 'A marvellous film with the young Jeanne Moreau.'

'I feel very differently about Fellini and his films. He used to call me "fratello mio". Once we were supposed to make a film together, with another one of my favourite directors, Akira Kurosawa. The idea was that we would each make a love story which would be a part of a film produced by Dino De Laurentiis. I wrote my story and I flew to Rome, where Fellini was finishing *Satyricon*. For three weeks we had a great time together while we waited for Kurosawa, who had just had a severe attack of pneumonia. Finally, De Laurentiis gave up and said that there would be no film. To be completely honest, it was difficult to get Federico to decide what story he wanted to tell. I had written and brought along a very detailed script, while Fellini had a three-page synopsis which he wanted to develop into a script with one of his regular collaborators. For all I remember, maybe they did actually write something, but everything fell through because Kurosawa couldn't travel because of his health. While we waited for him, I spent some time with Fellini at the studio watching him work on *Satyricon*. I'm very sorry that this project involving the three of us never saw the light of day. I liked Fellini a lot. I visited him and Giulietta Masina on the coast, and I had a memorable Easter dinner. We liked each other a lot. And I certainly

'I love *Amarcord* most of all.'

continue to look at his films. I love *La Strada* and, most of all, *Amarcord.*

'If we're talking of those film-makers whose work has really affected me and inspired me, we have to begin with Victor Sjöström, him first and foremost. Then there's Marcel Carné and Kurosawa, and Fellini. In no particular order. I just have a particular regard for them. I make an effort to see Sjöström's *The Phantom Carriage* at least once a year. It's become a tradition to begin my cinema season with *The Phantom Carriage* and to end it with *A Girl from the Marsh Croft*. I'm enormously attached to these two films. To see them again and again has become, in a way, a tradition. A drug. Or, if you like, a vice. When it comes to Victor's Hollywood films, people tend to mention *The Wind* first, which is certainly a marvellous work. But personally I find *He Who Gets Slapped* even more remarkable. Isn't it incredible how he could adapt to Hollywood yet still be innovative?'

Later, Sjöström became artistic adviser to Svensk Filmindustri (or SF, the big production company behind most of Bergman's features up to *A Passion* in 1969), when his then twenty-eight-year-old admirer directed his first film, *Crisis*, in the company's studios at Rasunda, near Stockholm.

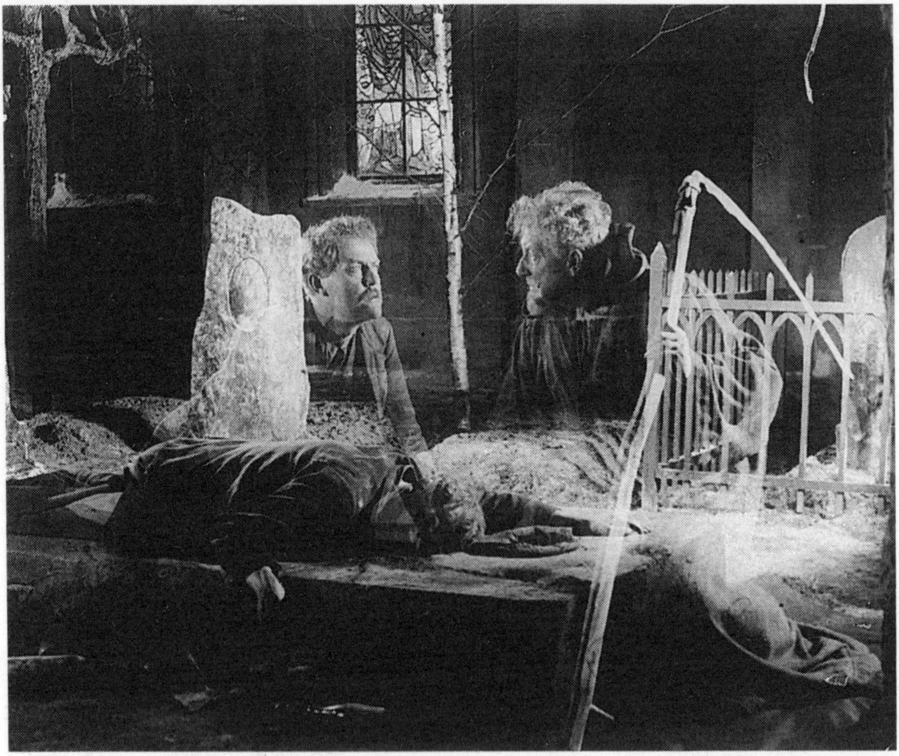

'I make an effort to see *The Phantom Carriage* at least once a year.'

'He was such a wonderful man,' Bergman continues, 'generous with his advice, simple but wise. "Don't make unnecessary trouble when you direct," he used to tell me. "Don't create too many problems for yourself and your crew. Elaborate camera movements – you don't know yet how to control such things, so don't bother yourself with them. Don't complicate things for the actors. Keep the sets simple and spare." Invaluable advice for a young iconoclast longing to experiment!

'I suppose I must have a particular weakness for silent films from the second half of the twenties, before the cinema was taken over by sound. At that time, the cinema was in the process of creating its own language. There was Murnau and *The Last Laugh*, with Jannings, a film told solely in images with a fantastic suppleness; then his *Faust*, and finally his masterpiece, *Sunrise*. Three astonishing works that tell us that Murnau, at the same time as Stroheim in Hollywood, was well on the way to creating a magnificently original and distinct language. I have many favourites among the German films of this period.

'I must confess a great weakness for the UFA films made after the First World War. But, when I began to work at SF as an assistant in the script department

Murnau's *Sunrise*: 'Astonishing'

(this was 1942, I was twenty-four), the main task for me and my five or six colleagues was to apply American dramatic principles to our material. On the floor beneath us there were three projection rooms that belonged to the distribution department, where they ran films non-stop, and whenever I had the time I used to go down there to watch. We had unlimited access to American films, and the result was that we became so used to the American approach to drama that it was impossible to write or to revise a script using different rules from Hollywood. When I directed my first films, I was pleased to have such strong foundations on which to stand. Later, of course, I got rid of them; but, at first, it was a firm and solid support.

'As far as American dramaturgy is concerned, none of its exponents mean more to me than that old Viennese, Billy Wilder. I can see the greatness of John Ford as a film-maker, but his films have nothing to say to me. With Wilder, it's the opposite. He has a genius when it comes to actors. He always makes the perfect choice, even in the case of Marilyn Monroe. I met him when he was filming *Fedora* in Bavaria; I was in Germany to prepare *From the Life of the Marionettes*. I've always loved his films.'

As a child and through his adolescence, Bergman went to the cinema as often as he could, particularly to Sunday matinees. He often used to watch the two afternoon programmes, the first at one o'clock, and the second at three.

'I'd have to beg, borrow or steal to get the money for a ticket, for after a while the price climbed well beyond my weekly allowance. But an even more difficult problem was that at home, after having listened to the Sunday sermon of our father, the pastor Eric Bergman, we children had to face the weekly ritual of "church coffee". It was understood that we would help out and be on our best behaviour. The trick was to slip off quietly in time for the first afternoon showing. If the second programme was too long, I'd run the risk of being late for another obligatory family ritual, Sunday dinner, which was at five o'clock. So, as a young film buff, I used to spend a lot of my time running. Luckily, at that time in Stockholm there were a lot of small cinemas relatively close to where we lived and that made it just possible.'

Did your passion for films bother your parents?

'Not at all. They both went to the cinema and loved it. I remember my mother getting cross with me only once. I must have been eighteen. It was because I had seen Julien Duvivier's last film. I told her: 'You must go and see it!' My parents remembered my enthusiastic recommendation and went off to see *Pépé le Moko*. Afterwards, my mother was furious with me: Duvivier's film was not a suitable entertainment for the pastor Eric Bergman and his wife. How could you like such terrible, immoral filth? After that, I stopped recommending films to them.

'This memory, which is still very fresh in my mind, reminds me of a little episode at a film festival in France during the sixties. I was there for some rea-

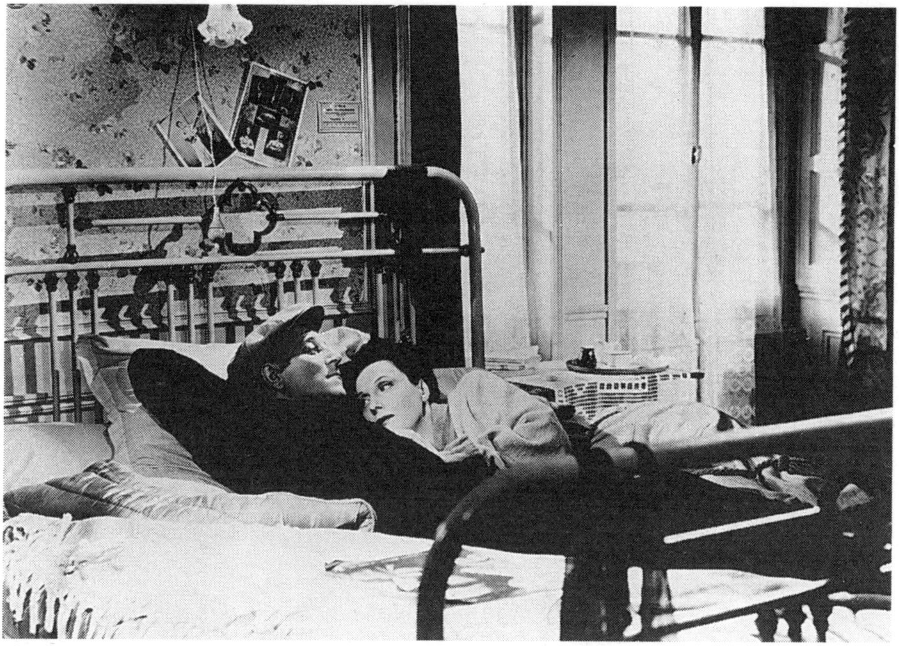

Le jour se lève: 'That was how I wanted to make films, like Carné.'

son I no longer remember, and someone in an audience of critics wanted to know what films had most mattered to me. I replied very honestly that Carné and Duvivier were decisive influences in my wanting to become a film-maker. It was between 1936 and 1939 when seeing Carné's *Quai des brumes*, *Hôtel du Nord* and *Le jour se lève*, and Duvivier's *Pépé le Moko* and *Un carnet de bal* had a huge impact on me. I told myself that, if I ever managed to become a director, that was how I wanted to make films, like Carné! Those films affected me enormously. But when I mentioned Carné and Duvivier at this French festival, the audience reacted with sniggers of scorn and disdain. I could read what they were thinking in the expressions on their faces: what a fool, a bit dense, this Bergman! If I had said Jean Renoir, it would have been OK. But how could someone who had really thought about it believe that Carné or Duvivier were any good?

'If I'm not mistaken, the supposed "*politique des auteurs*" was in vogue at the time, and the most influential of the French critics, following the path shown them by François Truffaut, had rejected what they called "le cinéma de papa". Jean-Luc Godard was worshipped as the new idol of the cinema and so on. So it was a terrible *faux pas* of mine to pay tribute to these two old clowns! But I still enjoy seeing their films. I watch them with enormous pleasure, find them extremely good. They possess a sadness, a tenderness and a sensuality that I find simply marvellous.'

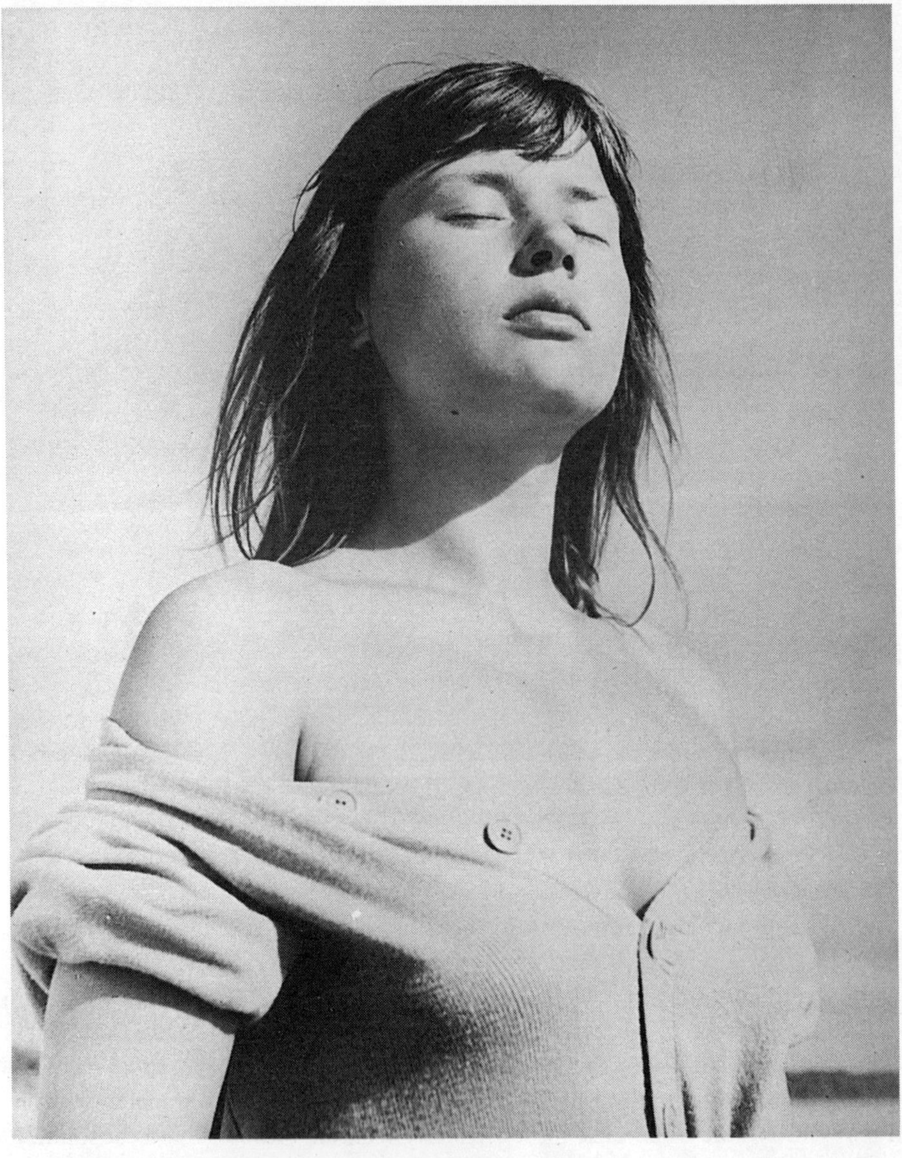

Monika: a revelation for Truffaut and Godard

As far as Truffaut and Godard are concerned, Bergman's *Monika* was a revelation for some of the young *Cahiers du cinéma* writers when they saw the fim again some years after its initially hostile reception in 1953. Afterwards, it became a sort of model for these writers, which they studied on their way to becoming directors themselves, as Antoine de Baecque points out in his book *La Nouvelle Vague: portrait d'une jeunesse* (1998). Godard wrote admiringly of *Monika*. Now, years later, the director of *Monika* adds: 'There's a symbolic scene in *Les Quatre cents coups* where the boys steal the film still of Harriet outside the cinema. I liked Truffaut enormously, I admired him. His way of relating with an audience, of telling a story, is both fascinating and tremendously appealing. It's not my style of storytelling, but it works wonderfully well in relation to the film medium. *La Nuit américaine* is a magical film. I can see some of Truffaut's films again and again without growing tired of them. Like *L'Enfant sauvage*. Its humanism made a huge impression on me.'

On the other hand, Bergman expresses an intense dislike of Godard and his avant-garde tendencies.

'I've never been able to appreciate any of his films, nor even understand them. Truffaut and I used to meet on several occasions at film festivals. We had an instant understanding that extended to his films. But Godard: I find his films affected, intellectual, self-obsessed and, as cinema, without interest and frankly dull.

'Endless and tiresome. Godard is a desperate bore. I've always thought that he made films for critics. He made one here in Sweden, *Masculin, Féminin* – so boring that my hair stood on end. No, I'd prefer to speak of the third of those directors from the peak of the New Wave, the one who specialized in crime dramas, Claude Chabrol. A marvellous storyteller in a specific genre. I've always had a weakness for his thrillers, just as I have for Jean-Pierre Melville, whose stylized approach to the crime drama accompanies an excellent sense of lighting a scene. I love seeing his films. He was also one of the first directors really to understand how to use Cinemascope in an intelligent and sensitive way.

'A French critic wrote, with regards to my film *Autumn Sonata*, that Monsieur Bergman has begun to make Bergman films.' It wasn't meant to be a compliment. But I still think it was a very intelligent and perceptive comment, which I really took note of because I knew exactly what he meant. He was absolutely right. And it's what a director must make an effort to avoid at all costs. Fellini made a few Fellini films, not many, mind you, he wasn't allowed to live long enough for that, just a few. But this was nothing compared to Andrei Tarkovsky. By that I mean, for him, leaving the Soviet Union was really an artistic disaster. Take *The Sacrifice*: it's a hopeless mess. Erland Josephson, his leading actor, wrote a marvellously funny radio play about a summer night on which Tarkovsky and his crew were filming exterior shots: funny and very revealing. In the end, it became a theatre play.

Andrei Rublev: Bergman was 'stunned and shaken'

'But Tarkovsky gave me one of the greatest and most forgettable cinema experiences in my life. Late one day in 1971 I was watching a film with Kjell Grede (a Swedish director) in a viewing room at SF. Afterwards, we looked in a cupboard which contained a pile of film cans. "What's that?" I asked the projectionist. "Oh, some crappy Russian film." But then I saw Tarkovsky's name and I said to Grede, "Listen, I've read something about this film. We must see what it's about." So we bribed the projectionist to show it to us – and it was *Andrei Rublev*. So, at about two-thirty in the morning, the two of us staggered out of the viewing room, with bloodshot eyes, completely stunned and shaken. I'll never forget it. And what was extraordinary was that it didn't have any Swedish subtitles! We didn't understand a word of dialogue, but we were still bowled over. Tarkovsky made another film which I like a lot, *The Mirror*. Erland Josephson was in two of his films, and he and Tarkovsky talked a lot to each other. I understand from Erland that Tarkovsky had a strange attitude towards actors: he didn't want them to act at all. Even so I think he was a wonderful human being. But I'll tell you something strange about my relationship with him. He was in Gotland filming the exteriors for *Sacrifice*. It would have taken only twenty minutes for me to go and visit him but I didn't. I've thought about that several times: here was someone who meant so much to me, who was such an important influence, perhaps even more in his attitude to life than as a film-maker, so why didn't I visit him when he was so close? I think it was a matter of language. He spoke neither English nor German, the two foreign languages in which I feel relatively at ease. He spoke a little French, a little Italian, and so we would have had to communicate through an interpreter. But for the sort of things I needed to talk to him about, an interpreter would have been useless. So we never met. To my profound regret, more so because he died so soon afterwards.'

When he was still making films, how did Bergman react to what the critics wrote? Did he ever worry about how his films would be received? He interrupted, waving his finger at me: 'You've had a go at me more than once! I thought of you as one of my enemies!' He then burst out laughing. 'But don't worry about it. You've kept a close eye on me over many years, which is good.'

But in the past there were some critics that Bergman recalled with less good humour and forgiveness, critics who caused some painful wounds.

'I had a very difficult start. No one appreciates it now. It was very hard. I can still recall some reviews word for word. Of *Sawdust and Tinsel* a respected critic on a daily paper commented: "I will not lower myself to consider the last bit of vomit by Mr Bergman." And then there was an influential literary critic, who had a big name in cultural debates, who deigned to go and see *Smiles of a Summer Night* and then warned his readers that it amounted to "the disgusting fantasies of a pimply young man. I'm ashamed to have seen this film". To see such responses in print wasn't exactly my idea of fun or encouragement. I've had to put up with many similiar comments.'

Critics from other countries seem to have been more perceptive than their Swedish colleagues in their evaluation of your films.

'Perhaps that's true. But at the same time you must understand something: this supposed celebrity attached to my name as a film director is completely and fundamentally alien to me. It's as if people were writing or talking about a distant cousin, about someone I had hardly anything to do with. For example, I hardly every see any of my old films.'

Because you don't like them?

'No, that's not why. It's because they disturb me too much. I'm swept away by a torrent of often very sad memories connected with their production. There's something wonderful about being a theatre director: you direct a play, it's shown to an audience so many times, and then it's gone. But films stay for ever. And that's sometimes very painful. Sometimes you discover that they've been cut to pieces by insensitive hands. As you know, each copy of a film begins with a length of leader and on this strip, in the case of *Persona*, I put an erect penis.

Just three or four frames. As the film passes through the projector at twenty-four frames a second, you can work out how long this penis was visble on the screen – a sixth of a second! It was a subliminal image. But it was discovered. The film caused a lot of interest outside Sweden and was shown just about everywhere – but, everywhere, this erect penis was cut! So I checked the Swedish negative and, believe it or not, the penis was no longer there either! Luckily, I was able to find a copy of the film where the leader was still intact with the three or four frames, and so I made a new negative from which new copies could be made. But this discovery really shook me.

'It's important for me, when people see a performance in the theatre here, at the Dramaten, for example, that they are completely aware that they are sitting in a theatre. Likewise, when they see a film, it's vital that they appreciate the great miracle of cinema, its unique quality, the human face. To arrange a scene so that it has maximum effect, so that it works in the most perfect way, is a very hard task for the director. The cinema is a fantastic medium because, just like music, it passes through your intellect and goes straight to your emotions. So the right close-up at the right moment can have an enormous effect. If a close-up is sensibly shot, well composed, adequately lit and focused on a good actor or actress, you can let it continue on the screen for as long as you want! While I was still active as a film director, my big dream was to make a whole feature in one single close-up.

'Returning to the distant cousin I mentioned earlier: I've never considered myself to be anything more than a craftsman, a brilliantly competent craftsman – if I can say that of myself – but nothing more. I make things which are considered useful, films or stage productions. I've never felt a need for – what's the expression? – *sub specie aeternitatis*. I've never worked with one eye on eternity. That sort of thing doesn't matter to me; what matters is to achieve a bloody good piece of craftsmanship. Yes. I'm proud to call myself a craftsman who makes chairs and tables that people find useful.'

Stockholm, March 2002

This interview first appeared in *Positif* magazine and appears courtesy of Michel Ciment.

Lawless Hearts:
Neil Hunter and Tom Hunsinger interviewed by Ryan Gilbey

Entire squadrons of researchers could be dispatched to unearth negative reviews of Lawless Heart *and still return empty-handed. This low-budget British drama, serious in purpose but with a seductive comic fizz, was one of the most widely admired movies of 2002. It begins at the funeral for Stuart, a restaurateur in the sleepy coastal town of Maldon, Essex, and traces the repercussions of his death on the lives of three men in his immediate orbit: his stifled brother-in-law Dan (Bill Nighy), who is stiffly flirting with the French florist Corinne (Clémantine Célarié); Stuart's boyfriend Nick (Tom Hollander), who finds his grieving unexpectedly disturbed by a bubbly checkout girl, Charlie (Sukie Smith), with whom, even more unexpectedly, he begins to fall in love; and Tim (Douglas Henshall), Stuart's chum, who returns home after eight years and walks slap-bang into the middle of a love triangle.*

What is immediately striking about the picture is its daring structure: each story begins afresh at the funeral, giving the writer–directors Neil Hunter and Tom Hunsinger the opportunity to replay identical scenes from contrasting perspectives, the better to solve the string of tender mysteries embedded in the narrative. As Hunter explains in the conversation below, this is a technique which audiences will recognize from Pulp Fiction, *not to mention* Go *or* Amores Perros. *But none of those films utilized it to quite such poignant effect. When the film finally discloses the rich and rewarding pay-off of each inquiry, or when the action in the third story plugs the gaps in the first and second, it as though an entire new dimension has just been revealed before our eyes.*

Hunter and Hunsinger have been collaborating ever since Hunter placed an ad in The Stage *in 1994 inviting actors to audition for his short film. He received a call from Hunsinger. 'I told him I was more interested in making the film than acting in it,' he says. They directed a short,* Tell Me No Lies, *before cobbling together £27,000 to fund their 1996 début feature, the sparky comedy* Boyfriends, *about the fluctuating relationships of six gay men cooped up in a country retreat for a long weekend. Hunter and Hunsinger occasionally work separately, but it is for their films together that they are currently best known. 'It's always been fun writing with Neil,' says Hunsinger. 'We sit around and improvise until he tells me to shut up.' 'Or wake up,' Hunter chips in. 'Sometimes I just let him sleep on.'*

We met at Hunter's London flat one tranquil morning in April 2003 to discuss their work to date, and the surprise success of Lawless Heart.

Tom Hunsinger and Neil Hunter (photo by Richard Sawdon-Smith)

Ryan Gilbey: Neil, when *Lawless Heart* won the *Evening Standard* award for Best Screenplay, you gave an acceptance speech thanking the critics, but you sounded slightly . . .
Neil Hunter: Embarrassed? I was thinking of all the film-makers who would be listening and going, 'What a creep.'

Tom Hunsinger: Actually, I thought the critics did do it for us. They really got behind it.

NH: It was fairly obvious that unless the critics supported it wholeheartedly, the film would go nowhere because we had only a small advertising budget. The broadsheets were naturally very important. In New York, they said it was fresh. A woman from the Condom League, which campaigns for condoms to be used in sex scenes, congratulated us. She gave me a little pendant with a rubber in it. That was a particularly favourable response.

RG: Did you recognize the good things people were writing about your film? Did it sound like they were describing the film you'd made?
NH: I was really thrown. I went for a long walk on the Friday lunchtime when it opened. I was trying to take it all in because it was so unexpected. Like putting a 5p in a slot machine and watching all these coins come pouring out.

TH: After the first reviews came out, someone said to me, 'Well, you and Neil are really set up now.' I thought: 'For what? For a fall?' I became rather scared, and I didn't want to hear any more. I was looking at the reviews thinking: 'This is ridiculous.' I was always convinced it was the film we wanted to make. I thought it was interesting, and that other people might think so too. But I didn't think it would be unanimous. There are so many films out there, and plenty of good work gets overlooked.

NH: I thought it was entirely possible that the critics would just shrug.

RG: Where did the film originate from?
NH: It came out of a story I'd written called 'Essex Weddings' – it has some resemblance to Tim's story, chronologically the third in the film. I still don't know how we decided to do three stories. The story of the gay guy falling for a straight girl came out of a conversation I had with somebody one New Year's Eve. But I don't think he was grieving initially. And the Dan story came, I think, when we had decided to structure it as three stories. We needed someone else. A guy deciding whether or not to have an affair. We asked ourselves what the gist would be. He would have to be married. It was important that he was happily married. His story should involve love. They're all half-stories of relationships that don't happen.

RG: Like *Eyes Wide Shut* – the sex that never arrives.
NH: Yes, that's all about frustration, isn't it? We're doing a linear story next.

TH: At the moment it's linear. Until we realize it doesn't work and we want to do something else.

NH: One of my interests or concerns with *Lawless Heart* is that gimmick. When our producer was raising the money, the fact that it was three stories rather than one immediately made it arthouse – that touched on the budget straight away. But if we had intercut the stories, it would have been just like a soap opera. On their own, they become far more intense. I realized on the shoot how hard it was for everyone to keep the time-scale in their heads. The costume designer would say to me, 'Which day is this supposed to be? Is it before or after they've slept together?' It was really inspired by Rohmer's *Rendezvous in Paris*, in which the first story is so much better than the others that you keep waiting for the characters to pop up in the subsequent sections, but they never do. We decided to do what Rohmer's film didn't. Our decision seemed very original to us, though it turned out not to be. A short time later, I suddenly thought, 'Oh – *Pulp Fiction*.' Although, commercially speaking, *Pulp Fiction* is regarded as the fluke. Now that we're doing a linear film, more people might see it. But I wonder if it will stand out as much for the critics as being fresh or interesting. *Lawless Heart* was always interesting for us to write because it felt different. Standing out is the thing. You're conscious of that because there's so many films, and why should people go and see yours?

TH: Our producer was constantly being asked: What's it about?

NH: Oh, I found the answer! Finally. I gave it to a journalist from the *LA Times*.

TH: Did you? What was it?

NH: It's about how our actions affect other people without us knowing. That was the most succinct description that was also believable.

RG: There's also the line early on in the film, which sets out your stall: 'The life you have: is it the life you want?'
NH: That line was written as a way of thinking about all three stories, but I don't think that's what the film is about at its deepest level. That's just the surface, the text. We threw the word 'change' into the script a few times. And 'courage'. The courage to change. Every film is about change, isn't it? We tend to love sitcoms as well, and the great thing about sitcoms is that no one ever changes. They never learn a lesson. Or rather, they learn it, but the next week they've forgotten it again. Frasier has been improved so many times and learned so many lessons that he has then managed to forget. Sitcoms really feel much truer to me than movies.

TH: They're stuck, aren't they? They can't move on.

NH: Which is life. Whereas in movies, everyone finally redeems themselves or has a significant, life-changing moment in which they become wiser. But I don't know of a single person of whom that's true. Don't people just repeat their mistakes?

TH: We must get a bit wiser. But it doesn't necessarily come down to big things. It comes down to things like: I've learnt not to invite people back whom I don't completely know!

NH: I think it's truer to say that people's lives get a crust around them, like hardened arteries. They narrow down, become more defined.

RG: This reminds me of Dan's speech in *Lawless Heart*, where he describes middle age as being like 'that moment in a whodunnit where you know who did it and there's still forty pages to go'.
NH: I think you just stop being curious. You become unwilling to be disappointed. I had this weird idea when I was eighteen that the state should force everyone to swap armchairs, so that we never got used to something. I have a certain nostalgia for that openness, that alertness, forcing people to be more alert as time passes. But I don't think people want to. It's too painful. Maybe that's what it's about: the avoidance of pain.

RG: Do you still like the armchair idea?
NH: Well, I wouldn't want it to happen to me. But yes, I think it's a good idea in principle. The other thing was that couples shouldn't go on holiday together.

RG: Given your dislike of those kinds of learning curves in films, do you actively resist them when you're writing?
NH: I think the fact that *Lawless Heart* was an ensemble piece allowed us to have the life lessons not in the lives of the protagonists but in the way that they mixed with each other.

TH: But you can't really avoid it in a linear story. In the one we're writing now, I'm finding that you have to hit things on the head a little bit harder. In *Lawless Heart*, it seemed easier to make little detours and get away with it.

NH: In a non-ensemble piece you're going to come up against the question 'What's it about?' And it's got to be about something happening to someone. What's that someone going to do? If that someone doesn't change then you've got a passive main character, and you can take a nought off your gross. We have had tendencies to write first drafts where there's no story. That's just how it comes out: character, pattern, incident, but no story. Because story is conflict. This isn't me spouting textbooks because I haven't read any. But I discovered that unless there's conflict, there isn't a story. I'm happy to go to the cinema and see something without a story if it's artfully done. But even in something like *Le Souffle*, there's story, there's conflict: the boy wants to escape.

TH: I often see films where I think the story isn't what we're seeing, the story is somewhere else, a sideline, a subplot, something that didn't get developed.

NH: We do get very distracted by secondary characters. In the new one we have two quite interesting characters who I suspect won't even be in the final draft. We've brought them down a lot already, because there's nothing for them to do. We've already got six main characters. You just have to be more funnel-like, things have to be narrowed down.

RG: That's becoming the motif for today.
NH: Yes. We could draw it.

RG: You've only made two films, but your working method has already become quite well known. It sounds a bit Mike Leigh.
TH: Basically, nothing's fixed before we bring the actors in. We have a loose idea of story and character, and we get them to improvise different situations around the kitchen table. Then we prepare a first draft, so that we're writing with the actors' voices in our heads. The idea of writing a script seemed so boring. That process would just have reproduced whatever feelings we happened to have, which seemed pointless. So on *Boyfriends*, we roped in a hundred gay actors and asked them about their sex lives.

NH: The improvisations go on and on, then you edit down the best stuff, and you can elaborate on the really nice things that the actors came up with.

TH: Sometimes it's just a word that an actor will say, and it can send you off in another direction. In the thing we're working on now, Bill Nighy said a word and it opened up a whole new idea for us in the script.

NH: It's opened a door. We haven't quite gone through it yet but we know it's open. For *Boyfriends*, we met all these men, took lots of notes. Initially the film was supposed to be more essayistic and would consist of people just shooting the breeze about topics of interest – threesomes, sleeping with your best friend, and so on. These were the stories that kept coming up, and which people were interested in. It was made at a time when these things weren't everywhere, they hadn't been done to death. Once we cast it, the discursive element got thrown out, and the film got tighter and tighter. It was entirely based on improvisations. We had a pencil outline of three couples in different stages of their relationship. We started with a guy trying to figure out how gay relationships work. We seemed to know the basic trajectory of each couple. Not that the trajectories are that complex. We knew who was going to be together at the end and who

The boyfriends: 'Nothing's fixed before we bring the actors in.' (photo by Boyd Skinner)

wasn't. The only discovery made in improvisations apart from character details was that two of the characters would previously have known one another. We didn't know that until we saw the actors together. They had a certain chemistry, and watching them for the first time made it apparent that there would be that twist. And because we had a twist, it suddenly felt like a real movie.

RG: The other conflict comes from Adam, who's a young, working-class guy in an otherwise very cosy, privileged setting.

NH: Yes, he's the outsider, and there was the class thing. Class is not something you really need to deal with on the surface because it always finds its way into every British movie I've ever seen. Adam needed to be superficially dumb but also perceptive. I met someone recently who told me he had auditioned for that role. He said, 'I was going to play Adam, the rent boy.' I said, 'He wasn't a rent boy!'

TH: He could have been.

RG: He can't remember how many men he's slept with, so that's as good as.

NH: One of the characters, Will, was supposed to be HIV-positive. That's one of the secrets of the film, but we never got it in. The scene in which that information was revealed got cut.

TH: It didn't fit, so we dropped it.

RG: Does any of the dialogue come from those hundred actors?
NH: Only the quotes that begin the film. I deliver some, Tom does one or two. They were hilarious. Very truthful, very poignant. Probably more poignant than anything in the film, actually.

RG: Isn't there a correlation in the film between what Paul is doing, videoing his friends talking about their relationships, and what your purpose was in making the film?
TH: In a way, yes. We were interested in how people conducted themselves in relationships.

NH: No one had done anything just about gay relationships at that point. People were doing films either about Aids or coming out. Those were the two types of gay film. *Beautiful Thing* came out the same time as us, and everyone loved it. We were the other gay film, the one everyone kept forgetting.

TH: *My Night with Reg* had also opened in the West End, and people were very big on that too.

NH: We were trying to discover what was different about gay relationships, and to our surprise the answer was: not much. It was about the same issues, and it gradually became less specifically gay and more universal. At the festivals now, there are always two French films that are definitely gay, but no one in this country seems to make gay films any more. The Americans do independent ones. And *The Hours* is amazingly lesbian, isn't it? When I saw it I thought: 'This is a mainstream film about lesbians and suicide – what's my mother going to think?'

RG: The use of title cards to introduce characters is very familiar now. Was that the case when you made Boyfriends?
NH: Well, again there was *Pulp Fiction*. We showed *Boyfriends* to some people, and someone sensibly suggested putting in cards to identify the couples. The reason I liked this was that it meant we could put in a card very late in the film when this new character arrives. It's so surprising. I love films that do that. I like new characters coming in late, or twists three-quarters of the way through – so long as it's not a film where you're expecting a twist. We watched *Reservoir Dogs* the other night. They have cards. But not for Mr Pink. I wonder if they shot a back-story for him. It's such a formally elegant film, you would think that every dog would have its dinner. A good way to have an afterlife for a film is to leave something hanging like that.

RG: There's a still from *Before Sunrise* in one of the flats in *Boyfriends*. Is that a reference of some kind?
NH: No, not from us. I find it excruciating when directors do that. It would have already been up because we were shooting in a friend's flat in Brixton.

Neil Hunter with clapperboard: 'We did absolutely everything.'
(photo by Boyd Skinner)

TH: We didn't have an art designer by the end of the shoot. He dropped out halfway through. I was left posting things up on walls. I even volunteered my fucking shirt, remember?

NH: Yes, those are our clothes. We were wardrobe.

TH: The art designer had had enough. He went off to be in a band.

NH: He was more interested in his pop career. He was in a band called Posh. Or perhaps Shop. Some configuration of those letters.

RG: Was *Boyfriends* a difficult shoot?
NH: It was a race. We were cutting corners.

TH: We worked from 7 a.m. until midnight. We did absolutely everything, it was a complete roller coaster.

NH: You were so exhausted by the end of it, you were actually giggling and high.

TH: I was sleeping on set and my bed collapsed in the middle of the night. I screamed, then fell straight back to sleep. That's how exhausted I was.

NH: What I liked about making *Boyfriends* – and this is something you couldn't do on a normal film – was that if the sun was shining, we'd switch and shoot outside. 'Oh, we're going off into the forest now. Which actors have we got with us?' And in half an hour, we'd be there. But as soon as you're on a budget of £1 million or more – as we were with *Lawless Heart*, which is still comparatively low – it becomes this huge machine that can't change direction. It's fixed on its course from 10 a.m. the previous morning. Whereas on *Boyfriends* we were running around, inventing scenes. It was very much a co-op. Actors and crew living on top of each other.

RG: And you were producing the film yourselves.

NH: Yes, it was complete freedom. No one interfering. When I'm directing, I'm very conscious of finishing the day, getting all the scenes shot, I really am. On *Boyfriends*, we were in charge of ourselves. But we didn't have a monitor, and we had a camera operator who was very tentative about what he'd seen, which wasn't a good combination. We'd say, 'Was that fine?' And he'd be like, 'Um, yes, except . . .' 'Except what?' 'No, it's fine.' Just enough to plant that seed of doubt. We didn't see any rushes either, until we'd finished. It was just a relief that the film had been exposed properly. There's a romance to thinking about all this, I tell you. Now we've moved on to proper films, proper budgets, but there'll be nothing quite so exciting again as making it all up. I think everyone involved looks back on it happily.

TH: I think I had a bit more stress than you when we were going to be shut down by the Loudwater Estate.

RG: Doesn't that get a mention in the end credits roll? You've got the traditional 'thanks' credits, then a 'no thanks' to the Loudwater Estate.

NH: This was in Rickmansworth. We had the permission of the houseowner, whose property we were using, but not of the estate. I have a feeling the houseowner had used us to annoy his neighbours because they wouldn't let him develop his house. We started filming on Good Friday, and they said they would call the law and have us shut down by Tuesday.

TH: I came out to see this huge man shouting at Neil.

NH: He was ex-BBC. He used to be a location manager. He knew the ins and outs.

TH: I told Neil to go back inside and continue filming. Myself and another crew member went and bought chocolates. Then we went round to the houses on the estate delivering chocolate and apologizing to all these people.

NH: You were on a charm offensive.

TH: It took up most of the day. After the chocolates, they backed off.

NH: I think they were worried we'd bring in articulated lorries. They didn't realize how low-budget we were. Every now and then they got annoyed with the way our cars were parked. People were forever re-parking their cars.

TH: They wanted us to re-park the cars in order of colour, remember? Starting with the red ones. It was so bizarre.

NH: They came on a set visit as well. We had to stop them seeing Danny because, if they saw him, they'd freak out.

TH: Danny was the make-up artist. He looked like a girl when I first met him. Twenty-two, in full drag, sweet, tiny, like a little girl.

NH: We were terrified they were going to find out we were making a gay story. We got all the women we could to come in, and we stood very close to them for the whole day.

RG: Even though *Boyfriends* isn't as polished as *Lawless Heart*, it has the same kind of rhythm: the gags are very sharp and snappy, as is the editing.
TH: I think jokes are very difficult. You go for a joke, and that's the easy answer to the character. It's easier to write a joke than to get to the truth of something.

NH: Sometimes instead of doing it as a cut, a reaction shot, it's better to do it as a two-shot and just let it play, so you're refraining –

TH: Allowing the audience to make their own judgement, to look where they like.

NH: In *About Schmidt*, I became very aware of how the director was timing the gags. The punchline was mostly Jack Nicholson's reaction shot. You'd see something and know right away what Nicholson's character would think of it, and then you cut to him and sure enough . . . It was slightly too much. That nail was hit too many times.

RG: In *Boyfriends*, you have the bonus of James Dreyfus, who's known as a sitcom actor in this country (*Gimme, Gimme, Gimme*; *The Thin Blue Line*), but who is quite abrasive here.
NH: He's a very talented actor who's got stuff in him that hasn't been used yet.

TH: He originally had the role of Nick, now played by Tom Hollander, in *Lawless Heart*, but he had other commitments. James worked on the improvisations, and we wrote it for him. He wanted to play that very straight role to get away from being the funny one.

NH: For *Lawless Heart* we came up with the idea that he could be in grief. James grieving seemed like a funny idea to us. All the comedy was in him being in this double act with a girl who really annoyed him. In the auditions, James

Lawless Heart: Sukie Smith with Tom Hollander (top) and Douglas Henshall (bottom) (photos by Nick Wall)

Clémentine Célarié with Bill Nighy: 'She's a temptress without knowing it.' (photo by Nick Wall)

had a preference for Sukie Smith, who eventually plays Charlie, and so that was very influential to us.

TH: Then when James couldn't do the film, we cast his replacement around Sukie. We had to find someone who could be witty, and Tom Hollander was ideal.

NH: Wit was the most important thing, otherwise Nick's story ran the risk of being very lugubrious.

RG: Besides James, there was another late casting change, when Jason Flemyng, who had developed the part of Tim, became unavailable.

NH: Jason had brought a real charisma and likeability to Tim. When Douglas Henshall came aboard, that character became much more intense.

TH: Sharper.

NH: You mean meaner?

TH: The good thing about Doug is he makes you unsure about whether you're going to like Tim. Doug had no problem with that from the beginning. Jason would have been more immediately sympathetic. You would probably have felt sorry for Tim right away. Doug plays it more egotistical. It's an intelligent choice.

NH: This is what you talk about while you're casting. What is the actor's essence going to entail? Obviously actors have a range, but there's also an essence that you have to figure out. We don't tend to look at someone's previous work, but on how they spark together as people.

RG: You go through a long process of improvisations, rewrites and public readings. How many of the actors you ended up with in *Lawless Heart* were there at the start?
NH: It was written for Bill Nighy, Ellie Haddington, Josephine Butler and Sukie Smith.

TH: I had acted with Ellie before. And she was well known from *Coronation Street*.

NH: It hadn't occurred to us that Ellie was our star. Then we were shooting on the Isle of Man, and she got recognized everywhere she went. Hollander could go shopping in Sainsbury's, but not Ellie.

RG: Is it fair to say that in your partnership Neil handles the technical side, and you, Tom, deal with the actors?
TH: More or less. If the crew have a question, they go to Neil. If it's the actors, they come to me. When we were in Essex, I stayed in the hotel with the actors, and Neil stayed in a separate one with the crew.

NH: If there's time, you rehearse them off set first, don't you? That's how it worked on *Boyfriends*. It was like a factory. That was a highly rehearsed film.

TH: There was more rehearsal on *Boyfriends* than *Lawless Heart*, even though *Lawless Heart* took four years to get made.

NH: There were three days' rehearsals for everyone. Some not even that. Bill Nighy came straight off the set of *Lucky Break*, which didn't matter too much because he knew the character inside out. But Douglas was cast very late and had a day's rehearsal, which is terrible – he's Scottish and we were asking him to do Essex.

TH: I had quite a few rehearsal sessions with Bill and Clémentine, who played Corrine, in the trailer.

RG: I read that you wanted Charlotte Rampling for the part of Corrine.
NH: I read that somewhere too. No, we never had her, or approached her even. The producer liked the idea of her, I think. But Clémentine was the only one we offered it to. We knew she was right. We did see Hal Hartley's actress, Elina

Löwensohn, who was over here doing an episode of *The Bill*. We loved her, but she was too slender.

RG: You can imagine a man like Bill being intimidated by Clémentine. She's got so much love.
TH: She's all woman.

NH: She's a temptress without knowing it. We always wondered what her character's motivation was. What's she after? Does she collect men? We talked a lot about that. She's obviously very bohemian for that town. She's a sophisticated person, so perhaps to keep herself amused she collects people or throws together odd combinations at dinner parties. The crowning irony of Dan's story is he's terrified of being alone with her, but it transpires to be nothing like that. Something about him must interest her. The whole idea of that funeral scene is for it to be a conversation where you become more interesting to yourself when talking about yourself to another person. In her eyes, he was finally becoming as interesting as he wanted to be, whereas in his married life he just has these roles – Dad or Husband. When he talks to her, he goes up a gear, and he's excited. But that excitement isn't something he can actually live with, which is why he hides from her.

RG: That's one of the recurring images in the film. Dan hides from Corrine, Tim and Leah hide from Nick, Leah hides from David at the party.
NH: I hide in my flat from people. If I'm about to go out and I hear a door open, I stay in. I'd rather wait five minutes; I'll get out more quickly in the end. I like it when Leah hides from David at the party. It's that first suggestion that something is going on. Like that moment in *The Son*, where you've been following this character and he starts to act weirdly whenever he sees this young guy. It really sucks you into the story.

RG: Another recurrent image in *Lawless Heart* is water. Stuart has drowned before the film begins; time-lapse shots of water divide each story; and this being Maldon, there's naturally water everywhere. It's like *Don't Look Now*, where the canals of Venice are a constant unspoken reminder of the child's death.
NH: Stuart's death permeates the film more than we knew. We didn't know we were going to open on that Super 8 film of Stuart. Simon Perry, an executive producer who used to be at British Screen, gave us some notes late in the day. Very good notes too, because he only gave us about three. One of them was to show Stuart up front, which wasn't in the script. It seems odd now that we hadn't thought of that. We were always going to show him at the end, in the film show, but his coffin was originally the first shot. Of course, now you see him and he puts his hand over the camera lens. It couldn't be clearer – it's death.

TH: I went off with David Coffey, the actor playing Stuart, and we shot loads of Super 8.

NH: A new reality kicks in when you're shooting. It has to do with the day you're shooting on, how the actors are on that particular day. It changes everything. When you're editing, it's not really the script any more, it's the material you've got. The fact that Tom shot so much good Super 8 made us re-evaluate its original place in the film. You can see why Malick shoots so much footage. You're going to get something you can use.

RG: The dislocation of sound and image in the funeral scene is also very inspired. You hear Dan talking and the camera drifts from face to face. Was that in the script?
NH: Yes, though I was never sure if it would work. It served a very banal function, which was to get from one location to another, and also to give the impression that Dan and Corinne had been talking for hours rather than thirty minutes. We were trying to stretch time. And also to make what he says particular to each character. For instance, when you're hearing that line, 'The life you've got: is it the life you want?', you're seeing Judy, who represents the life that Dan has.

RG: Do you write camera instructions into your scripts?
NH: Yes, and even if we don't write it, it's there between the lines. It gets very boring to write, and to read, so we usually take it out. But it's always there in your imagination. The idea of using different camera styles for each story hadn't really been articulated at script level. But when we came to think about what the camera should be doing, it seemed obvious that, for example, it should be hand-held during Tim's story, because that's very much in keeping with Tim's energy. The cutting is sharper in that story too.

RG: The sex scenes are unusual in that they feel messy and uncomfortable.
NH: All the sex has meaning. It reveals something about the characters.

TH: I quizzed the girls about what they wanted to do. We talked about favourite positions, and about how much flesh is really that exciting. I tried to make them comfortable. In one scene, the actress insisted that the guy playing her boyfriend had to wrap his dick in stockings.

NH: It was very low-budget. We couldn't run to a thong.

TH: Movie sex usually involves the same old positions. You know: girl on top, guy underneath.

RG: Isn't that the image on the US posters?
TH: Exactly! And it wasn't even in the film.

NH: I think people were a bit confused about the film in America where there's a greater awareness of *Boyfriends* than there is in the UK; the distributor had that audience to build on, though one article about *Lawless Heart* was headlined 'Not Really a Gay Film'. In America there's more awareness of *Boyfriends* than there is in the UK. There, we did a day of interviews with the gay press, whereas here we didn't do any. I approved of the film not being in the London Lesbian and Gay Festival because – and I've had arguments with people about this – I don't think films go down well at gay festivals if they're not really gay. In the US, the distributor didn't want it to be categorized as a gay film, but they did want gay people to go to it. One UK critic said to me, 'The film's very gay. But that's all right. It's not a bad thing.' I asked him to explain, and he said that it has a very gay sensibility. I felt like replying, 'Well, I've always felt your criticism's very straight.' Only it isn't.

RG: How do you think he was defining that 'gay sensibility'?
NH: My understanding is that he saw an off-kilter depiction of heterosexual relationships and sex.

RG: You could say the same about Rohmer.
NH: Maybe he's off-kilter in a straighter way. I'm not sure. It's hard to analyze what your own thought processes are, or where you stand in relation to 'normality'.

TH: It could have been to do with Charlie being quite ravenous and sexual, and that being the way gay men are perceived. But we worked on the script with those actresses, so . . .

NH: Once we work through the filters of the actors, the gayness gets knocked out of it. In the script we're writing now, those characters who aren't based on improvisation can get . . . I suppose they might end up as very strong women, or bitchy, and that would be the obvious gay sensibility.

RG: The film went through various false starts, financial problems and so on. How did that affect your spirits when production finally began?
NH: Ellie has said how important it was that it got made – that it was a big thing for her, not because it was a big film but because she had been with it for so long and felt very tenacious about it.

TH: We were all set to go a year before, and she had turned down a play in the West End. She'd made sacrifices.

NH: I had mentally abandoned it, I think. It's not like we spent those whole four years on tenterhooks. We were just doing the occasional rewrite prompted by a reading or by some new need to show it to someone interesting. We were dabbling.

TH: I was teaching. No one was rushing to commission us until after *Lawless Heart* came out and was a success.

NH: To go back to the critics, one thing I noticed in terms of the perception of us is that it was the critics who changed it. The industry had seen the film before it opened, and while there were individuals in production companies and funding bodies who liked it, there was no question that it was the critical acclaim which changed the opinion of us. When critics consider themselves powerless, they should remember that. It was a revelation to me. After the reviews came out, getting another commission was almost automatic. People don't really trust their instincts, so they wait to find out what everyone else thinks.

RG: So was that person right about you two being 'set up' now?
NH: Well, the people you go to for money in this industry all seem to want to work with us. We can get the money to write now, and people are asking us to direct scripts too. We've been offered television; I wouldn't turn it down *per se*, though I hear nothing but bad things from people who work in the industry.

TH: They say it's even worse than making a film!

NH: They're all desperate to leave TV to make films, but people in film don't seem any happier.

TH: I had an interview to do some TV, and they said [*assumes incredulous tone*], 'Why do you want to work in TV?'

NH: Which soap was it?

TH: I'm not saying which soap it was. What I would really love is to direct *Buffy*. I have very simple ambitions, you know.

RG: What stage are you at with your new script?
NH: We've just finished the first draft of *Sparkle*. At the end of the second draft, we might consider a public reading. I don't think anyone ever likes the projects we bring them. They just like *Lawless Heart*. They think that obviously something happens between the rough document we show them and the script we eventually write, even though they're not sure what.

TH: At least they're giving us the leeway.

NH: And they're just hoping what we come up with is nothing like what we showed them to start with.

TH: So are we.

Ryan Gilbey is the author of *It Don't Worry Me: Nashville, Jaws, Star Wars and Beyond*.

Offering Something Authentic: David Gordon Green interviewed by Jason Wood

If George Washington *offered a tantalizing glimpse of an extraordinary talent, the Sundance-winning* All the Real Girls *confirms director David Gordon Green as one of the most lyrical and distinguished voices in contemporary American cinema. Relaxed, confident and witty in conversation, could it possibly be that we might get through an entire interview without mentioning Terrence Malick?*

Jason Wood: I understand that you and Paul Schneider began writing *All the Real Girls* before your first feature, *George Washington*. Why did you wait until after *George Washington* to revisit it?
David Gordon Green: I wrote it with Paul when we were right in the heat of relationships and, like the characters in the film, going through a lot of 'stuff'. I was getting a little aggressive with the writing and being a little too self-indulgent with the material. I needed to step away from the absolute moment of it. At the same time, my goal was to make it at a point in my life where I could do it pretty quick so that it wasn't a guy looking back on a series of events or a point in his life without nostalgia or sentiment. I didn't want it to be an *American Graffiti* type of movie. I wanted it to be something that felt immediate. It was important to let the wounds scab over a little bit to be able to take more of a technical approach to it and more of an honest approach to the actors. Also, for a first film I needed to make a movie on which I could get away with a little bit more and make a little less narratively, and so we designed *George Washington* as a vehicle that if a reel got lost in the mail then a reel got lost in the mail; we really didn't need it. In my head, *All the Real Girls* was something that was so performance-based that I needed to be able to burn a lot of film to let the actors loosen up and improvise and let it feel real. They had to feel they could mess up whereas in *George Washington* they couldn't as we had to keep going; we couldn't do it twice as we couldn't afford another take.

JW: I understand that the collaborative process with Paul Schneider – who also appears in *George Washington* – was very important to you. However, was there resistance from the producers to having a relative unknown in the lead role?
DGG: We had several opportunities to make it beforehand if I wanted to look at other marquee-value actors. Paul was a guy I went to school with, where he was an editor, and he was the right man for the role. When the money was offered to make the movie, it was also suggested that I should look at X and Y

Top: Paul Schneider
Bottom: Zooey Deschanel

actor, and Paul commented that this might be the only opportunity to make the movie. We talked about it and Paul suggested that perhaps I should do it, but it just wasn't an issue. It never came up again as I made it clear that if you want to do this and you are interested in the script, great, but it is with Paul. The second that Sony and Jean Doumanian, one of the film's other producers, got in the room with him they recognized that Paul had a charisma, a voice and an approach to acting that isn't traditional and so decided to take the risk that nobody was going to lose their lunch if the film flopped.

JW: Again you cast a mixture of professional and non-professional actors, with the non-professional actors coming from the community in which you film. This is obviously very important to you.
DGG: Absolutely. To bring an authenticity to the texture it's always important to me to bring people with dialects and accents so that the words that come out of their mouths are what they would say. A perfect example is the scene between Noel [Zooey Deschanel] and her friend sitting on a porch, one shot, two girls talking, with Noel's back to the camera. It was two actors talking in a scene that was not scripted. I knew the other girl, Amanda, a lovely twenty-one-year-old with four kids, and wanted her to speak and tell her stories. I know that she comes from an amazing place and has an interesting background, and so we all sat down together to talk about what we wanted to do, which involved Zooey keeping within her professional understanding of what the scene needed to achieve and Amanda bringing a real natural life to the dialogue and the improvisation.

JW: It's unfair to pick out performances, but once again Patricia Clarkson really impresses. Was she someone you had wanted to work with for some time?
DGG: I had wanted to work with her since I had a real father/son bonding moment when my dad and I went to see *The Untouchables*. She walked on the screen and we looked at each other and went, 'Damn!' I was about seven but to have that 'Hey, you're my son' moment, that was cool. I finally brought my dad to the set fifteen years later. Also, I work with every actor in a different way but my approach is the same: to find out what they're willing to give and where they are willing to open themselves up and invest in the character. I then try to give them as much freedom as possible. Patricia and I came up with a lot of the characteristics that her character has, and I had a vague outline of what I want the character to achieve and how I want them to relate with certain people; then we come up with her background and the specifics together.

JW: Again with this film you ensured that your crew were fully integrated into the community where you shoot. Why is this so important to you?
DGG: It was particularly important on *All the Real Girls* because Paul lives there [Marshall, North Carolina] and my DP, Tim Orr, is from there, so I didn't

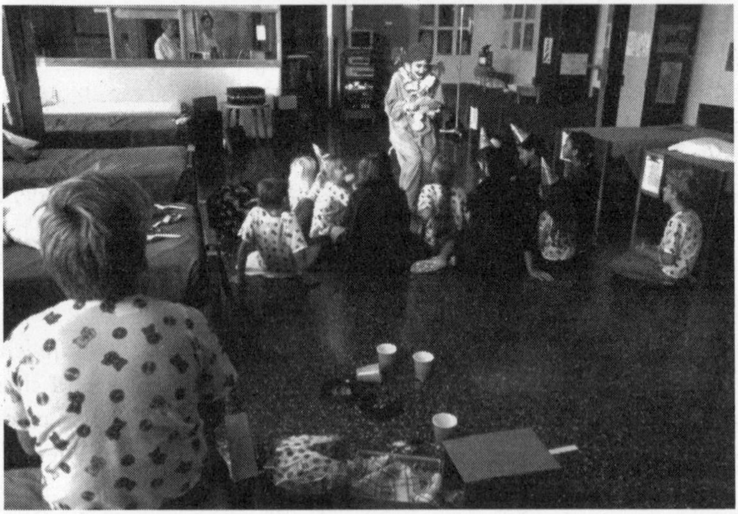

Stepping away from Southern stereotypes . . . Paul Schneider and child (top) and Patricia Clarkson dressed as a clown (bottom)

want to appear rude. We had a lot of ties with the community and that is always important to me. Being the outsider, I went there a year in advance and started working jobs, meeting people, understanding the place and discovering things, such as the richness that's in the back alleys of that town, which a normal film crew with its location scout just misses. A lot of the characteristics, the mannerisms and some of the dialogue that's in the movie I got from working in a factory and talking to people.

JW: Are you from those parts yourself?
DGG: No, I'm originally from Texas.

JW: You display a very good nuance for life in these Carolina towns.
DGG: Well, I went to school there and it's cheap to make movies there. The picture of the American south in my opinion is often caricatured and simplistic. Everybody is named Billy Bob, has missing teeth and rapes each other's cousins. Sure, that goes on, but we don't all do it. It was important for me to step away from the southern clichés of traditional Hollywood movies and show what I'm more familiar with and what is more interesting to me. The mission statement is to offer something that is a little less stereotypical and a little more authentic.

JW: You mention a desire to get away from hackneyed stereotypes in terms of depicting the people who inhabit these rural Carolina towns. Are there specific films and film-makers with whom you feel a kinship or draw inspiration from with regard to how you approach both physical environments and the characters your films create?
DGG: I think Alexander Payne draws a rich sense of place and characters in his films. Obviously Omaha, Nebraska, is a different animal than the rural south, and his style is quite opposite, but I feel that he approaches his subjects with all the honour and humour that a native would and the authenticity rings as a result of that. As for the south, I can't think of too many films that are grounded in a reality that I recognize. *Tomorrow* with Robert Duval might be one. *Deliverance* and *Mississippi Burning* are others rich with familiar texture. The irony is that those films were made by outsiders who happened to be more observant than their American film-maker counterparts.

JW: I understand that *Undertow* and, indeed, the upcoming *The Confederacy of Dunces* also have connections with the American south in terms of character and location. Do you intend to continue to explore this physical and emotional terrain? Also, do you intend to transpose your visions and techniques to other regions and/or countries?
DGG: I've worked fairly close to home because I know how to make films inexpensive using the resources of this region. I've chosen projects that I felt I could bring an authenticity to and were budgetarily realistic for me to get going. Most

of the concepts and projects in my head take place internationally, but at this point I haven't found investors willing to take a great financial leap with me. I fall in love with every country I visit and hope to have the opportunity to explore them with my films.

JW: Could you perhaps talk a little about the influence of Terrence Malick; for example, can you recall the impact of first seeing *Badlands* or *Days of Heaven*?

DGG: I recall seeing *Badlands* for the first time and the audience was very quiet. I found myself wanting to laugh and cry and swing punches and shake the crowd and wake them up. It had all of the excitement in the world for a film that worked within accessible genre conventions, but brought a pace and level of beauty and humour I had never seen before. I was told to quiet down by the woman behind me. I quoted the film for days.

Days of Heaven had such a meaningful voice, which carried the film so softly and unselfconsciously. I was moved by the visual element like everyone else, but the naturalism and quiet moments with the meditative editing and score really caught me by surprise. I was happy not to be beaten over the head with plot and high concept, twist endings and predictable convention. The ending was a perfect gift for a hungry audience tired of the traditional Hollywood scriptwriter's arrogance.

JW: You deal with the subject of youth and the travails of love without resort to cliché. The first shot of the film opens on Paul and Noel having already met. You avoid the preamble. Was this an early decision in terms of approach?

DGG: In a way, but it's also kind of frustrating. A lot of people come up to me and say, 'What a weird little love story, what a weird movie you've made.' Now, to me, what's weird is when you see a movie where people look great and have the perfect comeback when they've messed up their relationship and instantly know how to fix it all; the music swells and then they love each other. That's weirder, isn't it? I've had love at first sight certainly but never do the heavens open up and bathe me in light. Also, when people make out and they hook up and they stay up late, their stomachs growl and they fart to make situations awkward, funny and vulnerable. If I'm going to show people my work I want to show them something that they're not seeing every day, and in some situations they can fill in the blanks themselves. They met somewhere, that's cool; the exposition and the obvious notes you can fill in for yourself. We even shot a lot of clichés, some terrible stuff just to see what we really needed and what the bones of the structure needed to be. Our first cut of the movie was three and a half hours long and it was really about filing it down to the essential elements. We wanted to try something different; you can see people stumble into romantic situations in any video shop.

JW: Was there pressure from the producers and the distributor to make the film more conventional? I understand that you shot a lot of sex scenes.
DGG: From any financial entity there is a hunger to make a movie as marketable as possible, but that's understandable as it's their business and how they make their livelihood. At the same time, they do present you with creative ways to accommodate that. We did shoot a lot of sex scenes and nudity, but it took me out of the moment and replicated things I'd already seen before. It wasn't in any way interesting to me. I think of this film as being the scraps that the traditional romantic movie would leave on the cutting-room floor.

JW: You mention that you shot the film with more conventional elements, such as more sex scenes and more establishing shots or grounding between the characters. In what other ways did the film change during editing, and how relaxed are you during this stage? I get the impression that you are happy for – and indeed encourage – the film to find its own intrinsic rhythm.
DGG: Production is a discovery for me. I tend to put scripts down a month or so before we start shooting. Rehearsals and improvisations dictate where the characters will go and what interesting tangents we will take. Editing is an organic process for me. I begin with an image or word that I like, and I pay little concern to continuity or preconceived mechanics of the screenplay. *All the Real Girls* found its genuine moments in the eyes of the two main characters. We eliminated much of the introduction of the characters and jumped right to the moment when I thought their relationship became distinctive. The scene that now ends the film was written as the opening scene, etc. I give the audience a lot of credit for being able the fill in the blanks. I want everyone to spend their time wisely. I like to linger and not take an aggressive approach to plot. Many characters ended up on the cutting-room floor and virtually all of the plot did as well. I feel quite fortunate that we had creative threads weaving a narrative rather than development mechanics.

JW: It struck me when thinking about the film again how, as the idyll between Paul and Zooey is punctured, the real world begins to physically intrude on their more hermetic world. Could you talk a little about how you set about conveying this visually and what specific techniques you employed?
DGG: I think that any personal dramatic event deserves perspective, so I wanted to place these characters in an environment that showed how ultimately insignificant their personal happiness was. After the significant confrontation between the two main characters, I felt it was important to let the world continue spinning and their temporary hearts take a moment to breathe.

JW: In terms of specific scenes in the film, are there any that for technical reasons remain particularly memorable to you? I think that the way you hold the closing shot is mesmeric, but I wondered if there are other moments that give

you cause to think, 'Yeah, with that I really accomplished something.'
DGG: I like the part where the sound drops out of Noel's frantic break-up. So much of the conflict and miscommunication in my life has come from not listening.

JW: *All the Real Girls* has a timeless quality to it, making it very hard to date it.
DGG: A film like this doesn't have an immediate life. It's not *Terminator 3* opening on one day around the world and making $200 million at the box office. In the States, *All the Real Girls* opened in February and it's still playing, slowly travelling from place to place, and then it will open in Europe and other countries for the next couple of years. I don't want it to go out of style; I want it to go ahead and just be out of style. The other thing that frustrates me with many movies is that everything is so contemporary due to product placement. Sure I'm somewhat manipulating the environment because everyone obviously goes to Starbucks and Wallmart. I want it to be a movie in its own little capsule so that twenty years from now people can say, 'When and where the hell was this made?'

JW: Both *George Washington* and *All the Real Girls* are distinguished by their cinematography. How did you originally meet Tim Orr?
DGG: Myself, Tim and Erin [the film's costume designer, who recently married Tim] all went to school together. In fact, 65 per cent of the crew were at school together. Paul and I also worked at a film archive were Tim was the projectionist, so we all bonded over films whilst cleaning 35mm prints and enjoying illicit late-night screenings of *Deliverance*, a real love story! Tim and I have always worked together and share a similar sense of composition. I completely trust him, and the economic situation of the movies I make means that I don't have time to be running around doing all the stuff. I also want my friends to have a lot of fun doing their jobs.

JW: You pay a lot of attention to sound on the film, both the soundtrack – on which Will Oldham's 'All These Vicious Dogs' particularly stands out – and general sound design.
DGG: As much as the pictures, images and lighting are details that people absorb and make the movie something to look at, so sound – and, indeed, sometimes the lack of it – is also a huge part. Where we choose to have silence, where we choose to have music and where we choose to just have the ambience of the surrounding area, all that is very important to me. There is also experimentation within that. In the middle of a dialogue the sound will drop out and you won't hear the words the characters speak.

JW: I understand that the title is taken from a David Wingo composition that wasn't used in the film. What other titles did you consider?

DGG: I considered a lot of titles actually. *South of the Heart* was one, but people that didn't get the end thought that it was a TV-movie title.

JW: What future projects are you working on?
DGG: Well, as soon as I wrap *Undertow*, starring Jamie Bell, I'm going to be going down to New Orleans to tackle *A Confederacy of Dunces*. This will give a chance for me to do some comedic stuff. Steven Soderbergh is executive producing.

JW: Finally, people seem unable to mention your work without making comparisons to Terrence Malick. Are there other figures that you would cite as influential?
DGG: Well, I like movies a lot, and admittedly I do find the American cinema of the seventies to be a rich source of inspiration, but equally I find the *Dukes of Hazzard* TV series has had an influence on me. Frederick Wiseman, seventies Coppola and Robert Altman are all ballsy, brilliant film-makers. I like a lot of more obscure stuff too; Michael Ritchie is, I think, a very under-appreciated film-maker; equally, Charles Burnett's *The Killer of Sheep*, *Billy Jack* and James William Guercio's *Electra Glide in Blue*. I think there was a period between *The Graduate* [1967] and *Ordinary People* [1980] where things started to rock. People were taking chances on the narratives and the cinematography, and actors were throwing their careers on the line and doing very complicated work. Things weren't so on the nose and manufactured, which was inspiring for me as an audience member, and so I try to replicate that kind of enthusiasm through the films that I make.

George Cukor with Audrey Hepburn on the set of *My Fair Lady*

Designing Cukor
Gene Allen interviewed by Phillip Williams

During the course of a long and prolific career, George Cukor collaborated with many exceptional artists and craftsmen who made contributions both in front of and behind the camera. Few people worked with the director as long or as successfully as production designer Gene Allen. Joining the crew of Cukor's A Star Is Born (*1954*) *as an assistant art director, Allen quickly rose through the ranks to earn the production design credit on that picture. Over the next eighteen years, he collaborated with Cukor on seven films:* A Star Is Born, Let's Make Love, Heller in Pink Tights, The Chapman Report (*for which Allen also adapted the screenplay*), Bhowani Junction, Les Girls *and* My Fair Lady. *Nominated for an Academy Award for his work on* Les Girls *and* A Star Is Born, *Allen took home an Oscar in 1965 for his work on* My Fair Lady.

Gene entered the film industry as a blueprint boy at Warner Bros in 1936, when films like Captain Blood, Confession, The Private Lives of Elizabeth and Essex, The Prince and the Pauper *and* Jezebel *were making their way through the production pipeline – a great time to be gofering artwork around the Warner Bros lot.*

Taking art classes at night and rubbing shoulders with some of Warner's greatest art directors during the day, Gene quickly realized that he had much to learn. After serving four years in the Navy during the Second World War; he took advantage of the G.I. Bill to study fine arts full time at Los Angeles' Chouinard Institute, a breeding ground for some of the industry's most outstanding talents. Chouinard ultimately became the California Institute for the Arts (Cal Arts) under the stewardship of Walt Disney, but the school has always been more than a training ground for animators. In 1950 alone, four of the five Academy Award nominees for costume design were former Chouinard graduates, including Edith Head and Marjorie Best. Famed production designer John DeCuir was himself a Chouinard graduate. While a student at Chouinard, Gene first encountered DeCuir's work on display in the school halls.*

After completing his studies, Gene returned to work in the film industry with an arsenal of valuable skills at his command. He successfully charted his way through the ranks as an illustrator, assistant sketch artist, continuity artist, assistant art director and, ultimately, art director and production designer. Outside his collaboration with Cukor, Gene's credits include art direction for Back from

* *Chouinard, An Art Vision Betrayed* by Robert Perine.

Eternity (1956), Merry Andrew (1958) *and* A Breath of Scandal (1960), *and production design for director Gene Kelly's* The Cheyenne Social Club (1970).

Describing the production designer as part fine artist, part architect and part diplomat, Gene clearly chose a career path for which he was supremely qualified. His professionalism and dedication to his craft was put to further use as the two-term president of the Academy of Motion Picture Art and Sciences and as executive director of the Society of Motion Picture and Television Art Directors, a position he held for twenty-seven years. Gene also served as president of the Society of Entertainment Artists, a federation of the industry's pen, pencil and paper artists.

Though semi-retired, Gene remains a strong advocate for the rights of film artists and has given back a great deal to the industry that was his bread and butter for so many years. Though he spends a good deal of time painting, Gene also teaches two classes a year at UCLA-Extension: 'Production Design' – where, as a student, I first met Gene – and, on alternating semesters, 'The Art of the Storytelling Sketch'. As a student, I found Gene's enthusiasm for the craft of movie-making to be infectious, and I wanted to hear more about his experiences than he ever had time to relate in our weekly three-hour classes.

One of the qualities that makes Gene so rare is his desire to share what he has learned. Whatever one may feel about the relative merits of the studio system during the so-called Golden Age of Hollywood, there is no denying that it produced a level of craftsmanship that continues to inform and inspire film-makers and visual artists to this day.

Recently, Gene and his wife, Iris, graciously welcomed me into their Los Angeles home, where we spoke at length about what Gene calls 'the language of movie vision'.

Phillip Williams: George Cukor was known as a director who was very good with actors, but you've said that he was also a very visually oriented director.
Gene Allen: When you gave him the choices, he always made good choices. He did know a lot about camera, he knew a lot about architecture, he knew a lot about costume. He was very knowledgeable in almost all of the arts. He wasn't someone who said, 'Oh, whatever you think.' You had to sell him an idea.

He originally came out to Hollywood as a dialogue director for *All Quiet on the Western Front*, and before that he had his own stock company in Rochester, New York; he put on plays. Coming from the theatre meant that he already had great training in lighting, set design and staging. He had the theatre ideal already in his head, and when he came out here he had some good art directors working for him at MGM and at RKO. Then, during his time on *Gone with the Wind*, before he and Selznick had their falling out, he worked with William Menzies.

Incidentally, Selznick would come down on the set, which Cukor never allowed, and more or less try to extend his hand into the director's territory.

But Cukor was one of those directors who, when a producer came down on the set, would stop and wait until they left the stage. I think that there was a basic incompatibility there, no matter what's been said back and forth over the years about why Selznick fired him or why Cukor quit.

But as I say, it was on that picture that Cukor had a gentleman working with him named William Cameron Menzies, and Cukor found that what Menzies had to offer was what he really wanted. After that experience Cukor did a couple more pictures before he did his first colour picture, *A Star Is Born*,* and ran across a Gene Allen who thought like Menzies. I knew Menzies – I had certainly talked with him – but I was ready to direct a picture by that point. And Cukor by that time knew what he wanted to put in somebody else's hands. He wanted somebody who was there representing him, with a fine art background that had some innate sense of how to tell a story, where to place the camera, how to light the set, how to light individual scenes. So, in a very short time, that's what I was doing. *A Star Is Born* was my first movie with him.

PW: What was unique about Menzies as a designer that attracted Cukor?
GA: Menzies could really put together a motion picture frame by frame. It really takes a story mind and the ability to express your ideas visually.

PW: He did continuity sketches for the entire film. Was that practice common?
GA: Busby Berkeley had a guy named Phil Barber out at Warner Bros, doing all the sketches for all of his wild dance numbers. So there were illustrators being used. Menzies had a background all the way back to the silent era. He had a talent, which was to take the motion-picture frame and make these interesting divisions. He used a great many verticals; he was good at juxtaposing objects within the frame, and he could also put his ideas on paper and show them to you. He was the complete production designer. When *Gone with the Wind* was being made, Menzies saw himself as more than the art director. He had Lyle Wheeler in that role. He really wanted to direct. Selznick used one of his now-famous memos to the money people in New York, explaining to them how important Menzies was to the picture. He felt that Menzies was going to be the most important man on the picture, because he's not only going to lay out every scene, he's going to organize all the special effects, he's going to direct those, do the process shots . . . Selznick had a whole list of things to sell Menzies with. He suggested that Menzies' talents needed to be recognized with a new title: production designer.

PW: How did you become the production designer on *A Star is Born*?

* Although it was the first colour film he worked on, Cukor neither finished nor received credit for his work on *Gone with the Wind*. *A Star Is Born* is the first colour picture that credits Cukor as director.

GA: I started out as the sketch artist for the original art director, Lem Aires, a famous New York designer whom they hired to do the show. Cukor used to hold pre-production meetings with the heads of departments and various members of the creative staff. They'd sit and talk, go over any current or foreseeable problems – talk about costumes, make-up, hair, whatever. Cukor would ask Lem Aires questions, and Lem Aires, being a stage designer, really didn't know much about putting a movie together, so Cukor suggested that he bring along someone who knew the nuts and bolts of the process. Now I'd been at Fox as a sketch artist for quite some time, and I won't say I was fired, but I was laid off. Then I went to Warner Bros, met Lem Aires and did some sketches and continuity for *A Star is Born*. He saw what I could do, so one morning he asked me to come with him to Cukor's pre-production meeting, and I did.

I have to go back a bit here. When I was at Fox, as a sketch artist, I had become somewhat disillusioned with how my work was being used. I would normally do my continuities and give them to an art director: the art director would take them to the director, come back and perhaps request some more. But nobody ever gave me any feedback. I never knew what happened to my drawings once I passed them off, or if they were well received.

So one day I made an appointment to see a production designer on the lot, and I asked him, 'What happens to the sketches and continuities that come in from the art director?' He said, 'We usually just throw them away. They're generally not very useful.' So I said, 'If you were getting what you wanted, what would that be?' And he said, 'Well, most directors have a pretty good idea of what to do within a scene, but getting in and out of a scene can be difficult. Look for ways to create interesting transitions from one scene to another.'

That certainly influenced the way I worked in the future, but more than anything, I realized that I did not want to be a sketch artist – I wanted to be a director. And interestingly enough, the man I went to talk to about this was Harry Horner, a very talented production designer. He had worked for Cukor himself on a couple of pictures.

So, anyway, I went to Warner Bros to work for Lem Aires on *A Star is Born*, and I attended my first Cukor pre-production meeting. I had read the script, obviously, when I was doing the set sketches, and I did a couple of interesting backstage things for the film. Lem liked them and showed Cukor, who also liked them. Before Cukor closed the meeting, he asked if anybody else had anything to say. I raised my hand, scared to death – and I mentioned a scene in one of Cukor's earlier drafts. It was a great scene where the head of publicity, Jack Carson, tells James Mason that the studio is planning to have a big wedding for Mason and Garland. It's going to be in a big church. It's going to be a first-class event. And just as the words fall from Carson's lips, we cut directly to the couple being married before an obscure justice of the peace, with two drunks as witnesses and an old water tank in the background – not exactly what the publicity people at the studio had planned. In the script as it existed at that point, the film cut directly to the couple in their plush honeymoon suite.

So I suggested that we put this material back in the script, and Cukor said rather wryly, 'Oh, you think so, do you?' I learned later on that he was kidding me, but at that moment I wasn't so sure. But the next day, in came the B pages [the latest changes to the script], and that scene was back in. And it's in the version of the film that people see today. I think that showing the manner in which Garland and Mason elope helps to reinforce the tremendous animosity that developed between Mason and Jack Carson.

I went on to work with George Cukor for eighteen years. For just having that one idea.

PW: And from there you began to be given more and more responsibility on the film. Was there an overall design approach when you started?

GA: It grew on that picture. Later it became more defined. Remember: I'm just starting out now, filling in, stepping in, doing whatever I can to help, beginning to realize what had to be done. Right off the bat, we had that whole prologue to do, and Cukor turns that over to me. We took some footage of the opening night of *The Robe*, at Grauman's Chinese Theater on Hollywood Boulevard. We were on the roof across the street and shot a lot of footage that we later used in the prologue to *A Star Is Born*. Then we went down to the Shrine Auditorium and made a set. The Shrine Auditorium was the actual location for the scene within the script, but much of the exterior stuff – the streetcars and so on – came from Hollywood Boulevard. That took a lot of doing. We had three or four cameras going. And that whole opening on the stage at the Shrine with James Mason – all those camera set-ups, all that lighting – that was really something to step into. Anyway, I went from sketch artist to assistant art director, then art director and ended up with a production-design credit. One thing just led to another.

PW: What happened to the people filling those roles before you?

GA: Well, Mel [Malcolm] Bert had been the original art director under Lem Aires, so when Lem left and I was taken on, Mel stayed there for a while. I was his assistant, and then I became art director and I kept Mel as essentially my assistant, although he kept the title of art director along with me. I didn't knock him down. And as I say, I ultimately became the production designer.

PW: It's interesting to me that you mention Harry Horner, as he was someone who spoke very highly of Cukor's attention to detail. In your experience, to what extent did Cukor get involved in the look of his pictures?

GA: He didn't do too much visual during pre-production meetings. It was mainly the organization of the production overall that concerned him. He did work with individual department heads – the costume designer, the cinematographer, along with the production designer. But what he took from working with Menzies was the clear sense that he wanted that sort of person for himself. On *A Star Is Born* I was required to be on the set every day with Cukor – he wanted me there for every camera set-up. This was my first picture; I didn't know all the ins and outs. But there's no use being Irish if you're not lucky, so I did the right thing at the right time and I made a point of being there, available every minute and still designing all the sets. Though I had a good assistant to help me.

PW: Were you designing camera set-ups on the set?
GA: Every camera set-up on the picture I did from then on, and for the next eighteen years, in agreement with the cameraman. I would work closely with the cameraman.

PW: Who was the cameraman on *A Star Is Born*?
GA: We started out with one gentleman whose name escapes me, a Technicolor expert, because this was Cukor's first colour picture and he was concerned about colour. We ultimately ended up with Sam Leavitt who was the operator on the picture at the beginning. He had worked with Judy Garland at MGM, so they decided to take a chance with him. He and I became good friends.

PW: Were your designs conceived with some thought for the type of lens that the cameraman would be using?
GA: I'd done enough projections [drawings that illustrate how a particular scene will look through a given lens]. I knew every lens, the camera and what it would do because of my experience in the art department. We had all these camera angles – little plastic things – that we put on the plan when we were visualizing a scene. So I might say, 'Let's do this with a 50. What do you think, Sam?' I was there to make the cameraman's life easier. We collaborated.

PW: Since *A Star Is Born* was Cukor's first colour picture, can you talk a bit about the particular challenges that an art director faces when working in colour? Did you prefer colour to black and white?
GA: This was my first picture, so I had to enjoy colour. But we went from three-strip Technicolor to Cinemascope, so we made changes. That was about the time we eliminated one cameraman and brought in another one. Winnie Holk, who was a great cameraman, was with us for a while, but he was of the old school. We went down to look at the Coconut Grove for a set, and Cukor thought, 'Yeah, this isn't too bad.' Winnie Holk went out and stood in the middle of the dancefloor, and he put his arms out like dividing a pie; he gave Cukor one quarter of the pie and said, 'I need the rest to light this.' That was kind of the end of Winnie Holk. Cukor had done a lot of pictures but had never had a

cameraman tell him what part of the set he could have. I later built that set, the set that's in the actual picture – a very distinguished Coconut Grove, I think.

PW: Was the exterior real?
GA: Well, that was more of an insert, just to establish the scene. I think we put some neon lights or something in. I don't remember exactly what we did there.

PW: Was it the actual Coconut Grove?
GA: Could have been. At the old Ambassador Hotel.

PW: A nice scene.
GA: I think it's a terrific scene. And by the way, that's good staging by Gene Allen for George Cukor. Look at how it's shot – it really feels right, that slight movement we do, where James Mason kind of wanders through and we see the girl he's talking about and all that. Very delicate cutting and framing and placing of camera.

PW: There was some nice work with colour there, the way you focus the eye and lead us into the scene.
GA: Cukor brought in George Hoyningen-Huene as a sort of colour specialist on the film. Huene became a good friend of mine, though I didn't know him at the time. He had worked with Cukor before. His background was as a photographer on fashion magazines, but he had good taste and he knew museums and the world of fine art. He'd been run out of Russia when the Czar was kicked out. He'd just got out ahead of the Communists. His dad was head of transportation for the Czar – all those beautiful carrriages that were sent to Paris to be hand-painted. George grew up amongst all that, so he was a man of good taste. Cukor wanted him aboard. Now, he'd never really been a movie man. He'd never worked with movie colour before – he'd been doing black-and-white photography. And Cukor always appreciated the fact that I treated George very well because normally, when somebody comes in from the outside, he's not in the union, hasn't been in the studios, he gets a cold shoulder and disappears.

He was a terrific guy to work with. Every art book that I'd ever liked, he knew, and we'd sit and talk for hours on end. He'd bring his art books in. I'd bring mine, and we'd show the cameraman what we wanted in the way of lighting and all. It was a great combination.

So when we came to colour we decided that most movies were too colourful. So we decided to be selective in our colour to the extent that you could, we kept things simple. I would lay things out, suggest a colour palette, and Huene would pretty much agree with me. He was known as the colour co-ordinator, but with my background as a painter, I knew how to work with colour and I think I contributed a great deal. But we all agreed upon what we were trying to do. His job basically, on the set, was running around putting tulle on extras that would

A Star Is Born: the after-hours club

come in dressed in the wrong colour outfits, trying to control the elements as best we could. We wouldn't put blue books on a shelf because, under Cinemascope, blue popped out, so you had to be careful with what you did with decoration. It was a team effort to keep that colour under control. We aimed to be black and white with limited colour, because the film was so colourful to begin with: if you just shoot a white wall, it's got all kinds of colours in it.

PW: There were a lot of desaturated tones in that picture. Your primary palette seemed to consist of reds, blues and tans.
GA: That's true, but not always red and not always blue and not always mixed together. You used colour as an accent. Everything else was sort of warm and cool greys.

PW: Colours were assigned according to the mood or intent of a scene?
GA: Absolutely. Whatever the scene called for. There's the scene where Mason wakes and goes out to try and find Judy Garland. He goes to the Coconut Grove, she's not there: he's told she's playing in a little club down the street where all the musicians go after hours, and Mason finds her there singing 'The Man Who Got Away'. That was interesting; we shot that scene twice. She had a

costume that she looked lousy in, so we redid it. But the camera movement involved maybe fifty or sixty stops; essentially, we cut the whole thing in the camera. But if you look at that scene, it's all greys with just a wash of orange behind the bar. The first time we shot it the orange was too bright, so I put a scrim in front of it the second time and it made it smokier, and it looks nice. But everything else is black and white.

PW: The only real colour in the scene is behind her.
GA: The reason being that you want to sell her as a singer, as a performer, because she really impresses James Mason. In rehearsal I would ride the dolly to make sure that the framing was just what we wanted. She might make a movement, which we would then note, so that ultimately we could anticipate it on the next take, hoping the audience wouldn't become aware of the camera movement. All of this was intended to sell her as a singer and capture the mood of the band, the after-hours nightclub, introduce Tommy Newman again, her piano player, and, of course, to support Mason's attraction to her. To me it's a highlight of the picture.

PW: Did you begin to become aware of certain considerations involved in shooting a woman, particularly a woman who, in this case, is the focus of the film?
GA: It seemed to come naturally, Cukor always told people, though he never told me. 'I don't know where Gene comes up with all this. He hasn't got any background in movie-making, you know.' But I read, I went to a lot of movies, and I'd had my time in the art department. I guess my instincts are movie instincts. I think that I'm a terrific ideas person. I'd make my suggestions, and if Cukor didn't like an idea, I'd go off and come up with something else. I never gave up. I really worked hard at everybody else's job, whether it was the costume designer or the cameraman, lighting, camera movement, the sets, colour, decoration – I was involved in everything.

PW: The scene in *A Star Is Born* just before he kills himself, before he goes into the waves, is set at their beach house. That was a studio set, wasn't it?
GA: That was a standing set, I think, that we revamped for our purposes. There were two things we did that Cukor liked: making use of the silent wind machine to create atmosphere, and enlisting the use of process plates to create the reflection of the ocean waves on the glass windows which lined the house on the ocean side. Those two things actually created the illusion that you were out at Malibu by the beach.

PW: And it sets up what's about to happen to James Mason – that he will be engulfed by the ocean – because you feel the intense presence of the water and the waves.
GA: Yes, almost too much, but it works. There's some terrific acting there. The moment when James Mason hears Judy Garland's character talking to the

Exterior: Mason going into the waves

studio chief and he sees just what a mess he's made of her life – he plays that beautifully.

PW: On *Les Girls* you seemed to have a lot of fun with colour and the sets.
GA: That's what the story called for. It was one tale told three times – like *Rashomon*, but in this case we were just having fun. You could do things with cutting, moving from scene to scene in interesting ways.

PW: The costumes designed by John Kelly were wonderful. When working with your costume designer, how do you work out the colour palette? How do you work out the overall design scheme?
GA: Team effort. First of all, you talk to the director about it. He might have something specific in mind or when he's talking to the designer he may say, 'Talk to Gene, see what he has in mind for that.' So the designer comes in, you talk, and you have to be a diplomat. But you have to stay in control of it. That's all part of the picture.

PW: It must be a bit of a challenge on something like *Les Girls* to keep control of all that. There's so much colour coming in and out, yet at the same time, I'm sure that you want to lead the eye . . .

GA: You're back to fine-art principles. How do you lead the eye? That's all part of composition and design. In a painting you can literally trace the eye movement with arrows – you move the eye here, you go back in and through and into a picture and then back out. You never go down a tunnel and get stuck down the other end. Fine-art principles.

Colour is just one piece of the total. I always think of colour as warm or cool, and really its strength is as an accent. That's when you heat it up a little. Yellow, red, blue, whatever the scene is. But coming back to what we were talking about before – your transition from scene to scene is part of the whole thing. My procedure was to do a chart, not unlike the score that a musician uses. The important scenes, how high do they chart, up, down, are they quiet or loud? You establish that line to represent the arc of the story, then over the top you chart your colour. You run through a range of greys up to where the line is high, where there's an important point, and then you do something with the colour at that point in the story. To underscore your story points.

PW: They use this technique in animation. They create what is essentially a colour script.

GA: Absolutely. And that's how you keep it in your head.

PW: And that's something you work out with the costume designer and DP?

GA: If you were working for Cukor, he arranged it so that they were influenced by the production designer. You're not telling them they have to do anything, but if the concept is laid out and the director is pleased, and it works and it's giving some freedom to the DP to really light it within the range that's been suggested, then you end up with a team effort that in a sense starts before many of these people join the show. We're designing the mood of a scene before anyone else is in on it. You chart the mood of the picture. What's the mood in a given scene, in the previous scene, what's the mood in the next scene, how do we transition between those two scenes? Working with tone, value and colour. The language of vision, that's your vocabulary. Those are the elements you work with, so that you're never at a loss as to why something isn't lit. You have the basics to go back to, simple shapes, defined as you want them, depending on the story point being made. And if the point isn't being made, you know how to correct it. Talk with your team, do some quick sketches, maybe some tonal things, to show why A might work better than B.

PW: Did you find yourself learning how to appeal to Cukor's particular style and tastes?

GA: Yes, without intellectualizing it. It was sort of by osmosis. It got to the point where I didn't have to do as many sketches, I didn't have to talk as much. I'd do the set, and he'd come down and say, 'That's terrific.'

PW: When you were on *A Star Is Born*, as you say, you were on the set all the time. Did that remain true throughout the years?
GA: Never left the set. Not on anything I ever did for Cukor.

PW: Were you aware of Cukor's work before you started working for him?
GA: Not really. I saw his pictures. I read a great deal about all the directors. That's basic knowledge. As a sketch artist or an art director, I always thought that, if you're going to work for somebody, you ought to know what they do. What's their speciality, what do they like? So you can fit in; it's obviously teamwork with the director as boss.

By the way, though I'm speaking at some length about what I did as a designer, it was all for Cukor. He was very influential. Always bringing in new ideas. He'd come in the morning and say, 'You know, I had an idea.' Or he'd talk to Katharine Hepburn the night before and a whole approach to a scene would change, and you'd have to be able – within a few moments, because the crew is standing by – to rethink it. If the action had been rearranged, you'd start by redoing all the camera work, because perhaps Cukor had found a better way to lead the actors through the scene, from a story point of view – forget about the sets and so on. He might say, 'Well, it would be better if the actor entered the scene by coming down a platform rather than walking down a level.' He would see these things and come in with them, and so you'd throw out everything you did the day before, all the sketches and so on, and start again. He was that kind of a creative director, always.

PW: Did you plan and build your sets to accommodate potential changes?
GA: No.

PW: On *My Fair Lady* you put the set walls on wheels. Was that common practice?
GA: No, that wasn't common. But the reason they were on railroad tracks was because that big study of Henry Higgins, two storey, with all those books up high, was made of heavy, heavy walls. Cukor liked to shoot in continuity, so we had to be able to pull a wall out, reverse the angle and push the wall back in and go back to the other angle. That was a practical approach, which saved Cukor a great deal of money. It was expensive for me to build, but in terms of shooting time, it saved him a lot of money.

PW: That study was very beautiful. It reminds me somewhat of the panelled courtroom in *Les Girls*. Was that actual hardwood? Was there any illusion going on there?
GA: I found very early on that it often costs just as much to cheat as to build the real thing. You try it one way, then another and another until you get the effect you're looking for, and ultimately you realize you've saved very little. So on both of those sets, we used marvellous plywoods with all the finishes on them.

Rex Harrison as Higgins in his study

If you want walnut, use a walnut finish, and then try to keep the grips and electricians from scratching them when they're rigging the lights and everything else, because it's thin and you don't want a big gouge in it. Most of all that stuff would be real wood.

PW: Would you build your sets a little wide . . .?
GA: I'd build it to accommodate the camera movements that we had set up, knowing what we were going to do in my mind. I maybe wouldn't have sold it to Cukor yet, but I'd design the sets relying on my previous experience with camera angles, lenses and their various effects. I would work it all out, as I saw the picture, where the camera would be and so on. The set designs accommodated that. Rather than build an apartment, put actors in it and shoot it, my approach was to put the actors in a blank space, move the camera around them in my mind, seeing the picture, maybe making some sketches, so that the set we ended up with wasn't necessarily square, as a normal set might be, but was one that suited the action.

PW: So you designed the set around the people.
GA: Yes. Just stop to think how interesting that is: that you kind of see a scene

Cukor with Tania Elg in the panelled courtroom

in your mind, actors come in, try out various stagings, you start placing the camera, the set begins to take shape. You begin to see where the walls should go. You might want to see a lot of ceiling or you realize that you don't want to see any. You want scale, you want it narrow behind them or wide behind them. You take all these pieces and put together a room, and you end up with some interesting sets, places that look like they've been built for real people.

PW: When you did your continuity sketches, did you go so far as to detail the actual shot selection for the scene? And would Cukor follow those sketches?
GA: No, that was in my head, having gone over the material myself. So when I was working with the cameraman – like on *My Fair Lady* – after perhaps the

first week, Harry Stratling wouldn't turn to Cukor when we were through; he'd say, 'Gene, what's next?' And that was accepted by Harry, who, by the way, didn't necessarily like my design for the picture when he came aboard, though by the time he came on I'd already had the whole Higgins house up and all. When he first came in to view the set, he went in and said, 'Jesus Christ, George, I can't shoot that set – it's too black.' And Cukor said, 'Oh, Harry, I'm sorry to hear that. You would have been a terrific cameraman on this show.'

We didn't change anything, and Harry shot it beautifully. Never had any trouble with it. At first the cameraman was always looking for a sort of neutral set so that he could play with his lights easily. And our set was somewhat dark, but it really wasn't when you see the scenes; some of them actually look too bright when I see them now.

PW: I'm trying to visualize exactly what it would be like on that set, how you, Cukor and the cameraman would work out your shot selection, camera set-ups and so on. You're saying that was something you yourself did?

GA: For the most part. Normally the director does that. And some of it's just automatic. You get a good two-shot, you sort of get the placement, then you go over the shoulders. But Cukor always did the staging. We would often play through a scene together, the night before we shot it, putting ourselves in the actors' roles and finding the staging. And every once in a while, especially on *My Fair Lady*, I'd have an illustrator – Ed Graves in that case – come over to the rehearsals with us and jot down some of the general movements we had decided on in case I came down with the flu or something, so they'd have a record of what Cukor and I had worked out. Otherwise, I would usually just rely on my memory. Sometimes I'd do storyboards myself, especially on *A Star is Born*, but then I'd come in the next day and Cukor would have come up with something new, and I'd have to throw my boards out. And if you mentioned to him what had been decided upon yesterday he'd say, 'Well, yesterday I was drunk.'

And by the way, I never called him George in my life; he was Mr Cukor. In fact, I picked up very early on in working with him that when he called an actor on stage, such as Fanny Brice, he'd call her *Miss* Fanny Brice out of respect. A good friend of mine, Walter Bernstein, took me aside and said, 'Gene, you're never going to get anywhere in this business until you start calling the boss George.' But I never could.

Iris Allen: When Gene and Mr Cukor talked, they never finished sentences because they each understood what the other one was thinking . . .

GA: From the very beginning it was that way. Communication was never a problem. Part of the job of the production designer is that you've got to be able to use your influence in such a way that the cameraman is not offended, the costume designer is not offended, and the director is not offended.

PW: How did that work in your case, where you had so much input? Was there ever tension with the other department heads?
GA: No, because the results were good. If I didn't know what I was talking about, the first guy who could kill me would be the cameraman. He'd go to Cukor and say, 'This guy hasn't the faintest idea what he's doing.' But I did know what I was doing, and having suggested with sketches what sort of look we wanted, the cameraman was given the freedom to execute it. I never interfered. The lighting was the cinematographer's domain.

So what a good designer will do is try to give an indication of mood – which has maybe already been discussed with the director before the cinematographer came on. You back that up with some Goyas, a Rembrandt or something like that. But always suggestions; being a diplomat is very important.

PW: You did a picture with Cukor called *Bhowani Junction* [1956], which Freddie Young photographed. Did you enjoy working with him?
GA: Terrific cameraman. Loved working with him.

PW: Can you talk about your working relationship with him?
GA: Well, the same as with the others. When he found out I wasn't there to demean him and that I was an old friend of George Cukor's and that I can be helpful to Freddie Young, with the occasional suggestion – by being a troubleshooter – it makes for an easy relationship. You didn't have to discuss it. You just do it. You let the people you work with know what you think of them, that you respect them. But you had to tell Freddie very little of anything. You let him know what the next cut was then walked away. The cameraman doesn't necessarily care what Cukor's continuity was. I did. 'While we're here, we might as well get that.' So I'm doing a lot of the production work along with the unit manager.

PW: When working on location like that, to what extent might you alter the environments you were shooting in?
GA: Not much. If you're going to shoot the majority of your material in real sets, then, beyond choosing the location well, the best thing you can do is put light on them or take light away. But we took advantage of what was there. The light was white or it was grey. The main thing we tried to avoid on exteriors was Kodak blue – you have no control over your exterior skies. And we never used filters, Huene and I. We'd tell the cameraman right at the beginning, 'No filters.' We'd paint the walls the colour we wanted them. Material shot with filters felt phoney, not right. Bob Surtees used a filter in just one scene in *Les Girls*, and we didn't know it until we saw the scene at the rushes the next day. We decided not to reshoot but told Bob, 'Never again.' Film is colourful enough; work for the colour you want.

Bhowani Junction: shooting Pakistan for India

PW: How did you feel about *Bhowani Junction*? You went to India for that film?
GA: Went to India, got sick along with everybody else, every day.

PW: Did you go with Cukor beforehand to scout locations?
GA: We did the scouting. There were big banners, big signs: 'Cukor go home. Get out of here.' Many Indians didn't want us to do the picture.

PW: It's striking to me that the film actually got made by a studio at the time.
GA: It ended up being shot in Pakistan, because Pakistan didn't like India and didn't care what we did. The Indians wouldn't allow us back in the country after our initial location-scouting trip. We came back and decided on Pakistan. Shot it in Lahore.

PW: What was the source of the hostility?
GA: The picture dealt with the Anglo-Indian problem. Anglo-Indians were outcasts to some degree, neither fully accepted as Indians nor as Englishmen. The story was politically sensitive. One thing Cukor said was that a picture like that would have a difficult time finding success, because nobody cares about another nation's politics.

PW: You photographed some of the material on stages in England, didn't you?
GA: Yes, we went back to London and built some sets.

PW: I had a difficult time telling where the sets ended and the location material began. Can you recall which material was shot on stages?
GA: The train stations were shot in Pakistan. The office interiors were shot in London. While we were in Pakistan shooting the exteriors, I shot a lot of interiors. I had a great British set decorator, who was a former art director. He would just astound me. He would do more than I ever wanted. He made the sets so Indian that you could smell India. All the little details – the clutter, paper on desks.

PW: It doesn't feel like it's just been built.
GA: Again, it's where you put the pipes, things that make it odd. That's the only kind of work that Cukor would buy. He went through a set a friend of mine, Bill Creber, did for him at Fox, a picture about Africa [*Justice*]. It was a set of a hospital, and the way Bill told the story was that Cukor came in – and I think since Bill was new, Cukor didn't want to be too harsh right off the bat – and said, 'Bill, do you think that if we were in Africa to shoot this scene, do you think this is what the hospital would look like?' Bill looked at him and realized immediately what he had done: he had built a Hollywood set, not a hospital in the heart of colonial Africa. Bill said, 'Those words never left me.' It stuck with him throughout his career.

Cukor was not a writer, but there wasn't scene he couldn't improve. He had tremendous storytelling ability. He applied that same level of creativity to sets. I learned very quickly with Cukor that he liked the unusual, the unexpected. When putting together a set, I might take the reverse of a set wall and build another set on to it, often in effect bringing together elements that were not necessarily intended for each other, creating odd angles and different levels, maybe. And since you're in the same general location, you can perhaps use existing backdrops. I would put these little sets together, making use of bits and pieces. In *My Fair Lady*, where Higgins' mother gets into the car, that was all sort of added at the last minute. Never part of the original set. But I took advantage of the odds and ends we had. You see some nice long, white latticework there. But this was all built well into production. Cukor loved that; he thought that it was a great way to think. It forced you to do some interesting things.

PW: How might you deal with limited space on a set? You say you didn't like to use forced perspective . . .
GA: No. The only film I ever did that on was *A Star Is Born*. Judy Garland runs from office to office trying to get a job. That's all forced perspective. When you're out in the corridor, the very last time she crossed the screen, we had a midget dressed like her, because it was in fact a smaller, miniature set – all forced perspective. Every office interior in the sequence was designed to reflect the style

of one famous artist or another – Mondrian, for example. We worked with George Huene on those things, got out the art books for inspiration.

PW: This is her first day at the studio after James Mason gets hired.
GA: It's the number where she sings, 'I was born in a trunk in the Princess Theater in Coppocela, Idaho . . .' We see all the trials and tribulations she goes through to make it. It's the story of 'A Star Is Born' within *A Star Is Born*. That's what that number is. Cukor hated it. It was because of that number that they cut out a lot of other good material. Twenty minutes of good story material was deleted to make room for it. Cukor never saw the finished product. He never looked at the movie after the first preview.

PW: Were you able to put any of that material back when the film was restored in 1983? [While some of the original footage was recut into the 1983 version, the negative is yet to be properly restored. The last time Gene showed the film to a large group of people, he was unable to get his hands on a good print.]
GA: We tried to pick up some stuff. Everyone thought it was successful, but to me, having seen the original and having worked on it, I thought the restored version was a poor substitute. Nonetheless, there is an attempt there to try and bring back some of the story that they lost.

PW: How did you become involved in the 1983 restoration?
GA: Cukor asked me to stay on. He went to Europe and asked me to stay on and protect his interest in the picture.

PW: How did you become involved with the writing of *The Chapman Report* [1962]?
GA: With Cukor I became involved with the writing from the very beginning. I didn't actually do the writing, but I was always involved in working with Cukor on whatever script we were working with. He would bring me in early enough so I could work with him and the writers and make suggestions. As time went by, I did more and more of that. I would write bits and pieces here and there.

When we were doing *The Chapman Report* at Warner Bros for Zanuck, I had designed most of the sets, and Zanuck took me aside and said that he was going to have to shut the production down because Cukor was evidently not happy with the script. Cukor was given two, maybe three screenwriters, one after the other, and they were not coming up with anything. Cukor said he wasn't going to shoot what they had, so they asked me if I had any idea what Cukor wanted. I said I thought I did, and Zanuck said, 'Well what can you do about it?' I went home that weekened and wrote forty pages. I showed it to Zanuck to get his feedback, and he liked it. So we took it to Cukor, and he approved.

From that day on, I finished designing all the sets, continued to do all the camera set-ups, while running back to my little makeshift office whenever I could to work on the script. I was writing a day or two, maybe three days ahead of the company. I didn't work with any other writer; I didn't use anybody else's material. However, I was only doing an adaptation. This was not an original screenplay. I was adapting a book, *The Chapman Report*, for the screen. The book was based on the Kinsey Report. When I began to write, I simply went home, opened the book, started on page one and wrote a screenplay. In general, I followed the book faithfully. I had to invent all kinds of odds and ends, but the original writers on the project were trying to take the story away from the book, invent new characters. My approach was to more or less adapt what was there.

PW: Wasn't that film a little bit of a departure for a Hollywood film? [The film – with Jane Fonda, Shirley Booth and Claire Bloom – was based on the book by Irving Wallace, and dealt with a survey of the sexual habits of middle-class American women. The content ultimately was a little threatening to them.]
GA: Not too much. After I finished the screenplay, they submitted it to the Hays office, where they read the scripts, and the guy who read it wrote back to Dick Zanuck a short memo which said, 'Dear Richard, are you kidding?' Because I pretty much told them what was in the book, it was an interesting book. But I also added a bit. The rape sequence, I invented that. Cukor had wanted that in the script. Claire Bloom came to me and said, 'Gene, that's a terrific scene.' But I wasn't a seasoned screenwriter. I'd write 'dot, dot, dot' when I wanted a character to pause during their delivery. Still, it worked. The scenes played well, and what comedy I added came through. There was very little comedy in the book itself.

There were passages of internal dialogue in the book that couldn't easily be photographed. I decided to have one of the characters taking diction lessons. As she practises speaking into a recorder some of her inner life slips out. There were all kinds of little inventions I created to move it along, but remember: as I'm writing, they're shooting the damn picture!

PW: Without a completed script.
GA: Every day. I had a portable dressing room set up near the stage so that I could run down and go over the camera set-ups with Cukor, then run back into my office and keep writing. There was one scene which I placed on a boat moored down at the yacht club. And one day, as I was working at my desk, I overheard Shirley Booth yelling, 'Stop the piping, stop the piping!' I thought Shirley was joking around with someone. 'Piping them aboard the yacht' – the quartermaster generally does that with a little whistle. But as it turns out, Shirley was yelling, 'Stop the typing.' I was annoying her. She eventually came down and asked me to find another place to work. I said, 'You know, that's really a shame, I was working on a wonderful scene for you. It was really going well, but I stopped and threw it away.' Hard to imagine that I could be so cruel [*smiles*].

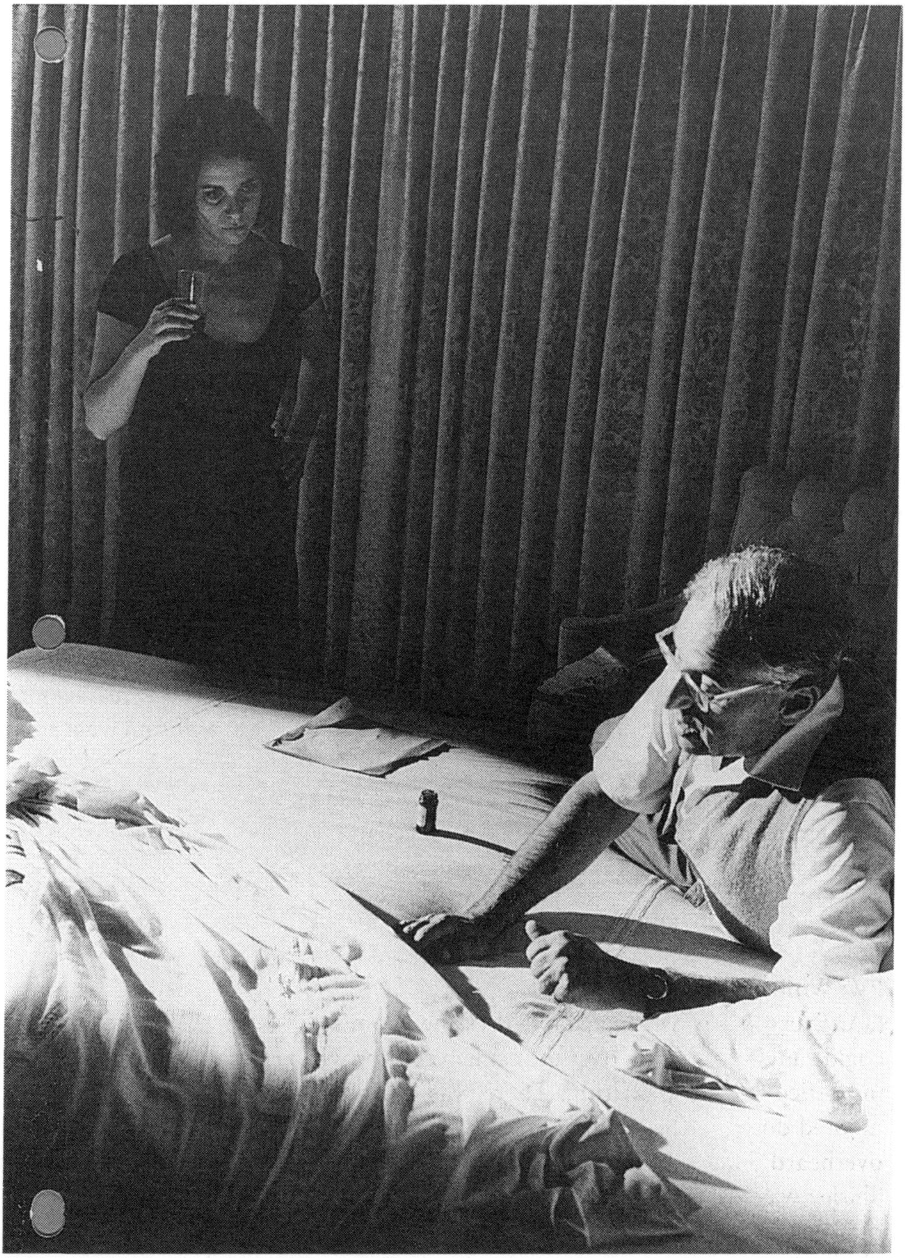

The Chapman Report: Cukor with Claire Bloom

I was so damn nervous. You know, it's one thing to fake being a production designer, it's another thing again to fake being a writer. I couldn't even spell. I remember one time Cukor and Zanuck were in the office throwing material back and forth: 'I think she'd say this.' 'No, I think she'd say this . . .' And I'm sitting there, terribly nervous, and I said, 'Get the hell out of here, both of ya. Get out and talk all you want out there.' I pushed them out the door. And afterwards, as I was going home. I thought, 'I've got to watch myself.' But Cukor and Zanuck laughed because they knew the sort of pressure I was under. I had helped out with story bits before, but this was the first time I worked through a script from beginning to middle and end.

PW: It's a challenge when adapting a novel, isn't it, to reveal what's going on internally with a character? What other methods were you using, other than the dictaphone?
GA: You use interesting conversation. The story took place in Bel Air, Brentwood, with middle-class housewives, and I understood that language. And what I learned from Cukor was to avoid a question and answer format, which is how many people would write. Character A asks a question, B responds directly, and so on. The characters aren't going to reveal themselves that easily. But some of the inner life of the character is brought out through the actor's performance, under the guidance of the director. It's not all in the script. It's what the character doesn't say sometimes that makes the point.

PW: Don't people generally talk about something other than what's going on?
GA: Exactly. And I guess I developed an instinct for that. Cukor always said, 'I don't know how he learned to write. I don't know where he gets it from.' But having me there saved Zanuck the embarrassment of having to shut down the production, throwing away a lot of money. He was always very appreciative, though I never asked a favour of him. He paid me no money.

PW: For the screenplay?
GA: Irving Lazar was my agent, and he was in Europe when I did *The Chapman Report*. I wasn't about to try and negotiate – I just did it. Irving had never gotten me any work to begin with. I set my own salary, and Cukor wanted me there all the time. But anyway, when Irving – or Swifty as he was called – returned from Europe, I told him the situation. He went to Zanuck, and Zanuck offered to give me $2,000, which I felt was ridiculous. I had saved the production, for heaven's sake. But Zanuck said that I was already making good money as the production designer. So I said, 'Fine, I'm not going to fight.' It was an emergency, so I did it. If they didn't want to pay me, that's OK. I liked Dick so much, I never made a fuss. But I told Lazar, 'I'm not going to pay you 10 per cent.' And he said, 'Oh yes, we have a contract. Your money comes to me and I take out my 10 per cent the way we always do.' And I said, 'But that's ridiculous, it's only

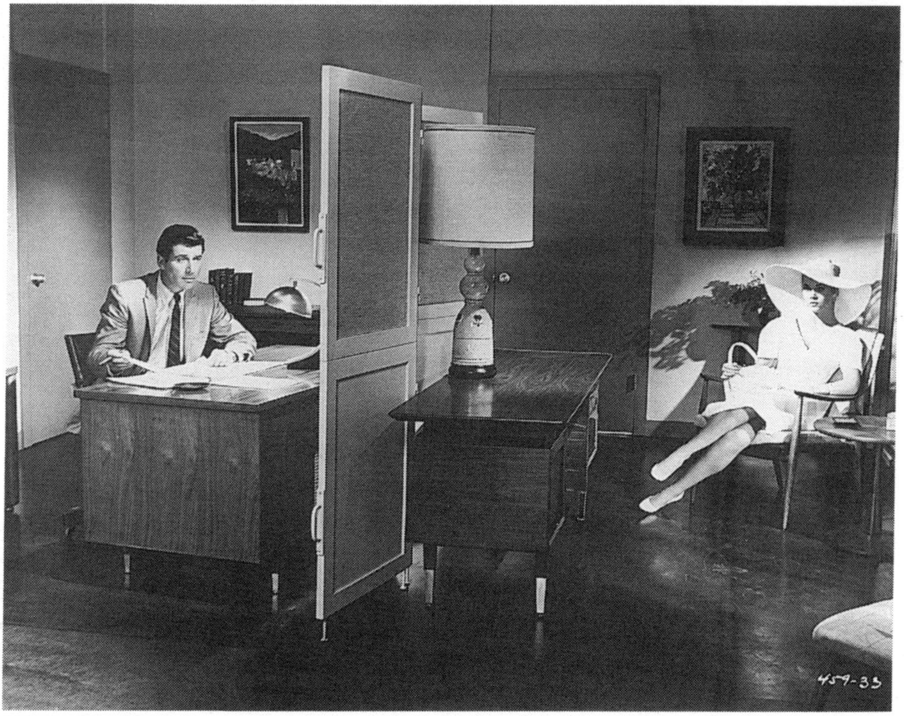

The Chapman Report: Jane Fonda as the frigid woman

$2,000. You're not going to take 10 per cent off. What does $200 mean to you? You're a rich, famous agent.' He said, 'You don't understand, Gene, there's telephone bills in the office' – smiling – 'All of this helps.' Nobody else that I know ever did it, but I fired Irving Lazar after that picture.

PW: You never really needed an agent.
GA: Not really. I had an agent and a business manager. You go through all that, and when you retire you wonder why you haven't got any money. But anyway, there was a dispute with the Writers Guild over screenwriting credit on *The Chapman Report*, and the credit was ultimately shared between myself and a couple of other writers. [Screenplay: Wyatt Cooper and Don M. Mankiewicz, from the novel by Irving Wallace. Adaptation: Grant Stuart and Gene Allen.] But it's interesting. Cukor's copy of the script, which is now kept in the Academy library, just says, 'Screenplay by Gene Allen.'

PW: Did you have much of a problem with censorship on that film?
GA: Not much. There were some things that had to go. The hardest character to write was the frigid woman, played by Jane Fonda. She did it very well, but overall I don't think we were terribly successful.

PW: Some of her material was cut out of the film in any case, wasn't it?
GA: Not much. I wrote in a way that wouldn't easily offend.

PW: Yet Cukor did express some regret over how that film was eventually cut and released by the studio.
GA: Something else in that period that you have to remember – one of the reasons *Bhowani Junction* wasn't terribly successful – was that in those days, it was very difficult to show a woman going from bed to bed. There was no acceptance for that sort of thing. And there were certain things that you didn't discuss, like the case of a frigid woman.

PW: And in the case of *Bhowani Junction*, the studio just took the film and recut it. Cukor's vision never really made it to the screen. They didn't think the public would tolerate a woman who went from the bed of one man into another's and then a third.
GA: Yes, that's right. There was even a scene in *Bhowani Junction* were Ava Gardner dips her toothbrush in Stewart Granger's whiskey glass and then brushes her teeth with it. [This scene was deleted from the final cut of the film.] And none of it today would mean a thing. But back then there were restrictions. There was a very wild, loose period in the early part of the century, then censorship came in and really knocked it down. It took a long time to come out of that.

PW: Given the cuts made to *Bhowani Junction* by the studio, did you feel that your design work suffered?
GA: I just thought that the story was not all there. The same thing happened with *Heller in Pink Tights* [Cukor, 1960]. It was a Louis l'Amour book called *Heller with a Gun*, a story about two men and, incidentally, a woman. They were in a location that wouldn't allow them to escape, held back by snow and ice. So anyway, the studio cast Sophia Loren, and now you have a movie about a woman and, incidentally, two men. And then the production company talked Cukor out of the sets I designed for the snowbound locale. They said, 'Every time you shoot, Mr Cukor, you're going to have to move the camera because their footprints will be left in the snow. And you like to do a lot of takes.' So now it's about a woman, incidentally two men, and the desert. We got so far away from the original story that it wouldn't work, no matter what we did. The French loved it, though, maybe because they liked what we did pictorially with it. We did some interesting things image-wise, but the story wasn't all that interesting to me. I think there were several writers on that picture, trying to make something out of it. Walter Bernstein did some writing, and I think even Dudley Nichols [who wrote *The Informer* for John Ford] was finally on it.

PW: Carlo Ponti [Sophia Loren's husband] was the producer on that picture. Was he active as a producer? Was he on the set?

GA: No, he worked behind the scenes, putting packages together. I did another picture with Sophia Loren, *A Breath of Scandal* [1960], which we did in Vienna and Rome.

PW: A Michael Curtiz picture. Was it much of a change for you to go from working with Cukor to Curtiz?
GA: Yes. Curtiz would say things like, 'If I want a horse's ass to do something, I'll do it myself.' That's an actual Michael Curtiz line. I used to think that he would stay up at night thinking of those one-liners so that he could use them the following day. He was a very famous director at the tail end of his career when I worked with him. But I missed working with Cukor.

PW: You didn't have the same amount of input?
GA: No, and the minute that I don't, I back off. You just accept the cards you're dealt. Do the sets and enjoy everything as it comes.

PW: Did you do much research for the film? Were you on the production for very long?
GA: I was on it long enough to do a lot. Went to Vienna, met with people, picked all those great locations inside the Schönbrunn Palace and the other palaces. Found the company that did most of the set decoration on the picture. It was a good-looking picture. Stupid story. It was based on a play by Molière called *Olympia*, about the caste system which existed during the Europe of his era, but by the time we made the film that issue was no longer relevant.

PW: How did Curtiz work with his production designer or art director?
GA: 'Give me a good foreground cutting piece' [a shape, an object, to compose with], he would always say. He's famous for using a grand piano on one picture over and over as his cutting piece. It started out in the living room, and he'd keep moving it, framing it again for the next shot, until he'd moved it from one room to another – still the same cutting piece. He knew that most people wouldn't notice it. He just needed a shape in the foreground, to create some visual interest, maybe break up the frame a bit. Mike was a real film-maker. Good with actors. Difficult to understand, though – he spoke half English and half German, and when we were shooting in Vienna, he spoke their language and they still couldn't understand him.

PW: But you went back to work for Cukor after *A Breath of A Scandal* was completed.
GA: It's a funny story, actually. While we were shooting in Vienna, a director on another picture which was shooting over there died [Charles Vidor], so they brought Cukor in to finish the picture [*Song Without End*], and he asked Harold Bernstein and me to leave the Curtiz picture and come and work for him. But, of course, we couldn't.

PW: Returning to *My Fair Lady*, what was it like working with Cecil Beaton? [Beaton received production design credit on *My Fair Lady*, but by all accounts it appears that he was only responsible for the costume design on that picture.]
GA: That's a whole lousy story. I didn't want to do the picture when I found out that he was going to be on it because I knew that he thought he would be designing the sets. But it turned out, in a meeting with Jack Warner, George Cukor and me, that I was to continue working with Cukor precisely the way I always had, no variation. Warner wanted me there because his production people said, 'You know, Cukor without Allen on a big picture like this could be time-consuming.' So I agreed to do the picture. I had already turned the picture down three times, and finally Cukor said, 'Do me a favour.' So I did the picture, and luckily so. But Beaton had absolutely nothing to do with any of the sets, the look of them or their lighting. He was never on the stage when we shot. He had a full-time job designing all those beautiful costumes. Giving him the production-design title was farcical. You can't be the production designer if you're never on the set.

PW: Was it his stature alone that landed him that credit?
GA: Well, he was promised that before Cukor and I came on the picture. His agent, I think, was Swifty Lazar, and the story is that they wanted [Vincente] Minnelli to do the picture. Anyway, Beaton was brought in and he let everybody think that he was designing the picture from New York. Now, he did design the costumes in New York, and Oliver Messel did the sets [for the stage play], but as far as Beaton was concerned, he did it all. I had to go to the press and clarify that he did the costumes and I did the production design. And that's the truth. I don't think there is much debate about that. By the time we were one week into production, Beaton and Cukor weren't even speaking to each other.

PW: I think that's been validated by Cukor himself in various interviews he did.
GA: He's done that. Jack Warner just didn't want any trouble, and he didn't want to lose Beaton because Beaton was going to bring a lot of publicity to the picture on the strength of his costumes. Beaton had the sort of ego that wanted to feel that he was in charge, but I never once took an order from him or consulted with him about sets. He says I did; I didn't.

One time I caught him in the art department. I had made a model of Covent Garden to show Cukor and Warner, and he was there with his easel and his oils, painting a picture of Covent Garden from my model. Years later, after the picture opened, I'm up on La Cienega, I go into a gallery and there's 'Cecil Beaton's design for Covent Garden'. But that's just a fact of life. When you read the history of Beaton and his ego, you see this. Still, he was terrific – his talent was recognized worldwide with his books, his photography and all that sort of thing. But I knew what I did, and so did Cukor.

Gene Allen and Jack Warner on the set of *My Fair Lady*

PW: You mention the use of models. Were models useful to you as a designer?
GA: For a complicated set like Convent Garden a model can help. Where to place the church, the back, side routes and so on. You see, I took a two-storey stage, then called Stage Seven, and I took the floor off, and under that, from Errol Flynn days when they were shooting maybe large pirate ships, was a huge tank. So I ended up with three storeys. Covent Garden was built down on that lower level. That's where we laid down all that cobblestone. The second level of the set was actually street level, so to come in with those horses and carriages we had to determine where the ramps would be placed so they could come in, circulate and leave. A model is good for that. But I didn't do too many models.

PW: Did you work with miniatures?
GA: No, we didn't. Cukor and I never really talked about it, but I generally refrained from using matte shots or shooting miniatures or forced perspective. I found other ways to create the illusion without resorting to that.

My Fair Lady: Covent Garden

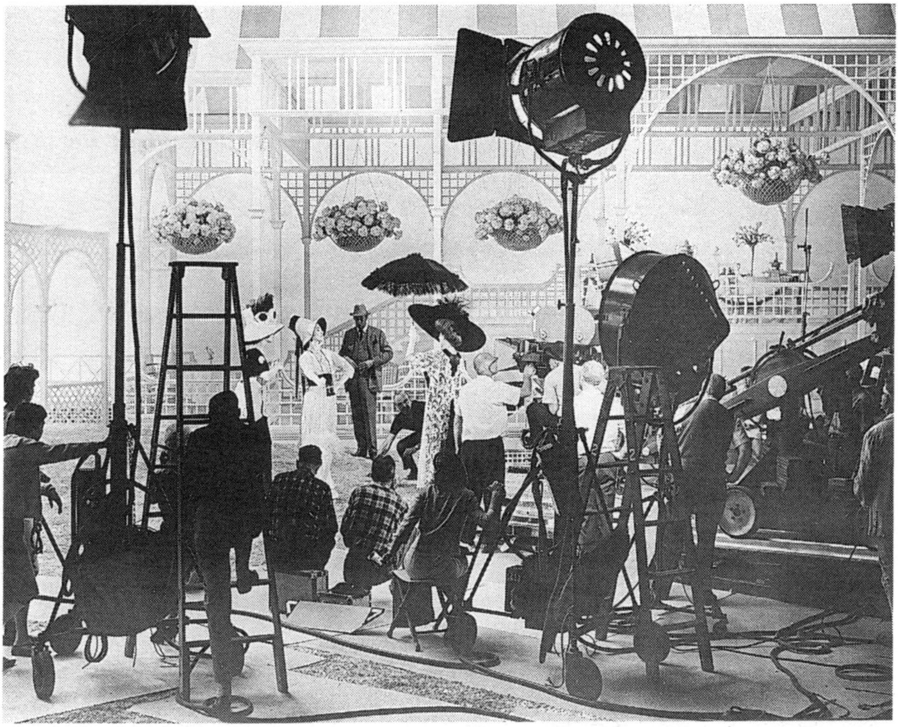

My Fair Lady: Ascot

PW: Rear projection?
GA: Sometimes rear projection.

PW: How did you arrive at the stylized approach to design on *My Fair Lady*?
GA: That started in the earlier discussions with Cukor. I don't remember what other picture we were going to do that involved translating a theatre piece into film, but I had a feeling from Cukor that you had to be very careful. How much do you open it up from the stage version? If you go too far, you end up with mere Hollywood spectacle, and you don't want to be accused of that. So when we came to do this, we wanted to do just enough to make it work for the story that was being told. There were no matte shots – you don't look out any window and see London. You don't miss it. Ascot was stylized in everybody's mind from what they'd seen of the stage play and all that black and white, the colours that were used because the king died, the colour of mourning or whatever. Beaton's costumes had that feeling. So there were some existing ideas that I built upon.

I directed the Ascot dance number. The scene where the crowd is looking through their glasses and the horses go by. I directed that scene up to where Rex Harrison bumps into his mother.

PW: 'Henry, what an unpleasant surprise.'
GA: Right. I also directed a lot of other business, such as the coming and going of the carriages in Covent Garden.

PW: Back to Ascot. We hear the horses, the camera is on the spectators and then the horses pass in front of the camera. Given that you were shooting on a sound stage, how was that accomplished?
GA: In real time. Today you might use a computer. No big deal. But I laid out the set, put the horses at one end, and opened the stage door at the other end. Now the first thing we realized, in talking to people who know horses, is that you can't use thoroughbreds because they could not stop or turn within the short distances we were working with. So, we got good-looking quarter horses. Anyway, we had large doors open on either side of the stage. On one side there was the Warner Bros commissary, on which we hung a big black [scrim] and painted railings on it. When the horses got to that point, which was actually off camera, they would turn and go north along the commissary wall.

PW: That's impressive. Those horses looked like they were really kicking.
GA: They were. The set was long enough to allow them to get up to full speed by the time they were in front of the camera. So it worked.

PW: Were you happy with the overall look of *My Fair Lady*?
GA: Oh yes.

PW: And A *Star Is Born*?
GA: They're so different that it's difficult to compare. I thought there was actually more work involved in getting *A Star Is Born* to look as good as it did.

PW: How so?
GA: The use of Cinemascope [on *A Star Is Born*.] When they changed from three-by-four proportions to the extra-wide frame of Cinemascope you lost a lot of the floor and ceiling. It's shaped rather like a letter slot on a mail box: long and narrow. You end up with a sort of band across the middle of your scenes with actors. So it meant finding new ways to create depth. There are generally three elements to work with in creating depth in a room: the ceiling, the floor and the walls.

PW: And lenses?
GA: With the lens we were pretty much limited to a 50mm. It was only the second picture done in Cinemascope. Twentieth-Century Fox established a set of rules for using the new format, but when Cukor read them he said, 'Gene, forget them.' They had one rule which stipulated that you needed to line your actors up and measure the distance back to the lens so that this actor and that actor are the same distance to the lens, and so on. Cukor said, 'I'm not gonna

Les Girls: 'I had all kinds of levels working there.'

do that. Just figure out how we can do it using our established techniques.' And we did.

They said you couldn't do big processes on little tiny screens. But the scene where Mason and Garland come out of the nightclub and into the parking lot was done with two huge screens to establish Sunset Boulevard in the background. We basically ignored what we heard. I looked through the camera on every set-up to make sure we had enough perspective working for us. So, to get the equivalent of the floor, you had to bring tables up into the shot, or chairs; anything to create new surfaces. You find new ways to make your walls work; we would drop the ceiling in the distance so you'd get that line down from behind heads. We were very selective though, so that we didn't get caught at it. Cukor had one rule for both Huene and myself: 'You can be as clever as you want, but don't get caught at it.' We were always pushing it up to that point.

George Huene and I looked at a lot of oriental prints, trying to find ways to compose within the exceptionally elongated Cinemascope frame. We found that some of the oriental scrolls used a lot of verticals, so we used that to break up the division of the space so that the audience wouldn't be so aware of this very wide frame. If you go back through the picture you'll see a lot of beams, posts and things that we utilized to make it work.

PW: You make use of that in the Coconut Grove, where James Mason first goes to look for Judy Garland. You dressed the set with these elegant trees. Then, in the after-hours place where he finds her, there are posts, beams and so on.
GA: Yes, and we put all the chairs on the tables. A lot of it was improvised right there. We'd get the set dresser to come over and we'd move chairs, get some sort of plan going. If you look at *Les Girls*, that was really well designed for Cinemascope. I had all kinds of levels working there. I put the camera in a fixed position in the kitchen [of the girls' apartment], and from there we see the raised centre area that you can look through into the living room; then there is the stairway that they climb to enter the apartment, which can be seen to one side, with a window on the other side with a view of the outside, so that overall we have several levels within eyesight. Again, Cukor hated to see artificial backdrops, so there's very little of that sort of thing seen through the windows on the apartment set.

PW: And these design elements were tailored to the Cinemascope format.
GA: To make things visually interesting, to take your eye away from the outside borders and provide some interesting places for the actors to play out the sort of French farce that the picture called for.

PW: You put some of this to work in *Let's Make Love* [1960], didn't you?
GA: Not as much. By then we were quite confident using Cinemascope. It's a very simple picture. I made sure that Cukor was never restricted in so far as where he could place the actors. The other thing that Cukor insisted on and taught me was the importance of research. He always said, 'You know, if I'm going to do a picture about New York – although I was born in New York and I know everything you'd think a native might know about New York, I would start a picture as though I'd never been there. Show me some research.' So we would make folder after folder of research. He would have one, the assistant director would have one and we'd have one in the art department. I learned very early on, when creating an environment, to place in it things that don't necessarily belong there – a pipe in the wrong place, a window that should be there but has been bricked over. Cukor liked that sort of attention to detail. He'd walk on to a set like that and say. 'Hey, I like it.' I learned a lot from him through the amount of research he encouraged. When we did the western [*Heller in Pink Tights*], I didn't look at the west but instead went back and looked at places like Pittsburgh, New York, Philadelphia and Chicago, from that period, because the people who came out west – the carpenters, the plumbers – all came from back east, so that's the sort of look they would produce, adapting it somewhat to the sort of materials available in the west. A

building made out of stone in the east might be made out of wood and so on. But Cukor just loved to do research. Loved it. When we'd go location scouting I'd have two cameras clicking as fast as I could.

PW: Were you involved with scouting locations for all the pictures you did with him?
GA: I went to London with him for *My Fair Lady*. He sent me to Paris alone for *Les Girls*.

PW: But they were both ultimately shot on the studio lot in Los Angeles.
GA: With *Les Girls*, Paramount was doing a picture in Paris at the same time with Fred Astaire and Audrey Hepburn – *Funny Face*. They were going to shoot on location, and so here we are, this little picture over at MGM, which would come out more or less at the same time. So they sent me over to Paris to find locations, and I came back and sold Cukor on the idea that we didn't need to shoot on location for our picture; we could do it all from the inside looking out. Let the competition do their picture out in the streets and we'll do ours on the lot, Cukor sold the studio on the idea and so that's what we did. But the exteriors in London were shot on location. The London courtroom was a studio reproduction of an actual court in London, which I went over and photographed for reference. George Huene and I also did the main titles for that picture and for the Marylin Monroe picture, *Let's Make Love*. I did the whole prologue to that one.

PW: How was your experience working with Marylin Monroe?
GA: I liked her. She gave me a cigarette box with the inscription 'Gene, I have designs on you.' She did it with her own handwriting with one of those electric engraving devices. But anyway, we got along fine. That was a very simple picture to design and do. A kind of 'theatre in the square' environment.

PW: Did you prefer to shoot in the studio? What were the advantages to you?
GA: There were definite advantages for the designer, such as the ability to move walls so that you could put cameras where you wanted them. The studio gave us a bit more control over the lighting, the overall look. And I believe there is actually a built-in realism that isn't there on a location set; you can make your moldings deeper, wider, darker, lighter – things that may be more difficult to achieve on a real location. You do have a lot of old movies where you know they're on sets, but I like it. We always tried to disguise it, though people were amazed that every shot in *My Fair Lady* was shot on the stage, except for the number, 'With a Little Bit of Luck', which I did on the Warner back lot. Everything else was built for the picture.

PW: In *Les Girls*, how did you create the illusion of Paris outside their apartment?

GA: You look through the window and see a couple of chimneys.

PW: And the far background is out of focus anyway.
GA: You don't do too much. We were only trying to suggest it. The courtyard was a copy of one that I shot in Paris. You know you're in Paris; you don't have to see the Eiffel Tower.

PW: I thought the courtyard was nicely done. And again you're playing with levels; there's a lot of visual variety. It does break up the frame . . .
GA: That's what we needed, working with Cinemascope. You want to focus the eye. Once in a while you might call attention to the edges, but generally what you do is cover up one fourth of that frame with something. You play it back in the old proportions.

PW: You didn't like Cinemascope.
GA: Lousy format. Great for the business. It was at a time when they were looking for a new gimmick. But it was lousy. The best colour was three-strip Technicolor, and the best proportions were Menzies proportions, three-by-four.

PW: Can we talk for a moment about film restoration? To what extent did you get involved with film preservation when you were president of the Academy? You were involved with the restoration of *My Fair Lady*, weren't you?
GA: Yes.

PW: Is there a general reluctance on the part of the studios to restore their films?
GA: Well, what are studios run on? Money. And it's expensive. There are several people that do it now, some that restore films cheaper than others, some that do it better than others. The two guys who restored *My Fair Lady* [Robert A. Harris and James C. Katz] I think are the best. They called me in to look at some of the footage because the print was so bad; they couldn't tell if it was day or night in some scenes. They do a terrific job.

PW: Going back to Cukor for a moment: any additional thoughts about him?
GA: What I think about Cukor is that he was first of all a terrific guy. Great sense of humour. Great depth of knowledge, both with respect to the theatre and the motion-picture business. Good taste in all things. When you came to work for George Cukor, you were delighted to go to work that day. He was very inventive, always kept you on your toes. Bob Surtees once said, 'You know, when working with Cukor, it's as though he goes home every night, takes his brain out, washes it out with alcohol and comes in fresh the next day with a thousand new ideas.'

He was always throwing ideas out, and I had to learn in working with him to listen, then go and do the practical thing – whatever was needed to make it work. But you can't overemphasize his ability to harness the talents of others.

He'd listen to what the people around him had to say and take the best of whatever he wanted. One day a unit manager took him aside and said, 'George, it doesn't look good for you to have Gene Allen in there giving all these ideas in front of the group. Why don't you send him back to the art department where he can draw all these things up and give them to you?' Cukor said, 'I don't care who gives me ideas. I'm satisfied knowing that when I want to I can fire them.' You could have heard him a mile away, he was so angry at this guy. At that moment I knew that even if he didn't want me on the stage he'd keep me there just to show the unit manager. I don't think any production designer, including Menzies, had the privileged position that I had with Cukor. Still, I was clever enough, or Irish enough, to handle the work, to be able to design all those sets, get everything done on schedule, on time. I was rarely constrained by a tight budget. But Cukor was very professional: he never spent money just to spend money. If you could show him a way to take something and get a good shot, he was all for it. Loved it.

PW: Do you think there were advantages to working within the studio system?
GA: Oh yeah. First of all, the studio system trained you. You worked in an art department for fifteen years and then you might get to be an assistant. I worked probably close to that. But I had friends over at Fox who worked for another eight to ten years before they became art directors. I had this lucky break with Cukor and got there a little earlier. Very seldom was anybody allowed to have the title of production designer. Very seldom. The studios didn't want it. Certainly Cedric Gibbons didn't want it. Lyle Wealer didn't want it. They were heads of the art departments. In their contract they got top screen credit on every picture – every Fox picture, every MGM picture. That's why they had so many Oscars. They didn't necessarily do the pictures, but they got the credit. Hal Pereira did the same thing over at Paramount. When I became head of the art directors' union, the first thing I did was to cut that system out. I was executive director of the art directors' guild for twenty-seven years.

PW: What did that involve?
GA: I was essentially a business agent, a mother hen for 800 art directors. Negotiating the contract, enforcing the provisions of the contract, promoting their general welfare.

PW: And you held the job of Academy president at some point.
GA: I was head of the Academy for two terms. Each term is a year. I was really pleased to get that job. It usually went to producers, directors, actors or writers. I believe I was the only one out of the ranks, so to speak, who got the job.

PW: What does the president do?
GA: The first thing you do is put on the Academy Award show. I picked the

producer for the first year, and the second year I co-produced it with Bob Wise, Gregory Peck and Larry Gelder. I put together a team, so that was a great experience. The rest of the time you're travelling on behalf of the Academy. I went behind the Iron Curtain for a trip, to China for a trip. We represented the arts side of the industry. It was more or less to generate good will. They all want to make contact in order to find out how the Foreign Film award is given out and how do you win it.

PW: [*laughing*] How do you win it, Gene?
GA: Nothing special. It's the most honest organization I've ever known. I was president of the Academy, and until they opened the envelopes the morning they announced the nominees. I hadn't heard a word. Nobody in the Academy knew a thing. They work it out so that two accountants know the score, and they come in separate cars in case one of them is kidnapped or whatever. But nobody believes that in Europe. It's hard for them to believe that that's the way it is.

IN MEMORIAM

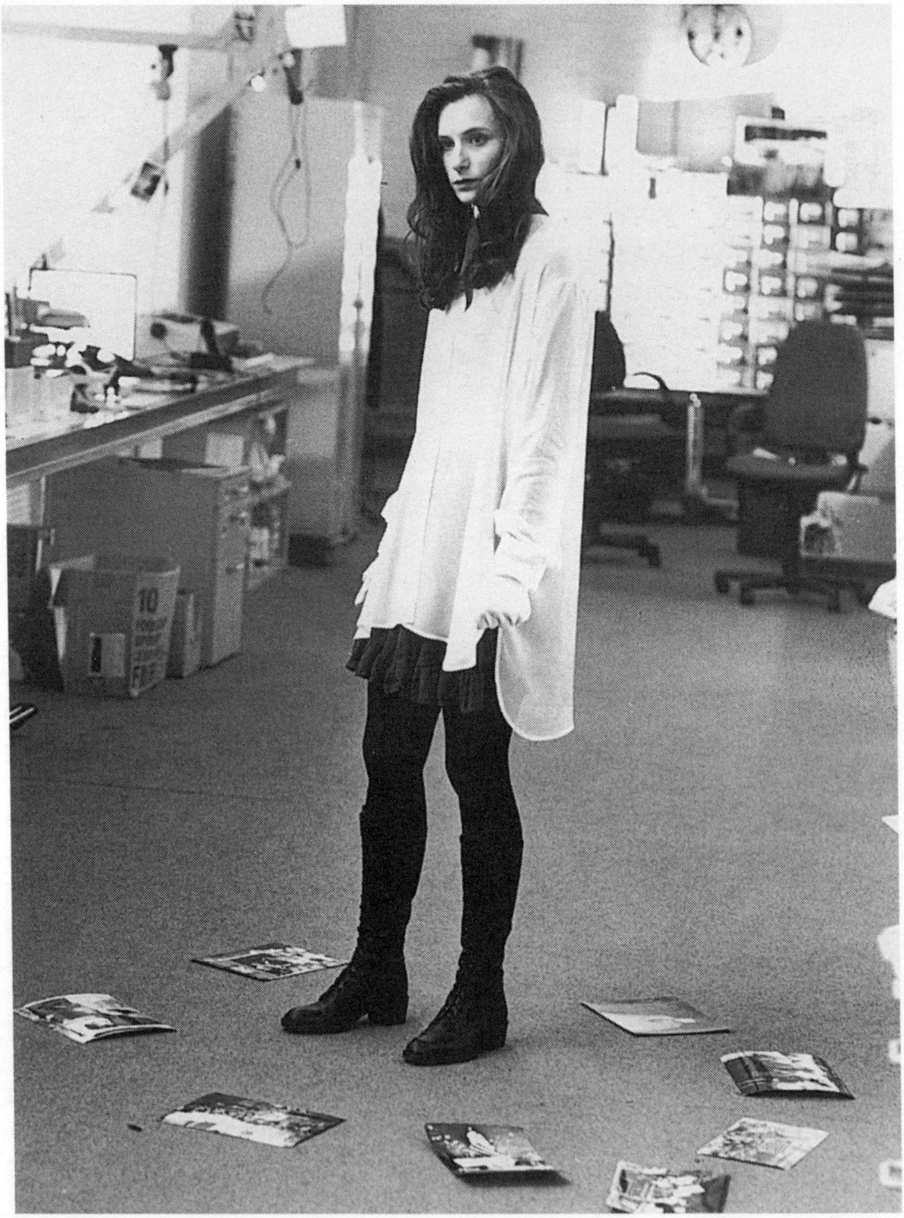

Katrin Cartlidge in *Before the Rain*

Katrin Cartlidge by Mike Leigh

I was at the Toronto Film Festival when the dreadful news of Katrin Cartlidge's untimely sudden death spread like a shock wave. We were all utterly stunned. Many of us knew her personally, others only from her many screen performances. Yet everybody felt they knew her, and everybody loved her. It happened to fall to me to tell Juliette Binoche. I was unaware she was soon to start work with Katrin on Walter Salles' new film. She was bereft: she had not yet even met Katrin. At the question session after our own film, a member of the huge audience asked me about Katrin. The audience was palpably shocked.

Film festivals are not all like Cannes or Venice. They come in every shape and size. Many of the best are modest, uncompetitive affairs, where audiences and film-makers mingle intimately. Katrin loved these especially, and attended many of them: she was always a popular participant. Some of us were lucky enough to spend time with her at the friendly film festival at Sarajevo only a couple of weeks before. Her work on Manchevski's *Before the Rain* (1994) made Katrin a Balkans heroine long ago, but since *No Man's Land* last year, she has become a veritable star in Bosnia-Herzegovina.

And here she was in Sarajevo, where they idolize her, radiant and sunny, with her long hair and famous infectious laugh, and her little rucksack on her back, chatting with members of the public, avidly watching all sorts of films, having genuinely serious, spontaneous discussions with young film-makers. She was fascinated and ever-inquisitive about the city, the recent war, and above all the people; endlessly enthusiastic about everything, not least the food; and characteristically happy pottering around the old town, rooting out cotton scarves and leather slippers.

One of our joint duties was to introduce the late-night open-air screening of *Naked* to an audience of 2,500. Much to Katrin's amusement, the interpreter asked me what I was going to say (Katrin knew that I always improvise). I told the woman not to worry, I wouldn't say anything she couldn't translate. While waiting to go on, Katrin suggested I say something untranslatable. I volunteered, 'Twas brillig, and the slithy toves (etc.).' Katrin said that if I'd recite that, she would utter a long sentence in Serbo-Croat, picked up while shooting *No Man's Land*, which she duly demonstrated. This turned out to be the foulest of obscenities; but the great joy of Katrin's delicious sense of humour was that we didn't need to bother with the dare itself – just savouring the wheeze was enough.

Naked: her first leading role (photo by Simon Mein)

I adored her twinkling anarchy. During the Sarajevo trip, we attended a reception given in our honour by the British Ambassador in the garden of his official residence. From time to time, as we chatted with various film-makers and diplomats and their wives, I would catch sight of Katrin giving me a naughty, conspiratorial, anti-establishment wink, as if she was about to perform some dastardly republican deed.

Katrin was occasionally given to sophisticated practical jokes. When she was on the jury at the Edinburgh Film Festival, she sat in the row in front of another jury member and made enthusiastic noises throughout the screening of an obviously atrocious film, much to her colleague's bewilderment. As the credits rolled, she jumped up, turned round and chortled, 'Gotcha!'

It is my privilege to have worked with Katrin on the film that led to her career, unique amongst British actors, in independent European and American films. *Naked* was not her first film, but Sophie was her first leading role. I had known her for a number of years and had admired her theatre work. (She always recalled my visit to her theatre studies class at Parliament Hill School, where, typically, she remembered her delight at the short shrift I gave her unfortunate teacher.)

She had often told me how much she wanted to act in films, especially in mine. Of course, lots of actors say that sort of thing, but it was only when I started to work with Katrin on *Naked* that I began to realize that there was more to it. She took to the improvisation and character work instantly, easily and with extraordinary commitment and imagination. Other than at the Royal Court Young People's Theatre, she had had no formal training, but you would never have guessed it (Drama Centre London turned her down, and that put her off). And my abiding memory during the long rehearsal process is of her endlessly exclaiming, 'This is such a gas.'

On the whole, even the most intelligent actors don't pay much attention to the filming itself, and far less to the nature of film performance in relation to the whole process. But, as Simon McBurney said in his moving obituary in the *Guardian*, Katrin believed 'in the process of cinema as well as the product'. It turned out that she had originally wanted to go to film school to direct, but had decided early on that she should first find out about acting. And, despite her inspired, genius ability to lose herself in the character and to behave as an actor should, she also had the objective eye of an artist. For that is what she was, in the broader sense of the word and in the way that most actors are not. She drew her inspiration not only from life and people and experience, but also from painting and sculpture and much else, including world cinema. She often talked to me about her eventual move into directing. I am in no doubt that we have lost not only one of our greatest actors but also one of the most interesting new directors of the future.

But the depth, scope, range and sheer electricity of Katrin's acting was phenomenal. Had she continued, she would most certainly have become, over the next forty years or so, one of the true greats. Her tastes and sensibilities were both classical and yet alert to the contemporary pulse. And her acting was always informed by her compassion, her courage, her humility, her gravity, her humour, her sexuality, her sense of justice, her acute observation and her deep-seated suspicion of all forms of woolly thinking and received ideas.

We worked together only twice after *Naked*. In *Career Girls*, her remarkable achievement, for which she won the *Evening Standard* Best Actress award, was to play the immensely complex Hannah at both twenty and thirty. Others in the cast had to do this too, of course, but Hannah's behavioural complexity made Katrin's characterization phenomenal.

She was mostly unavailable for *Topsy-Turvy*, but was desperate to take part, in however small a role, 'just for the gas of it'. So at the last minute, she came in and played her delicious madame in the scene where Sullivan visits a Paris brothel. And when she showed up to contribute her cameo, she had been to Paris to do some pretty thorough research.

Her co-lead in *Career Girls* was Lynda Steadman, who was very ill during the shoot. Naturally, everybody was as helpful as possible, but Katrin took total responsibility for her comrade and, without compromising her own work, was

Career Girls: Hannah at twenty with Kate Byers (top) and thirty (bottom)
(photos by Joss Barratt)

Top: *Topsy-Turvy* – 'a delicious madame' – with Allan Corduner (photo by Simon Mein)
Bottom: with Emily Watson in Lars von Trier's *Breaking the Waves*

As *Claire Dolan* (photo by Lodge Kerrigan)

so caring and so very strong that Lynda was able to deliver a beautiful, flawless performance. For, as has been said of her often, Katrin was a truly loyal friend, and was universally loved.

I still find it impossible to believe she is gone, that I will never again meet her for lunch and have that special free-flowing Katrin conversation, at once profound and hilarious. But the hardest thing of all is to face the unbearable truth that Katrin Cartlidge will never again make her magical contribution to my films. This devastating fact leaves me very sad indeed. It is a terrible loss.

Conrad Hall
by John Boorman

In 1968, being young and foolish I elected to shoot *Hell in the Pacific* on a remote island in the Palauan Archipelago. It could have been made in comfort in Hawaii. I persuaded Connie Hall to shoot it for me. He was born in Tahiti and he knew the light on those latitudes. In fact, he got his first job in the business on Brando's remake of *Mutiny on the Bounty*. Connie's father had co-written the book on which it was based. He had an 'in'.

When Connie saw my little island, he couldn't stop laughing. 'Boorman, you're out of your mind. I love it.' We lived on a Chinese ship and most of the crew were Japanese. It was a volatile mix.

Connie was more than a colleague. He was an ally. He didn't just agree to do a movie; he plunged in, gave it his all and stood with you, shoulder to shoulder.

We plotted the look and style of the picture. We planned the lighting and character of every scene. Connie favoured a lush, rich, luminous style. I wanted something harsher, bleaker. We wrestled with that. Even his black-and-white work in *In Cold Blood* looked velvety and sensual. Richard Brooks had been a powerful influence on him, and what he had learned he passed on to me – if there is a delay, always have an insert or an alternative shot standing by. Once a shot is completed, go straight to the next set-up. Don't allow people to chit-chat: keep the tension up, the concentration high. Move with speed and stealth and urgency. The exception, I learned, would be Connie's lighting. He was notorious for stealing time from the actors and director for setting his complex lights. As I would become impatient, he would encourage me by looking in the camera and letting out orgasmic cries of delight at his own work. I have always used the Mitchell side-finder to set up my choice of lens and composition. Connie would seize the finder and try to pull it towards his choice of shot. I held firm. He would finally set up the camera where I wanted it, but could not resist moving it six inches to the left or pushing it in a foot when I was not looking. He needed to make the images his own. As we fought over each shot, we would laugh and giggle and argue and embrace each other. Connie could shout and holler, but he never got angry or irritable. He loved our tussles. We only saw rushes once a week when the Dakota light aircraft arrived on the dust strip on a neighbouring island. We screened them in the ship's saloon, and Connie and I would take a few drinks beforehand. The whole film crew watched, while the ship's Chinese crew stood at the back, impenetrable and implacable, Connie cheered each shot

Top: *Hell in the Pacific* – Conrad Hall (left) at the edge of the frame
Bottom: *In Cold Blood*

Oscar-winning cinematography: *Butch Cassidy* (Paul Newman and Katharine Ross)

and gave himself a standing ovation at the end. The next morning, as we went to work in our tank landing craft, he would have a tight little smile on his face and say, 'We should reshoot that tracking shot.' 'Why?' I said. 'Didn't you see that highlight on that rock? I should have sprayed that down.' 'It doesn't matter. Mifune's performance was superb.' 'Everything matters or nothing matters,' he replied using his oft-repeated mantra.

After *Hell in the Pacific*, Connie was slated to shoot *Butch Cassidy and the Sundance Kid*. He was planning to shoot one sequence overexposed. To gauge the effect, he overexposed each of our slates so that he could see the effect in different lighting conditions. He tried one stop, two stops and three stops.

As advances in emulsions and film speeds came along, and refinements to the camera, he was the first to explore them and press them to their limits.

Whilst making *Butch Cassidy* he fell in love with Katharine Ross and determined not to work as a DOP anymore. He wanted to direct. He spent several years trying but it didn't quite work out. After I had made *Deliverance*, he remonstrated with me. Why had I not asked him to do it? 'But you have stopped being a cameraman.' 'But I couldn't have resisted that one. The only thing that attracts me these days is the impossible.'

Sam Mendes was quoted as asking Connie how he knew where to point the camera. Connie said he pointed it at the story. He liked working with first-time directors who let him call the shots. He would deliver their visions, the relationship like a Renaissance painter's with a pope. His lighting in *American Beauty* was wonderfully balanced and mature. The prettiness that he sometimes slipped into was mostly held at bay.

His final film, *The Road to Perdition*, was a *tour de force* of cinematography. Technically, it astonished. This was a master in utter command of his craft. He left behind his own obituary on film. It was the best and worst of Connie. Why was he drenching these criminals in romantic beauty? Where was the harshness the subject demanded? There were many shots that resonated wonderfully with the story, but for the most part the actors were smothered by the cinematography and it gave the subject a portentousness. There was a gap, a disparity between the narrative and how it was framed.

Connie's romanticism was modified by his scepticism and his dark humour. And when these elements came together, as in *American Beauty*, he was at his best.

He will be remembered for his courage, his humanity and the urgent, burning enthusiasm he never lost in all the vicissitudes of his career.

American Beauty: pointing the camera at the story (Mena Suvari and Kevin Spacey)

The Rebel Inside
Gavin Lambert remembers Karel Reisz

When an old and loved friend of mine dies, someone usually asks when we first met; and usually I can't remember, because we seemed to have known each other for ever. All I know for certain is that I met Karel Reisz a year or two after I started editing *Sight and Sound* in 1950. Like Lindsay Anderson and Tony Richardson (whom he later joined to form the gang of three behind Free Cinema), he contributed some of the best film reviews to the magazine.

But what did I know about him then? Not much more than that he was a Czech-Jewish refugee, whose parents managed to evacuate him to England in 1939, when he was twelve, and German troops had just occupied Prague. And although he spoke English with no trace of a foreign accent, he had a beautiful, unmistakably Slavic face that reflected the various strains, from Greece to Mongolia, of the ethnic history of the Slavs. The face seemed even more unique because Karel's behaviour was so English: the quiet, understated manner, sly humour and reluctance to discuss his personal life.

Although he told me he'd taught for a while, he never confided that soon after the end of the Second World War he learned that both his parents had died at Auschwitz. I heard about that several years later, I think from Karel's first wife, Julia. And in that context, I remember someone who'd recently lost a beloved friend quoting the Talmud: 'The greater the sorrow, the less tongue it hath.'

Karel and I soon discovered that we both admired Edith Wharton's novels, and in 1953 he suggested that *The Children* would be a good subject for Max Ophüls, whom I knew fairly well at the time. We collaborated on a screenplay, and Ophüls liked it. Ophüls also produced some fascinating ideas, but as usual was juggling various projects and didn't commit. He finally opted for *Lola Montes*, and we didn't meet again until he'd finished shooting the movie. This was in Paris, in late 1954. He said that he was still very interested in *The Children* and was going to propose it to Alexander Korda. A year later, Korda was dead of a heart attack, and the following year, after accepting an offer to direct a film about Modigliani, so was Ophüls.

By this time Karel had made two documentaries, *Momma Don't Allow* (about a jazz club, co-directed with Tony Richardson) and *We Are the Lambeth Boys*. Free Cinema, oriented towards social realism, may seem a far cry from Edith Wharton, but in fact Karel, Lindsay and Tony approached working-class life from widely divergent personal points of view, and as Karel once remarked:

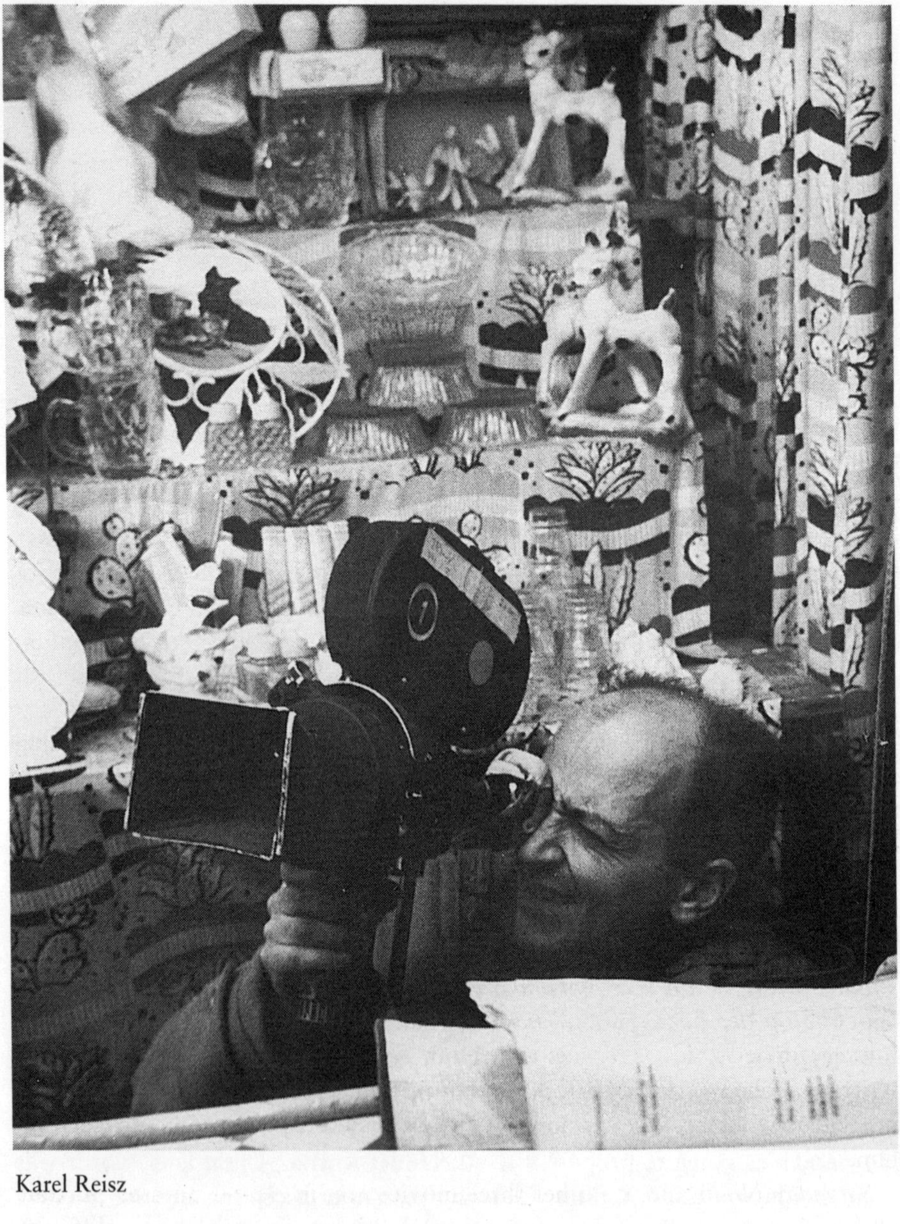

Karel Reisz

The Gambler (with James Caan)

'There are certain things you simply can't do with documentary, like getting inside character.'

Getting inside character, in fact, became Karel's major preoccupation as a director; and the kind of character that interested him provides a clue to his own, which he always guarded so closely. On the surface he seemed (and in many ways was) exceptionally reasonable and balanced. But he was also a passionate underground subversive, something that emerges in all his most personal movies – *Saturday Night and Sunday Morning*, *Isadora*, *The Gambler* and *Who'll Stop the Rain?* (a.k.a. *The Dog Soldiers*). It also accounts for a private mystery. In her vivid and engaging memoir, *The Memory of All That*, Betsy Blair writes that she fell in love with Karel not just on account of his charm, wit and intelligence, but because 'I know I'll always be interested in him, intrigued by him.'

Saturday Night and the other three movies are, in Karel's phrase, 'portrait films'. They're constructed around a central character, in each case a different kind of adventurer; and adventure, as William Bolitho wrote in *Twelve Against the Gods*, is 'the irreconcilable enemy of law'. (One of Bolitho's twelve, by the way, was Isadora Duncan.) Adventure, he added, is 'the vitaminising element in histories, both individual and social'. And although it's an element that clearly attracted Karel, he maintained an open-ended attitude towards it.

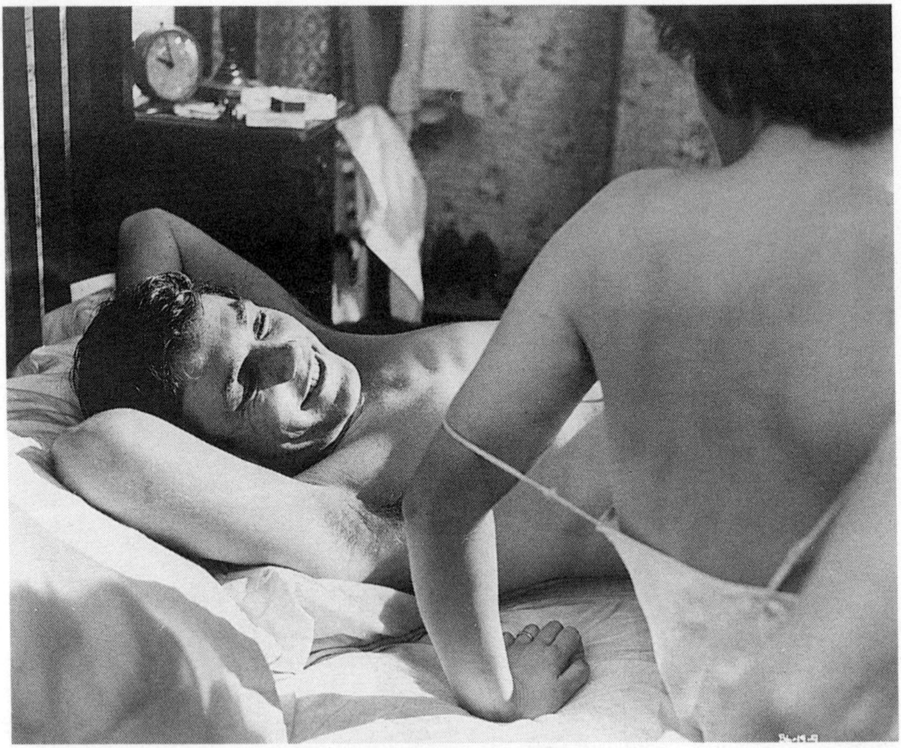

Top: *Saturday Night and Sunday Morning* (Albert Finney)
Bottom: *Who'll Stop the Rain?* (Reisz with Michael Moriarty)

Isadora: Reisz with Vanessa Redgrave

Arthur Seaton, the protagonist of Alan Sillitoe's novel *Saturday Night and Sunday Morning*, is really a mouthpiece for the rage and longing of a young man of his class and time, like Jimmy Porter in *Look Back in Anger*. But in Karel's movie he's also a prisoner of his class and time; and by implying that he may finally become a prisoner for life, an extra dimension is added to the character – whom Albert Finney makes alternately desperate, funny and touching, and sometimes all three at once.

The first half of *The Gambler* (until James Toback's script lapses into conventional melodrama) is a riveting study in compulsion. A college professor (James Caan), balanced and 'respectable' in one of his lives, becomes dangerously addicted in the other: a self-destructive yet heroic loser who can't resist upping the ante against chance. *Isadora* is the story of one of the great self-expressionists, a tireless rebel in dance, politics and sex, whose bizarre accidental death seems like a cue for laughter from the gods.

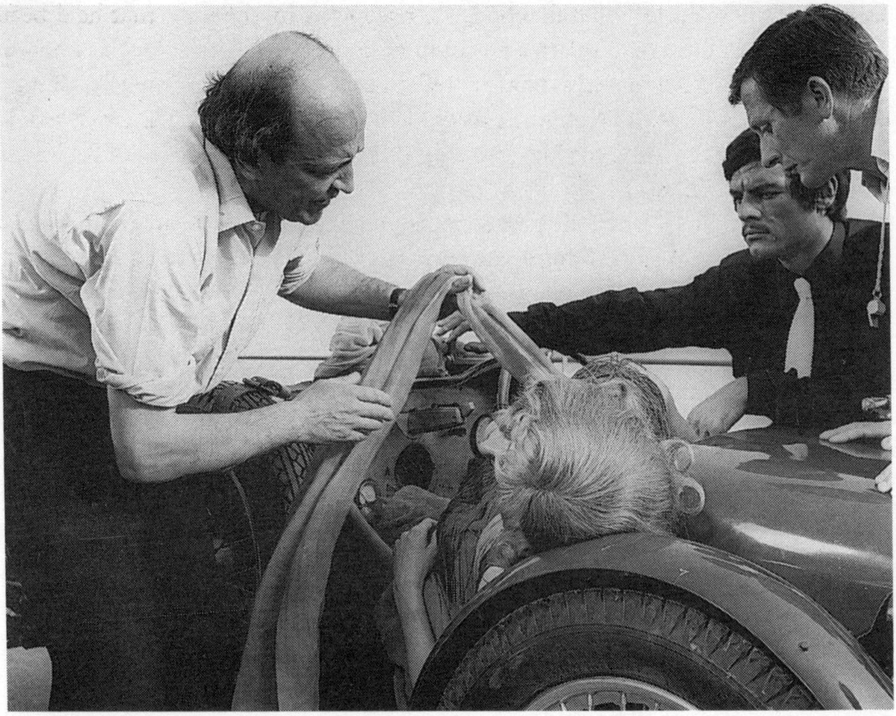

Isadora: making the challenge more heroic

This exceptionally ambitious movie was probably Karel's greatest disappointment. The studio chopped more than thirty minutes from his original cut and rearranged parts of a narrative never intended to be linear. Fortunately, his original cut is available on American video and, in spite of a flawed script and the synthetic Russian scenes, its central portrait is unforgettable, with Vanessa Redgrave charting a flamboyant descent from the sublime to the absurd.

Finally, *Dog Soldiers/Who'll Stop the Rain?*. Karel's grittiest movie centres on his most violently antisocial outsider, the war veteran (Nick Nolte), who is involved in smuggling heroin from Vietnam to the US. The portrait embodies all the sad and horrible confusion of that war and that time, but as usual the comment lies in an absence of comment, by someone who has witnessed or felt the best and worst of life and remains undiscouraged by despair or hope.

Which brings me to one of our last meetings, when I was in London during the autumn of 2002. Karel was suffering from a blood disease that necessitated regular transfusions, and he asked me to visit him at the Royal Free Hospital and keep him company during that long and dispiriting process. As usual, he talked very little about his own situation, but wanted to hear my news. News of

America, the remains of Hollywood. He felt lucky, by the way, that he'd been able to work in the theatre after he could no longer make the films he wanted. Then, before I left, he said, 'When you talk to Betsy, tell her how well I'm doing.' This was important, he explained, because he worried that she might become too involved with caring for him. He didn't want that. He didn't want his illness to take over her life.

His concern, it seems to me now, typified 'the vitaminising element' in Karel's life as well as his portrait films of adventurous outsiders. He had an unshakable regard for the free individual, and it was the challenge this individual represented, not its outcome, that mattered. The likelihood that Arthur Seaton would get trapped by the conformism he despised, or the certainty that the fringe of Isadora's scarf would get trapped in the wheel of a fast-moving Bugatti, jerk her head forward and snap her neck, only made the challenge more heroic.

Gavin Lambert is the author of *About Lindsay Anderson.*

Acknowledgements

Photographs courtesy of BFI Posters, Stills and Design and the Kobal Collection. Copyright for the stills are held by the folllowing: Focus Features (*Laurel Canyon*); Lions Gate (*Lovely and Amazing*); Gramercy Pictures (*Fargo*); Miramax (*Tadpole*); United Artists (*Personal Velocity*, *Dog Soldiers*); Jasmin Productions Inc (*All the Real Girls*); Thin Man Films (*Naked*, *Career Girls*, *Topsy-Turvy*); Zentropa Entertainment ApS (*Breaking the Waves*, *Open Hearts*); MK2 Productions (*Claire Dolan*); Columbia (*In Cold Blood*); Twentieth Century Fox (*Sunrise*, *Butch Cassidy and the Sundance Kid*); Paramount Pictures (*The Gambler*); Paramount Pictures/Mandalay Pictures LLO (*Sleepy Hollow*); Dreamworks (*American Beauty*); Woodfall Films (*Saturday Night Sunday Morning*); Les Films Georges de Beauregard (*The Little Soldier*); Rome Paris Films (*A Woman is a Woman*); Anouchka Films (*Band of Outsiders*); De Laurentiis (*Pierrot le Fou*); Jean Renoir Estate (*Rules of the Game*, *The Lower Depths*, *The Golden Coach*, *Grand Illusion*, portraits of Renoir); Warner Bros (*Strangers on a Train*, *My Fair Lady*, *A Star Is Born*, *The Chapman Report*); Nepi/Sofitedip/Silver (*La Notte*); FC Produzione/PECF (*Amarcord*); Svensk Filmindustri (*The Phantom Carriage*, *Summer with Monika*); Sigma (*Le jour se lève*); Mosfilm (*Andrei Rublev*); MGM (*Les Girls*, *Bhowani Junction*); ABC/Henry G. Saperstein Entreprises Inc. (*Hell in the Pacific*); Essex Features (*Boyfriends*); Aim/British Screen (*Before the Rain*); Fidelite Productions (*Under the Sand*); Martin Pope Productions (*Lawless Heart*).